The Presidency of
JOHN
ADAMS

AMERICAN PRESIDENCY SERIES

Donald R. McCoy,
Clifford S. Griffin,
Homer E. Socolofsky,
General Editors

The Presidency of
JOHN
ADAMS

by

Ralph Adams Brown

THE UNIVERSITY PRESS OF KANSAS
Lawrence / Manhattan / Wichita

Library of Congress Cataloging in Publication Data

Brown, Ralph A.
The Presidency of John Adams.

(American Presidency series)
Bibliography: p.
Includes index.
1. Adams, John, Pres. U. S., 1735-1826.
2. United States—Politics and government—1797-1801.
I. Title.   II. Series.
E321.B84   973.4'4'0924 [B]   75-5526
ISBN 0-7006-0134-1

12.00
3-17-76 —

Editors' Preface

The aim of the American Presidency Series is to present historians and the general reading public with interesting, scholarly assessments of the various presidential administrations. These interpretive surveys are intended to cover the broad ground between biographies, specialized monographs, and journalistic accounts. As such, each will be a comprehensive, synthetic work which will draw upon the best in pertinent secondary literature, yet leave room for the author's own analysis and interpretation.

Each volume in the series will deal with a separate presidential administration and will present the data essential to understanding the administration under consideration. Particularly, each book will treat the then current problems facing the United States and its people and how the president and his associates felt about, thought about, and worked to cope with these problems. Attention will be given to how the office developed and operated during the president's tenure. Equally important will be consideration of the vital relationships between the president, his staff, the executive officers, Congress, foreign representatives, the judiciary, state officials, the public, political parties, the press, and influential private citizens. The series will also be concerned with how this unique American institution—the presidency—was viewed by the presidents, and with what results.

All this will be set, insofar as possible, in the context not only of contemporary politics but also of economics, international relations, law, morals, public administration, religion, and thought. Such a broad approach is necessary to understanding, for a presidential administration is more than the elected and appointed officers composing it, since its work so often reflects the major problems, anxieties, and glories of the nation. In short, the authors in the series will strive to recount and evaluate the record of each administration and to identify its distinctiveness and relationships to the past, its own time, and the future.

Donald R. McCoy
Clifford S. Griffin
Homer E. Socolofsky

v

Preface

John Adams is seldom emphasized as one of the great Americans. When he is accorded such an accolade it is almost always as a revolutionary and not as a president. There are numerous reasons for this. Americans often think of their great men in terms of contrast or opposition: Jefferson versus Hamilton, Marshall versus Jackson, Lincoln versus Douglas, Grant versus Lee—the list is almost endless. John Adams, on the other hand, stands alone.

During the 1790s Adams's decisions and policies ran counter to the wishes of strong, ambitious, and verbal elements in his own political party. The Arch Federalists favored alliance with Britain, war against France, seizure of territory from Spain, a strengthening of the power of the central government, and vigorous action to weaken the political opposition. Thus as early as 1796 some of them were in bitter opposition to Adams, and the number continued to mount.

Another and perhaps even more important basis for the tendency to denigrate President John Adams is the influence his enemies and critics had on the contemporary press and publications of the time. Alexander Hamilton, who had watched his chance for glory and perhaps for power disappear in the wake of Adams's shrewdness and determination to prevent war with France, branded Adams as vain, temperamental, unpredictable, and incompetent. James McHenry, whose intellectual and administrative limitations were only exceeded by his disloyalty, told of Adams's temper, his vanity, his lack of administrative ability. Timothy Pickering, stubborn and intractable and often lacking in understanding and vision, continually undermined Adams's position.

Over the years historians like George Gibbs and Henry Cabot Lodge did their able best to perpetuate the ascribed weaknesses, faults, and mistakes of America's second president. Even reputable scholars, perhaps unwittingly, accepted the portrait of John Adams as first drawn by Hamilton, Pickering, Wolcott, Sedgwick, Cabot, and other political enemies and then engraved on the pages of American history by Gibbs and Lodge.

As a result John Adams, alone, of the many who created our nation and led it through the first difficult years, has become known largely in terms of the descriptions and evaluations left to us by his enemies and his detractors. As Joseph Charles has noted, "It is customary when writing of the presidency of John Adams to speak of him as a man of great gifts and great shortcomings, and then to concentrate upon the latter."

Moreover, until the very recent past the great bulk of Adams's manuscripts—letters, diaries, memoranda that might be used to clarify Adams's beliefs and policies, or to reveal his human qualities —has been shut up, first in Quincy and then on Boyleston Avenue in Boston, where few, even among scholars, had ready access. With the release of the 608 reels of the microfilm edition of *The Adams Papers*, a decade ago, this has been corrected and new light has been shed on many national problems between 1797 and 1801.

Awareness of the role of Adams's opponents in influencing the judgment of history does not imply that he had no weaknesses. When tired or overworked he could be irritable and aggressive. At times he procrastinated, doubting his judgment, though when sure of the rightness of an action he persevered despite the opposition of friend or foe. He admitted his tendency to write and speak hurriedly, and with too little regard for the impression his words might make. He was overly critical, frequently prone to exaggerate his own faults and those of others.

Gilbert Chinard, who overemphasized Adams's impulsiveness, neverthless recognized his concern for his country and its people: "he was to the last day ready to sacrifice his personal interest and to fight for the rights of his fellow beings. A self-made aristocrat, he led a simple life, never gathered a fortune, and never thought of building a palace for his old days. A regular and orderly citizen who never broke a law, he never hesitated to speak his mind and to criticize unreservedly the institutions of his country."

Gradually, during the past two or three decades, our second president has begun to emerge as a shrewd assessor of the dangers and problems of his time; a sensitive, experienced diplomat; a man of fiery beliefs tempered by superior insight and judgment; a man who, despite his love of freedom and his enthusiasm for the American Revolution, feared war and mob violence; a man who favored broad social reforms and change of government by due process.

An examination of the opinions of John Adams's political supporters, in the years after 1790, reveals that they had great faith in him; that they considered him as able as he was kind; that they trusted his leadership. In spite of his defeat for reelection in 1800, it appears that he may have had even greater popular support than he received while winning the presidency in 1796. Common people, especially in New England, considered him honest, sincere, loyal both to friends and to country, intelligent and dependable in his leadership. That they were more nearly right than the critics and opponents whose opinions for so long have colored the verdict of history and that his administration was marked by wise and unselfish decisions and by courageous actions is the central thesis of this study.

When direct quotations from Adams and his contemporaries have been used I have retained the spelling and capitalization typical of the time and have not deemed it necessary to burden the reader with the use of *sic*.

Much of the data used in this book has been taken from primary sources, but except for the *Adams Papers* these have been taken from printed collections. Readers who care to check these sources will note that various editors have often modernized spelling and punctuation; the sources become more confusing because different editors have sometimes handled the same manuscript source in different ways.

In writing this book, I am indebted to many persons. Friendly and helpful librarians at Stetson University in DeLand, Florida, at Cornell University in Ithaca, New York, at the New York Public Library in New York City, and at the Cortland State College Memorial Library have been of inestimable assistance. Curators and guides at the Adams houses in Quincy, Massachusetts; members of the staff of The Adams Papers at the Massachusetts Historical Society; dedicated and efficient typists, Mrs. John Gorman, Josephine Kiernan, and Mary Stack; all encouraged and gave assistance. My wife, Dr. Marian R. Brown, was an editor, a consultant, a research assistant, and a morale builder.

Ralph Adams Brown

State University of New York
State College at Cortland

Contents

1

★★★★★

JOHN ADAMS BECOMES PRESIDENT OF THE UNITED STATES

It was the eighth day of February 1797. The Senate of the United States was meeting on the second floor of Congress Hall in Philadelphia. Presiding over its session was the vice-president, a man of sixty-one years. About five feet eight inches tall, he was alert and impressive despite his weight. He had a round face, graying hair that was fine in texture and thin in quantity, and blue eyes that could crinkle with laughter or blaze with anger.

His teeth were bad, a condition that gave him much pain. It also caused him a certain amount of mental anguish, for he was often fearful that his speech would not be clear. Yet twenty years before, while Adams was a dynamic leader of the Continental Congress, a colleague had written that he "was a most sensible and forcible speaker. Every member of Congress in 1776 acknowledged him to be the first man in the House. Dr. Brownson (of Georgia) used to say when he spoke, he fancied an angel was let down from heaven to illumine the Congress."[1]

This was an important day for the United States of America, and a day of great personal significance for the vice-president, John Adams of Quincy, Massachusetts. The preceding September, George Washington, having nearly completed his second term as the first president of the young nation, had announced his forthcoming retirement. This first change in the presidency of the new nation was alarming to many citizens. The Federalists had agreed to support John Adams for president and Thomas Pinckney of

1

South Carolina for vice-president. Their political opponents had selected Thomas Jefferson for the first post but without agreement as to their nominee for the second post. Presidential electors were chosen in each state. Each of these electors then voted for two persons to become president. Whoever received the majority of the votes would become president; the one with the second largest vote would be the new vice-president. By midwinter it was rumored that the number of presidential electors who would vote for Adams outnumbered those intending to support Jefferson. On this day, February 8, 1797, the ballots of the electors were to be opened and officially counted.

The tellers brought the ballots in sealed envelopes to the desk of the vice-president, and John Adams began the official count. One by one he opened the envelopes, read and announced the designee. A hush fell over the chamber as the returns were read. Those present sensed that this was a historic moment, signifying the end of one administration, the start of another, the first change of command in the history of the young nation.

When all the ballots had been tallied, the vice-president announced the final result. Federalist John Adams had been chosen to succeed George Washington. His margin of victory, however, was narrow—seventy-one to sixty-eight. Thanks to the maneuvering of Alexander Hamilton, who had sought to eliminate Adams by promoting Thomas Pinckney for president, John Adams's support was less than he had hoped it would be. Furthermore, his opponent, Thomas Jefferson, garnered more votes than Pinckney and thus would become the new vice-president.

This was the day to which John Adams had looked forward since the outcome of the various state elections had been generally (though unofficially) known. He would have been less than human not to have felt a certain elation, a thrill of victory. But he had long trained himself to conceal his feelings. Only in times of great stress, deep sorrow, or sudden anger did John Adams wear his emotions on his sleeve.

Up in Quincy, Massachusetts, in the small farmhouse that had been their home since 1787, John's "Dearest Friend," Abigail, was conscious of the significance of this day and of what it meant to her beloved husband. Taking pen and paper, she wrote, "You have this day to declare yourself head of a nation. . . . My thoughts and my meditations are with you, though personally absent . . . . My feelings are not those of pride or ostentation upon the occasion. They are solemnized by a sense of the obligations, the important trusts and numerous duties connected with it. That you may be enabled to discharge them with honor to yourself, with justice and impartiality to your country, and with satisfaction to this great people, shall be the daily prayer of your A. A."[2]

A month later John Adams was inaugurated as the second president of the United States.

It may have been just before noon on March 4, 1797, when John Adams dressed for the ceremony at which he would assume the responsibility for leading the nation. He had selected a new suit of pearl-gray broadcloth, a full sword, and a cockaded hat. There were no buckles on his shoes nor other ornaments, but his hair was well powdered. He had purchased a new carriage for the occasion. "Simple but elegant enough" was the way he described it.

March 4, 1797, fell on a Saturday. President George Washington had summoned the Senate to meet in its chamber at ten that morning. Assembled on the second floor of Congress Hall, Senator William Bingham of Pennsylvania, president pro tem of the Senate and perhaps the wealthiest and most successful merchant in the land, swore in the new vice-president. Wearing a long, blue frock coat buttoned tightly down the center to his waist, with his hair lightly powdered and tied tightly in the back with a black ribbon, Thomas Jefferson took the oath of office and began his four-year term as the Senate's presiding officer. Newly elected senators were sworn in, and the members then filed downstairs to the chamber of the House of Representatives where the new president was to be inaugurated.

John Adams left his house on Fourth Street, entered his new coach, and was driven to Congress Hall, which was located at the corner of Chestnut and Sixth streets. To the delight of observant Republicans, he dispensed with some of the pageantry of Washington's inaugurals. Marshals did not march ceremoniously before his carriage, and he did not affect a court uniform as some of his critics had suggested he would.

Adams had not slept well the night before and, as he wrote Abigail later, he was worried that he might faint during the ceremony. His palsy, he thought, was worse than usual, and he feared he could not make himself understood. It seems probable that John Adams suffered from stage fright.

It is possible that the descending senators and the new vice-president reached the chamber of the House on the first floor before John Adams's carriage came to a halt outside of Congress Hall. The president-elect stepped from his carriage, entered the chamber of

3

the House of Representatives, and walked to the elongated dais at the front of the room. He took the chair usually occupied by the Speaker of the House. On his right hand sat the vice-president, and just beyond Jefferson, the secretary of the Senate. On Adams's left was the Speaker of the expired House of Representatives. In front of the dais sat the justices of the Supreme Court and certain foreign emissaries. With them, erect and impressive in a plain, dark suit, and with well-powdered hair, sat the retiring president. Slightly over a hundred members of the House of Representatives occupied their usual seats in three semicircular rows. Chairs had been brought in for the senators and the visitors. Many ladies were present and every available space was filled. No member of either Adams's or Jefferson's family was present, however.

Unlike the inaugurations of the present day, John Adams gave his address before taking the oath of office. His nervousness disappeared as he launched into his presentation. Historians have generally agreed that it was a moderate, balanced, sensible speech; that John Adams established his respect for the Constitution, his faith in the new government, and his hope for a united and peaceful nation. Writing to Abigail, after the ceremonies were over, the new president indicated his belief that he had done a creditable job.

At the conclusion of Adams's address, Chief Justice Oliver Ellsworth stepped forward and administered the oath of office. This was the first time the oath had been so administered. Thus John Adams became the second president of the United States.

Theodore Sedgwick, senator from Massachusetts, was among those present. Long an acquaintance and sometimes even a social intimate of John and Abigail Adams, Sedgwick was to become, after 1798, one of Adams's bitterest critics and opponents. A few days after the inauguration, however, he wrote to Rufus King, U.S. minister to England, describing the proceedings in Congress Hall on March 4: "The inauguration of the President was a scene the most august and sublime I ever beheld. Mr. Adams behaved with dignity. The company was numerous, respectable, and behaved with that decent gravity which the solemn occasion demanded . . . ."[3]

The next day John Adams wrote to Abigail concerning his inauguration, "Your dearest friend never had a more trying day than yesterday. A solemn scene it was indeed, and it was made more affecting to me by the presence of the General [Washington], whose countenance was as serene and unclouded as the day. He seemed to me to enjoy a triumph over me. Methought I heard him say, 'Ay! I am fairly out and you fairly in! See which of us will be happiest.' When the ceremony was over, he came and made me a visit, and cordially congratulated me, and wished my administration might be happy, successful, and honorable."[4]

By means of a generally peaceful, reasonably democratic process, the people of the young nation had determined how the government would proceed and who would lead it for the next four years. The first change of administration had been accomplished.

2

★★★★★

THE ROAD TO THE PRESIDENCY

As a shaper of the American tradition, a revolutionary agitator, statesman, treaty-maker; as America's first vice-president and second president, John Adams left his stamp on the new nation and its government. Poised between the strong, conservative, Federalist administration of Washington and the more democratic years of Jefferson, Adams bestrode a period of rapid change, of internal discord and personal opposition, as well as the continual threat of foreign war. Throughout his four years as president he was above all a lawyer, and guided by his Puritan sense of duty and a deep concern for the rights and welfare of the people, he emphasized the responsibility of each individual and the importance of law and order in government. If any one aspect of his personality exceeded others, it was his all-pervading sense of responsibility.

Born on October 19, 1735, in the small Massachusetts village of Braintree (soon to become Quincy), Adams was descended from land-owning yeomen of Somerset County, England. A century earlier his grandfather, Henry, had settled south of Boston and within sound of the ocean. His father, a farmer and cordwainer, served as a deacon in the church, a selectman, and a lieutenant in the local militia. He was loyal to England and had great respect for his king. He married Suzanna Boyleston of Brookline, granddaughter of a physician who immigrated from England in 1656. John was their first child.

The Adams family lived in a small, low-ceilinged, frame house, heated by fireplaces. Young John Adams loved to ride and hunt, to fish, and to walk in the fields, play ball, and watch the ocean. He was assigned the usual chores around the house and barn. In haying season and at harvest time, he breakfasted at sunrise and worked long hours in the fields. Both John's father, who had left school at twelve, and his mother believed in education and, despite their limited means, decided that their first son must go to Harvard and become a clergyman. John attended Dame School, the Public Latin School, and had two private tutors, but preferred his work on the farm.

At Harvard, however, Adams won honors as a scholar although many of his classmates later became famous men. Seated according to his family's social rank, Adams was fourteenth in a class of twenty-four. Academically he was among the top three. While he enjoyed his studies, joined a play-reading group, and worked diligently, he was strongly attracted to the opposite sex and found much pleasure in their company. He had a ready tongue, a quick wit, a sense of humor and could laugh at himself, his plumpness, and his mistakes. He graduated at nineteen, having demonstrated to his professors an unusually keen and original mind and a deep intellectual curiosity. His classmates believed he "had a voice and a tongue as well as a face and a front for a public speaker."

Looking back on his education, Adams wrote:

> Under my first Latin master, who was a churl, I spent my time in shooting, skating, swimming, flying kites, and every other boyish exercise and diversion I could invent. Never mischievous. Under my second master, who was kind, I began to love my books and neglect my sports. From that time I have been too studious. At college, next to the ordinary routine of classical studies, mathematics and natural philosophy were my favorite pursuits. When I began to study law, I found ethics, the law of nations, the civil law, the common law, a field too vast to admit of many other inquiries. Classics, history, and philosophy have, however, never been wholly neglected to this day.[1]

Few have ever questioned Adams's scholarship, his depth and breadth of intellectual interest. Dr. Rush once noted that John Adams "possessed more learning probably, both ancient and modern, than any man who subscribed the Declaration of Independence. His reading was various. Even the old English poets were familiar to him."[2] A generation later Theodore Parker commented that "with the exception of Dr. Franklin . . . no American politician of the eighteenth century was Adams's intellectual superior."[3] Es-

7

mond Wright, a British historian, has noted that "as a political thinker he [John Adams] was perhaps the most original and, with Madison, the best read in constitutional history and law of all the Founders."[4]

John Adams did not become a clergyman, as he was unwilling to accept the rigidity of the theological doctrine. Instead he taught in a log schoolhouse in Worcester. Adams found the people in this frontier community much interested in politics and in the developing country to the west. As his own interest in government and politics increased, he decided to become a lawyer. He studied in the office of James Putnam, then returned to his home in Braintree and was admitted to the Boston bar on November 7, 1758.

Three years later John's father died and he inherited a house and small farm. He was now a freeholder, a man of local importance, and was promptly elected to his first public office, surveyor of highways. That fall, after practicing law for the required three years, John rode to Boston. Wigged, powdered, and gowned in black, he was sworn in as a barrister at a session of the Superior Court.

John had done his share of courting in Worcester and Braintree. Only his firm ambition, his determination to read and study rather than be confined by the need to support a family, seem to have kept him from matrimony. Now his good friend Richard Cranch was courting Mary Smith of Weymouth. John often rode over from Braintree with him and he was soon captivated by Mary's younger sister, Abigail. Daughter of a well-known clergyman and his socially prominent wife, Abigail Smith was neither physically strong nor beautiful. As saucy as John, she was widely read, spirited, affectionate, and soon deeply in love with the young lawyer. She resented her mother's attempts to prevent the marriage.

Six days past his twenty-ninth birthday, John Adams married the nineteen-year-old girl. The Quincy family, to which Abigail's mother belonged, had long been active in the political, economic, and social life of the colony, and this marriage extended John's connections with prominent Massachusetts people. Abigail herself was to prove a match for her husband in courage, loyalty, and in acuity of mind. In the next decade four children were born to the couple: Abby, John Quincy, Charles, and Thomas Boyleston.

John Adams had no meteoric rise as a lawyer. His practice grew slowly as he became increasingly involved in local affairs. Those were turbulent times. The Stamp Act, the Townshend Acts, the continuing efforts of Parliament to find revenues in the colonies and to enforce its control over commercial matters aroused more and more opposition. Consideration of the political relationships between England and the colonies consumed much of Adams's time. He wrote articles for the newspapers in which he discussed the question of Parliament's authority to pass various acts. He attended meetings called by the leaders of colonial opposition; he read widely in history, law, government, and philosophy, ordering books from England and building up the best law library in New England. As long as he lived, John Adams would search for more knowledge, for deeper understanding of the meaning and role of government.

In 1768 John moved his family to Boston and became closely associated with the leaders of the Patriot movement. He rejected a lucrative appointment to the Court of Admiralty. Coming at a time when his family was growing and his law practice was still small, this proffered appointment to a politically important and well-paying position must have presented a real temptation to an ambitious young man. John Adams, however, correctly ascribed the offer to an attempt on the part of the supporters of the crown to divert his activities away from association with the Revolutionaries.

Throughout his life John Adams was to remain an independent thinker who put law and justice before partisanship, made his own decisions, and steadfastly did what he thought was right. When asked to defend the British soldiers accused of murdering colonists in the Boston Massacre, he felt morally obligated, as a lawyer, to do so. Rejecting his cousin Sam Adams's warning that such an action would ruin his budding political career, Adams accepted the case and won their acquittal.

Annoyed by the Loyalists' assumption that his defense of the British soldiers meant he favored their side in the dispute, and disturbed because so many of his friends misunderstood his motives in accepting the case, Adams concentrated more and more on his law practice and his own family. In 1773, however, both Massachusetts Governor Thomas Hutchinson and the British Parliament took actions that Adams would not ignore. First, Parliament decreed that the five judges of the Massachusetts Superior Court should have their salaries paid by the crown. Appointed by the king, the only colonial control over these judges had been the power of the colonial legislature to vote their salaries. John Adams was incensed at this action of Parliament. He at once began the preparation of eight essays, widely published in colonial newspapers, denouncing the action of Parliament and asserting the need for some colonial control over the judiciary.

Second, Governor Hutchinson, alarmed at the favorable reception given Adams's essays, appeared before the colonial legislature to defend Parliament's action. He asserted that either Parliament had complete and total control over the colonies or the colonies were in fact independent of the mother country; there could be, he declared, no halfway status. John Adams at once denounced Governor Hutchinson's position and argued that a colonial congress was desirable.

A third action was Parliament's passage of the Tea Act. Rifts among the Patriot leaders were at once healed as their anger at this act united them against England. After 1773 John Adams became an increasingly energetic speaker and worker for colonial rights and independence.

Elected a delegate to the First Continental Congress on June 17, 1774, Adams became the recognized leader, the most effective promoter and organizer of those who favored independence. It was he who nominated Washington for commander in chief of the Patriot army and he who led the fight against Galloway's Plan of Union, an attempt to avoid independence. The fiery Adams became a member of the committee of five and the subcommittee of three to write the Declaration of Independence.

Between 1774 and 1778 he served on more than eighty committees of the Continental Congress, and chaired twenty-five of them. Writing many years later, Thomas Jefferson noted that John Adams "was the pillar . . . [of the movement for independence] on the floor of Congress. its ablest advocate and defender against the multifarious assaults it encountered."[5] A New Jersey representative to the Congress referred to Adams as the "Atlas of American Independence."

Yet despite his leadership in the American Revolution, John Adams never wavered from his belief in law and order and constitutional government. Essentially he was a prudent man who disliked mobs and violence. He believed that it was possible, however, to "establish the wisest and happiest government that human wishes can contrive." During the next decade, a decade marked by violence and rebellion, Adams played a major role in encouraging the thirteen colonies to unite and establish a new identity. His oratory and written polemics made him known from New Hampshire to Georgia. It was his hope that each colony would map out its own government, write its own constitution, and then unite into a confederation for mutual strength and protection.

In 1778 the Continental Congress sent Adams to France to assist Franklin in gaining recognition and aid from European countries. The ten-year-old John Quincy accompanied his father. (By the time this lad was eighteen he had visited most of the capitals of Europe.) Active, energetic, conscientious, John Adams's role was important both in negotiations with European governments and in liaison with Congress.

In the summer of 1779 Adams returned to Massachusetts and immediately assumed major responsibility for drafting a new constitution for his own state. In November, this time with his two older sons, John Quincy and Charles, Adams returned to France. In the summer of 1784 Abigail and their daughter joined the men. Influential in the negotiations that led to peace with Great Britain and the latter's recognition of the independence of the new American nation, Adams also journeyed to Holland and obtained financial assistance.

On February 24, 1785, Adams was appointed diplomatic envoy to Great Britain; on the twenty-sixth of May he was in London. On June 1 he was received by King George III. Abigail much preferred the English to the French countryside and she enjoyed her house on Grosvenor Square. Soon Adams's daughter, Abby, was being courted by Lieutenant Colonel William Stephens Smith, who had served under Washington and was now secretary to the American legation in London. On June 12, 1786, the young couple were married.

Bitter over the loss of their former colonies, those in power in England grudgingly accepted John Adams as America's ambassador and made it plain that they resented his role in the American Revolution. Thus his work at the Court of Saint James was often unpleasant and equally unproductive. At the end of 1787 he asked to be recalled.

Both John and Abigail missed the United States and welcomed word from home. They were upset by news of Shays' Rebellion and the defiance of law and government in their own state. There was also trouble on the national scene. People were clamoring for changes in the government. Both in Europe and in America there was talk of the advantages of a government with a unicameral legislature. Adams was appalled. Dr. Franklin approved of the unicameral legislature and Adams was fearful lest state governments adopt this form.

11

Retreating to his study, Adams directed Abigail to allow no one to interrupt him. Surrounded by books and notes he read and wrote from sunrise long into the night. Entitled *A Defense of the Constitutions of the United States of America against the Attack of M. Turgot,* his book emphasized the need for representative government, for the separation of powers, for a system of checks and balances, for a bicameral legislature and a strong executive with an absolute veto. It included masses of information on ancient and modern governments. It was hurriedly written, and Adams's grandson was to list its main defect as a "want of methodical treatment of the subject."

Published in England just as the French Revolution was getting under way, the first volume is said to have been widely read by the delegates to the Constitutional Convention of 1787, and to have had considerable impact on the acceptance of that document by the people of Massachusetts.

When Adams arrived in Boston in the spring of 1788, the people of his state promptly elected him to a seat in the Congress of the Confederation. Before he could take this seat, however, the new constitution was ratified. Presidential electors were chosen, and met in each state to cast their votes for president. As expected, George Washington was their unanimous choice, receiving 69 votes. John Adams received 34 votes; John Jay, 9; John Hancock, 4; and 22 were scattered among various men. As soon as John Adams heard that he had been chosen vice-president, he started for New York City, the temporary seat of the new government.

Four years later, in 1792, both Washington and Adams were reelected for second terms. George Clinton of New York actively sought the vice-presidency, but the electoral vote was as follows: Washington, 132; Adams, 77; Clinton, 50; Jefferson, 4; and Burr, 1. Even though the two men disagreed about the fundamental nature of government, Thomas Jefferson gave considerable support to John Adams in this election.

During the mid-1790s America's relations with Britain worsened and a second war with that powerful nation seemed imminent. Britain was not complying with terms of the Treaty of Paris (1783). She did not withdraw from forts along America's northern boundary, she was often blamed for Indian disturbances on the frontier, and her continued impressment of American sailors caused constant friction. Sent to England to attempt a solution to the disagreements, John Jay returned with a treaty so unfavorable to the United States that it was vigorously opposed. The resultant debate drew clearly definable and irrevocable lines of disagreement between the Federalists and the supporters of Jefferson and Madison. The battle over the Jay Treaty was fought twice: first in the Senate over ratification, and later in the House of Representatives over the appropriation of the necessary funds to carry out the provisions of the treaty.

Presiding over the Senate, John Adams refrained from participation in the public debate, though it is apparent that he had strong feelings about the matter. He felt the Senate should ratify the treaty because it was, he believed, the best solution that could be obtained at that time and because it would at least postpone war. Once the treaty was ratified, he had no patience with the efforts of the Jeffersonians in the House to prevent the appropriation of the necessary funds.

The Senate had ratified the treaty; therefore, John Adams believed, the nation was morally bound to put it into effect. The House of Representatives, he felt, had no right to render impotent both the Senate and the chief executive. Yet it is significant that, feeling as strongly as he did, John Adams made no public pronouncement nor any effort to persuade the House to act. He believed in the separation of powers.

While it is true that Vice-President Adams tried to be nonpartisan in the sense that he was fearful of deep political partitions among the people, and while he consistently supported the independence of the executive's position, it is equally true that he usually followed and supported the Federalist party line. Because of the multiplicity of the political arguments and the nearly equal strength of the two parties, John Adams, as presiding officer of the Senate, had more opportunity to break tie votes than any other vice-president in American history. Twenty times, during the three sessions of the First Congress, John Adams cast the deciding vote.

At the close of the year 1795 one question was on the minds of most public figures in the United States: would George Washington accept another term? He had wished to retire in 1792, but had yielded to the pleas of many, including both Jefferson and Hamilton, and had agreed to serve again. As the year 1796 opened, the best-informed public figures assumed that Washington would retire, yet neither political party (and party lines had been tightened by the debates over the Jay Treaty) could make any definite campaign plans until the president had spoken.

On January 7, 1796, John Adams wrote to Abigail, who was in

Quincy: "In perfect secrecy between you and me, I must tell you that I now believe the President will retire. The consequence to me is very serious, and I am not able, as yet, to see what my duty will demand of me. . . . But I think, upon the whole, the probability is strong that I shall make a voluntary retreat, and spend the rest of my days, in a very humble style, with you. Of one thing I am sure—it would be to me the happiest portion of my whole life."[6]

Throughout the next months John Adams seems to have been alternately steeling himself to accept neglect and reconciling himself to return to private life, while constantly dreaming that he might actually succeed to the presidency. It was only natural that some people saw in the vice-president the logical successor to Washington. On January 20 he wrote to Abigail that he was "quite a favorite, I am to dine today again. I am Heir apparent you know."[7]

Assuming that he might be passed over by the Federalists, he later wrote to Abigail: "I believe I have firmness of mind enough to bear it like a man, a hero, and a philosopher. I might groan like Achilles, and roll from side to side abed sometimes, at the ignorance, folly, injustice and ingratitude of the world, but I should be resigned, and become more easy and cheerful, and enjoy myself and my friend better than ever I did."[8] Reading his letters, Abigail recognized her husband's mental turmoil and knew he hoped for the presidency.

In 1794, after the resignations of Jefferson and Hamilton, and Washington's loss of confidence in Randolph, the president turned more often to John Adams, both for advice and for companionship. John's letters to Abigail relayed greetings from Martha, mentioned her invitations for both of them to visit Mount Vernon, and spoke of going to the theater with the president and his wife.

From the letters that passed between John and Abigail in the winter and spring of 1796, it is apparent how much the former wished to succeed Washington. Yet John Adams believed that positions of trust and power should seek the man and not vice versa. In common with many of the leading public servants of his generation, Adams believed it was unethical to admit desire for a position of power. The people, rather, should approach the person whom they wished to lead them, should summon him forth from routine tasks—tasks to which the leader should retire once his service was completed.

In the summer of 1796 John Adams attended to his duties at the farm in Quincy, read avidly, and thought deeply. Rumors spread that Washington would refuse another term. David Howell, of Rhode Island, and Theodore Sedgwick, Arch Federalist of Massachusetts, both made their way to the Quincy farmhouse to pledge their support to Adams. While courteous, he was noncommittal to both of them. Such a reception did not mean that John Adams was indifferent or lacked interest. When it was reported to him that one of the toasts at a rally in New York City had been "To John Adams, inflexible to preserve, virtuous to pursue, and intelligent to discern the true interests of his country," he was both pleased and deeply moved. "God grant they may never be belied, never disproved," he commented.[9]

Perhaps no single incident is better indicative of John Adams's independence of action and seeming indifference to the outcome of the election than his open attendance at a lecture given by Dr. Joseph Priestley. He admired the man's mind, and his disagreement with Priestley's religious thinking had not prevented pleasant conversations in Europe. Priestley, a deist, while visiting America was hailed and admired by the Jeffersonians and was openly supporting their position. Yet John Adams, without concealment or apology, went to hear Priestley's public address.

With the release of Washington's Farewell Address on September 19, the presidential campaign of 1796 began in earnest. The Federalists supported John Adams and Thomas Pinckney of South Carolina; the Republicans chose Jefferson and some selected Burr for the second spot. Neither Adams nor Jefferson, however, made the slightest effort to influence the outcome of the election, as both considered it unethical for a candidate to campaign in his own behalf. Adams, who certainly hoped for victory, was therefore as seemingly indifferent as Jefferson, who was a most reluctant candidate. Although largely confined to newspaper polemics, pamphlets, and political rallies, the campaign has been termed one of the most violent and scurrilous in American history.

The Federalists branded Jefferson as an atheist, a nonbeliever who would destroy all organized religion. He was, they said, a friend of France and the French Revolution. He would draw the United States into the European conflict against Britain. William Cobbett, in his *Porcupine's Gazette*, and John Fenno, editor of the *Gazette of the United States*, attacked Jefferson's philosophy, criticized his alleged religious beliefs, belabored his friendship for France and his opposition to Hamilton and to the Jay Treaty.

Bache's *Aurora*, seconded by dozens of smaller and usually less effective journals, branded John Adams as a monarchist, a friend of

Britain, a man who neither believed in democracy nor respected the federal constitution. They made fun of his physical appearance —"His Rotundity"—and they charged him with having deserted his former support of democracy.

The Jeffersonians attacked the Jay Treaty and denounced the economic centralism of Alexander Hamilton. They scanned the writings of Adams—especially his *Defense of the Constitutions* and his *Discourses on Davila*—seeking sentences or even phrases that, often taken out of context, made John Adams appear to favor monarchy, to admire the British form of government, and to applaud ceremony and ritual.

In Boston the Jeffersonian supporters printed and distributed a handbill that quoted many of these carefully selected excerpts from the writings of John Adams and then closed by urging "the independent Citizens of America . . . [to] determine how far Mr. Adams has apostatized from his former sentiments in favor of American liberty and independence, by writing his Eulogium of Monarchy and the British Constitution, and consequently, how far he is to be regarded as a fit person to be elected President of the United States."[10] As with many such charges, this was widely reprinted in Republican newspapers.

One of the important aspects of the campaign of 1796 was the interference by the French government's agents. It became perfectly apparent that the French Directorate hoped Jefferson would win and that its members were willing to do anything possible to defeat Adams. This attitude was at once the result of the French reaction to the Jay Treaty and of their belief that Jefferson and his friends would favor France. The French minister to the United States, Pierre Adet, was especially active in public circles. He wrote letters urging the election of Jefferson and issued pro-Jefferson proclamations, all widely reprinted. He urged those Americans who supported France to make public announcements to that effect. He assured Americans friendly to France that the French government did not intend to allow the Federalists to turn the country over to Great Britain.

In the summer of 1796 Pierre Adet made a trip through New England, continuing his exertions in Jefferson's behalf. In late October, Adet sent Secretary of State Pickering a decree of the French government declaring that France would, in the future, treat all American ships and cargoes "in the same manner that they suffered the English to treat them." Adet also released this threat to the newspapers. Then, on November 15, the announcement timed to be a possible influence on the presidential electors as they prepared to cast their ballots, Adet notified the American government that he had been recalled because the French government considered the United States to be pro-British. It later developed that Adet had received his recall weeks before but had held the news for this dramatic announcement. In his statement Adet appealed to the American people to honor the alliance of 1778 with France and to renounce the pro-British Jay Treaty of the Federalists by casting their votes for Jefferson.

Federalists, of course, were furious. On Monday afternoon, October 31, Washington arrived in Philadelphia. Two days later he wrote to Alexander Hamilton: ". . . I arrived in this City, and among the first things which presented themselves to my view, was Mr. Adet's letter to the Secretary of State, published by his [Adet's] order, in the moment it was presented. . . . There is in the conduct of the French government relative to this business, an inconsistency, a duplicity, a delay, or a something else, which is unaccountable upon honorable ground."[11]

Federalist newspapers accused the Republicans of responsibility for Adet's statements. As a matter of fact, Madison had feared that Adet's undiplomatic utterances would anger Americans and cost Jefferson votes that he might otherwise receive, and it seems probable that Adet was solely responsible.

The role of Alexander Hamilton in the campaign of 1796 has been the subject of much disagreement. It seems apparent that in 1796 Hamilton would have preferred almost any Federalist to John Adams. Adams had often disagreed with Hamilton's economic views, and he was a stubborn and independent man who would resist control by the ambitious Hamilton. The latter soon realized, however, that John Adams not only had the prestige that came from having been second to Washington for eight years but that he was so popular with the rank and file, especially in New England and Maryland, that it would be impossible to ignore him. Sometime in the spring or early summer of 1796, well before Washington's official withdrawal, Hamilton seems to have developed the idea of relegating Adams to another four years in the vice-presidency. The plan that he developed was to pretend to support Adams for the presidency while actually arranging for the vice-presidential candidate to receive more electoral votes than Adams. He had toyed briefly with the idea of selecting Patrick Henry for the vice-presidency but finally settled on Thomas Pinckney from South Carolina.

Hamilton felt that Pinckney's selection as the nominee for vice-president would draw certain southern votes away from Jefferson. Also, if northern Federalists could be persuaded to vote solidly for both Adams and Pinckney, the few additional southern votes that the latter might be expected to receive would make him the new president rather than John Adams. Hamilton apparently believed that the election of Pinckney would place in the executive position a man less experienced, less stubborn and independent than Adams, a man Hamilton could more easily influence and perhaps direct.

The Hamilton-inspired technique was to announce admiration and support for John Adams but to raise the specter of a Jeffersonian victory and insist that such a calamity could only be prevented by a solid vote for both Adams and Pinckney. Writing to an unknown correspondent sometime in the fall of 1796 Hamilton suggested, "We have everything to fear if . . . [Jefferson] comes in. . . . there can be no doubt that the exclusion of Mr. Jefferson is far more important than any difference between Mr. Adams and Mr. Pinckney."[12]

According to Robert Goodloe Harper of South Carolina, most prominent and active of all Arch Federalists in the South, the original plan to elect Pinckney president was the work of Hamilton and Rufus King. Writing to Ralph Izard of his state, on November 4, Harper pointed out that Hamilton's plan had always been to make Pinckney the first choice. "It is not Pinckney or Adams with us," he wrote, "but Pinckney or Jefferson."[13]

Did John Adams know of Hamilton's plotting? Were Adams's supporters aware of it? And if so, how early? As the campaign progressed, Hamilton's scheme became apparent to members of the opposition party, evidence that it was probably known to John Adams and his close friends. As early as October, John Beckley of Pennsylvania, possibly the shrewdest political organizer of the decade, wrote to Monroe that "Adams, if Hamilton can prevent it without danger, is not designed as Washington's successor—Pinckney from London is the man."[14] On December 5 Madison suggested to Jefferson, "This jockeyship is accounted for by the enmity of Adams to Banks & funding systems, and by an apprehension that he is too headstrong to be a fit puppet for the intrigues behind the screen."[15]

Certainly John Adams was warned of Hamilton's scheming no later than November, although he may have been reluctant to accept the latter's intrigue as aimed exclusively at him. On December 1 the vice-president wrote to Abigail, "I can tell you nothing about elections . . . . There is some anxiety lest Pinckney should be smuggled in, unintentionally, to the first place." On the twelfth he wrote, "If Col. Hamilton's personal Dislike of Jefferson does not obtain too much Influence with Massachusetts electors, neither Jefferson will be President nor Pinckney V.P. of U.S. . . . . Hamilton and Jay are said to be for Pinckney."[16]

By mid-December, Adams was convinced that Pinckney would be chosen president. On the sixteenth he wrote to Abigail that the South Carolinian would win and that "the English Party [Hamilton?] have outgeneraled the French and American both. That is the Construction I put upon it, though others would make me believe if they could that it is an insidious Maneuver of Hamilton's individual ambition."[17] Only two days later John Adams thought he might be the winner, and his letter to his wife included this illuminating paragraph:

> There have not been wanting Insinuations to make me believe that Hamilton and Jay have insidiously intrigued to give Pinckney a Sly slide over my head. . . . I do believe that both of them had rather Pinckney should come in P. than Jefferson be either P. or V.P.—one of them might believe he should have more Influence with Pinckney than with me—Both of them might think that if I was out of the way, one or other of them might have a better chance to come in at [the] next Election into one or the other office. Both of them may have designs or desires of closer Connections with England than I should approve. But whatever cause for these surmises may exist, that shall make no Impression on my Friendship for those Characters. . . . Jay at least had probably no active share in the Business. H. certainly had.[18]

The same letter also contained a note of confidence: "I am much mistaken if I do not remove many Prejudices both at home and abroad before the fourth of March. There are many ways of correcting Errors, that all men don't perceive. These are confidential Communications."

One week into the new year, Abigail received a letter from their old friend Elbridge Gerry, in which he wrote, "the insidious plan to bring a third person into the presidential chair arose from a corrupt design of influencing his [Pinckney's] administration."[19] A month later the same writer addressed John Adams to indicate that while Hamilton was certainly the author of the scheme to bring in Pinckney as president, he believed Jay to be innocent because he was "a person of too much honor."[20]

A few days later John Adams received a long letter from Elkannah Watson, detailing not only the role of Hamilton in the election but also the evidence of the hostility of Hamilton and his friends towards Adams. Adams's grandson, Charles Francis Adams, believed it was this last letter that finally convinced the president-elect of the personal animosity of Hamilton. Yet the fact remains that only six days after John Adams's inauguration, he wrote to a friend:

> That Hamilton is displeased with Jefferson's Election may be true. That he had rather Mr. Pinckney should have been P. and the four years passed without any Vice president, [than] that Mr. Jefferson should be Vice President may be true. But my opinion is that he wished me to be P. and Mr. Pinckney V. P. If he did not I can account for it on no other supposition than this, that he wishes for Closer Connections with Britain, than he believes me disposed to[.]   This I know to be the Case with the Essex Junto.[21]

It would seem that John Adams was well aware of the scheming to "bring in" Pinckney but did not want to jeopardize his administration, at the very start, by recognizing and thus widening the schism within his own party.

Some of the Arch Federalists, as well as most of the moderate or Adams Federalists, disagreed with Hamilton and remained loyal to John Adams during this 1796 campaign. Writing to Oliver Wolcott, Sr., on December 6, Uriah Tracy, later one of the most bitter of Adams's opponents, expressed the hope that Adams would win and declared that he would rather have Adams and Jefferson than to have Pinckney defeat Adams. Less than a week later, perhaps motivated by Tracy's letter just cited, Wolcott wrote to his son, the secretary of the treasury, indicating both his strong support for John Adams and his serious doubts about Pinckney's qualifications for the office. A few of those who followed Hamilton steadfastly maintained their position was caused by fear that Jefferson would win, rather than by opposition to Adams. On March 12, for example, Theodore Sedgwick wrote to Rufus King regarding the previous election and maintained that he and his friends had worked for Pinckney as president only to defeat Jefferson.

Throughout the early winter of 1796 the electors sent in their votes. On December 8 John wrote to Abigail, "I can say nothing of [the] election. I have received to-day the votes of New Jersey but know not for whom they are, as they are under seal." In this same letter he mentioned, "I feel myself in a very happy temper of mind, perfectly willing to be released from the post of danger, but determined, if called to it, to brave it, if its horrors were ten times thicker than they are. I have but [a] few years of life left, and they cannot be better bestowed than upon that independence of my country, in defence of which, that life has ever been in jeopardy."[22]

Not till December 30 did John Adams feel sufficiently certain of victory to risk disappointing Abigail. On this next to the last day of the year he wrote of the problems and perplexities that would confront him and then added, "I think a man had better wear than rust." One paragraph of that letter is especially revealing of Adams's basic optimism and determination: "John Adams must be an intrepid to encounter the open assaults of France and the secret plots of England in concert with all his treacherous friends and open enemies in his own country. Yet I assure you he never felt more serene in his life."[23]

Finally, on February 8, 1797, the votes of the electors were opened and counted, and the results announced: John Adams, seventy-one; Thomas Jefferson, sixty-eight; Thomas Pinckney, fifty-nine.

3

★★★★★

JOHN ADAMS BEGINS
HIS ADMINISTRATION

As John Adams entered the presidency the young nation had completed eight years under the Constitution of 1787. The jubilation over freedom from England, the excitement of military and diplomatic success, and the tremendous feeling of confidence and achievement stemming from the writing of a constitution and the setting up of a new and challenging form of government had largely disappeared. George Washington, slightly tarnished by partisan animosities but still widely respected and revered, had retired to his plantation on the Potomac. Jefferson stated in 1797, "The President [Washington] is fortunate to get off just as the bubble is bursting, leaving others to hold the bag."[1]

There were few common issues or actions behind which Americans could unite. Some desired a stronger government, even as others feared the strength already established. Some looked to Britain for leadership and aid; others found hope in the revolution that had shaken France. The booming prosperity of the late 1780s and early 1790s had given way to a wave of speculation and then to economic depression. Life was a struggle. Jealousies and power plays were emerging. The violent disputes over the Jay Treaty had heightened partisan differences. The New West, those Americans who had crossed the Appalachians and settled in the river valleys beyond, was suspicious of established America and often felt no real loyalty to the national government. Even such an old hero of

22

the Revolution as George Rogers Clark was not above foreign intrigue.

The country had changed little in the last fifty years. The total population was under five million, two-thirds of whom lived within a hundred miles of the seacoast. Half the people beyond that distance lived in log cabins, the others in houses made of thin wooden planks.

Much of the land was wilderness. Roads were poor and existed only along the coast or between important villages or cities. Light stagecoaches carried up to twelve passengers, baggage, and mail three times a week from Boston to New York. Leather flaps attached to sides and roof were the only protection from rain, snow, and cold on the three-day journey. The coach left New York for Philadelphia five times a week for the two-day trip. Between New York City and Albany passengers traveled by sloop. There were no regular sailings. When a departure was advertised, individuals embarked, carrying their own bedding and supplies. Communication was slow between sections of the country, and it took weeks for a message to cross the Atlantic.

Europe was at war. With the American army consisting of less than two thousand men and the navy a single, unarmed custom boat, the new nation was helpless to protect either its citizens or its commerce. Accredited diplomats to the U.S. conspired against her, and unofficial foreign agents worked to change the political climate.

France, bitter over the Jay Treaty and America's seeming surrender to Britain, and annoyed at Washington's recall of America's pro-French minister, James Monroe, was rumored to have refused to accept General Pinckney as Monroe's successor. American merchants reported the loss of ships to French privateers. Britain continued to impress American seamen, deny the right of naturalization, and interfere with cargo ships sailing out of American harbors. It was indeed a dangerous, uncertain, and troubled time when John Adams took the oath of office as America's second president.

There were many problems and adjustments for the new president, yet eight years as vice-president had given him personal acquaintance with most of the nation's representatives who gathered in Philadelphia. His law practice in Quincy and Boston and his activities during the Revolution had familiarized him with the leaders in New England. He knew the royal courts of Paris, Saint James, and The Hague.

Perhaps equally important, Adams understood the leadership and machinations of the Federalist and Republican parties and was conscious of both their weaknesses and strengths. He knew the country, its resources, the differences between life in the city and in the country, between North and South, aristocrat and poor farmer. He had taught in a log schoolhouse on the frontier; he had had audiences with the sovereigns of three foreign countries, had lived in New York City, Philadelphia, Boston, Paris, and London, as well as in the tiny town of Quincy. He understood and had tried cases concerning the fisheries, farmers, and the rights of individuals. Now, in the first position in the land, he felt that he was the advocate and counselor for all the people; that, within the framework of the law, he must lead, communicate with, educate, guard, and protect all Americans.

Adams believed all men were subject to passions and emotions that had to be disciplined and controlled. For this reason government was essential and laws must be made and enforced to protect the rights of all individuals and to help guide each person in his growth toward mature citizenship.

Despite Adams's idealism and dedication to his country, however, he had been attacked, during the campaign for president, as a monarchist and as vain, irascible, and irresponsible. He considered any defense beneath the dignity of his office, but he was sensitive and the falsehoods hurled at him cut deeply. As a young man he kept a diary, as did Franklin, in which he attempted to list his shortcomings and record his progress in overcoming them. At twenty-one he noted in this diary, "Oh! that I could wear out of my mind every mean and base affection, conquer my natural Pride and Self Conceit, expect no more deference from my fellows than I deserve, acquire that meekness, and humility, which are the sure marks and Characters of a great and generous Soul, and subdue every unworthy Passion and treat all men as I wish to be treated by all."[2] Now at sixty-one what type of man was the new president? Like many modern psychologists he recognized the need for self-love and self-respect. He called such feelings "vanity" but accepted them as a necessary part of a healthy personality. Yet he has come down to us, through the pages of history, as a roly-poly little man whose stiff-necked pride rendered him unfit for effective public leadership and whose insufferable vanity made him vulnerable to the flattery and chicanery of unscrupulous men. Nothing was farther from the truth.

Honest and forthright, John Adams accepted his "vanity" but maintained that he kept it under control. The men to be watched and distrusted, he believed, were those who denied any vanity and pretended to absolute humility. Writing to Benjamin Rush in 1807, he said, "Vanity is really what the French call it, *amour-propre*, self-love, and it is an universal passion. All men have it in an equal degree. Honest men do not always disguise it. Knaves often do, if not always. When you see or hear a man pique himself on his modesty, you may depend upon it he is as vain a fellow as lives and very probably a great villain."[3]

Between five feet seven inches and five feet eight inches in height and overweight, Adams was nevertheless an impressive figure in courtroom, Senate, or levee. Broadshouldered and erect, he carried his weight well. Possessed of great physical and psychic energy and drive, he was intelligent, well read, and widely traveled. He was destined all his life to be in the forefront of movements and controversies where his honesty and judgment catapulted him into positions of leadership.

Driven by ambition, intellectual curiosity, a feeling of responsibility and concern for the welfare of mankind; aware of his ability, yet often filled with doubts and questions—Adams never backed away from a problem and made great demands upon himself. While he enjoyed guests and good conversation, he could clarify his values, organize his time, and isolate himself for periods of intense work. Never greedy but often impatient, frustrated by the slowness or ineptitude of others, he was capable of great compassion and understanding but also of quick retort and sudden anger. In the presidency, however, he was to be an unusually patient and, at times, amazingly tolerant man.

As emotional as he was intellectual, Adams loved his family deeply, wrote openly to Abigail of his passion and longing, respected her intelligence and advice but was not dominated by it.

At times persevering to the point of stubbornness, Adams's personality was leavened by a strong strain of optimism, a sense of humor (including the ability to laugh at himself), and the capacity to write with clarity and force. He was to need the last three to help him through his next four years in the presidency, for not all Federalists and Republicans were as devoted to representative government or as nonpartisan as Adams.

While it was expected that the Republicans, or Jeffersonians, would oppose many of Adams's ideas and suggestions, the Federalists were often as recalcitrant and as bitter toward the president. One of these frequent critics was Alexander Hamilton; others were Timothy Pickering, Uriah Tracy, Theodore Sedgwick, Robert

Goodloe Harper, George Cabot, Fisher Ames, and Oliver Wolcott, Jr.

After he resigned as secretary of the treasury in 1795, Alexander Hamilton maintained his influence in the cabinet and in the national government. His relationship with Washington was warm and close. The latter repeatedly sent to New York to ask Hamilton for advice or information. When Adams became president, Federalist leaders in Congress, such as Sedgwick, Tracy, and Harper, continued to look to Hamilton for leadership. This was also true of three members of the cabinet.

The president's cabinet had developed through use and custom. The Constitution simply provides that the president "may require the Opinion, in writing, of the principal officer in each of the executive Departments, upon any subject relating to the Duties of their respective Offices." By 1797 four such departments had been established by act of Congress: State, War, Treasury, and the Attorney General. By the end of Washington's first term the heads of these four departments had become a council of advisers to the president and the name "cabinet" was occasionally used.

It was generally accepted that these department heads should be in sympathy with the president's basic views and policies. Washington frequently turned to them for advice, addressing questions to them and expecting written responses. He sometimes sent such questions to Chief Justice Jay and to Vice-President Adams. At least once, on April 4, 1791, Washington wrote from his home to request his secretaries to meet together in the event of an emergency and to include John Adams if the latter were in Philadelphia. Such a meeting was held just a week later, with Adams present. Washington occasionally scheduled a meeting of the group, but there is no indication of any regularity or frequency of such meetings.

The understanding and support of his advisers can lighten the burden of responsibility and increase the effectiveness of any president. This, however, was not to be the case between 1797 and 1800. Few chief executives have endured as devious and disloyal maneuvers from their cabinet or as rabid and continuous personal attacks as did John Adams. Charles Lee, the attorney general, seems to have been loyal to Adams, as was Benjamin Stoddert, who joined the group with the establishment of the Navy Department. The secretary of state, Timothy Pickering; the secretary of war, James McHenry; and the secretary of the treasury, Oliver Wolcott, Jr., on the other hand, were ardent disciples of Hamilton and in differing degrees were subservient to the latter's opinions and wishes.

Adams's relationships with the cabinet were precarious from the start and his decision to retain Washington's advisers has been questioned by many historians. Why did Adams continue them in office? A year before he left the presidency, President Adams wrote to Benjamin Lincoln on March 10, 1800: "When I came into office, it was my determination to make as few removals as possible[—] not one from personal motives, not one from party considerations. This resolution I have invariably observed."[4]

In 1797 there was no precedent about the change of personnel with a change of president. John Adams believed that good government depended on the labor of a body of skilled and experienced administrators. Undoubtedly he felt that the men who had been conducting the affairs of a department knew more about its functioning than a newcomer would.

The president was also aware that Washington had had great difficulty in persuading competent men to accept appointment as head of a department. He knew the salary was low and that little prestige was attached to the positions.

Another fact dictating Adams's retention of Washington's cabinet was the precarious political situation in which he found himself on March 4, 1797. He had been chosen president by the narrowest of margins. Thomas Jefferson, leader of the political opposition, was now Adams's vice-president. Hamilton's attempt to make Pinckney president in 1796 had resulted in division and animosity among the Federalists. John Adams would have been extremely obtuse not to have sensed that an effective administration would require more, rather than less, party harmony. He must have feared that changes in the cabinet in March 1797 might split the Federalist party wide open.

Of the four "advisers" whom Adams inherited, Timothy Pickering was the most difficult to deal with. A tall, thin-faced, long-nosed, balding man, Pickering was more interested in military affairs and music than in diplomacy. Formerly secretary of war, he had accepted his present position only because Washington could find no one else. Outspoken, overbearing, loud, and often sarcastic, he antagonized others by his excessive self-confidence and righteousness. He angered easily, and would not take suggestion. A Harvard graduate, he had been admitted to the bar but disliked law and was not a successful practitioner. Opinionated and rigid, he was financially honest and a hard but unimaginative worker, often performing tasks that one of his clerks might have done. Fiercely loyal to his own concept of right and duty, he did not hesitate to betray, or deceive, when he felt the occasion demanded.

Originally friendly toward the French Revolution, by 1797 Pickering had turned against France and brought to his new-found love for Britain all the zeal of a recent convert. He was convinced that France plotted trouble and that in alliance with Britain lay the hope for national survival. He repeatedly opposed Adams, whom he disliked. He withheld information from the president and revealed government secrets to Adams's critics. Convinced of his superior judgment, he saw himself as a policy maker rather than an adviser and aide to the president.

Without great political prestige, without wealth, burdened by a family of ten children and frequent debts, he apparently attempted by his constant espousal of the Arch-Federalist position to ingratiate himself with such powerful men as Hamilton, Sedgwick, Tracy, Harper, Cabot, and King. John Adams has been criticized for believing that he could work with Pickering. Yet there is evidence that, especially during the first year and a half, Adams effected a rather satisfactory relationship with this rigid man.

President Adams seems, however, to have been quite aware of Pickering's undependability, for less than three months after his inauguration he wrote to his oldest son, "You have wisely taken all Europe for your theatre, and I hope will continue to do as you have done. Send us all the information you can collect. I wish you to continue your practice of writing freely to me, and cautiously to the office of State."[5]

John Adams's reservations were certainly warranted, for Pickering's dislike and distrust of Adams, his interest in an alliance with England, and his admiration for Hamilton were all revealed in a letter he wrote on June 9, 1798. Bewailing the president's lack of interest in an alliance with England, Pickering assured Hamilton, "I wish you were in a situation not only 'to see all the cards,' but to play them. With all my soul I would give you my *hand*, and engage in any other *game*, in which I might best cooperate on the same side, *to win the stakes*."[6]

The secretary of war, James McHenry, was born and educated in Ireland, came to America in 1771, and studied medicine. Enlisting at the outbreak of the Revolution, he saw service in the medical department of the army and later as a secretary to Washington. Washington, Hamilton, and Wolcott were all to complain of McHenry's incompetence as an administrator.

McHenry's subservience to Hamilton, his treachery to Adams, and his lack of integrity are all spelled out in a note he sent to the former on August 6, 1798. Accompanying copies of secret government papers which he had made for Hamilton, the note read in part as follows, "Do not I pray you, in writing or otherwise betray the confidence which has induced me to deal thus with you or make extracts or copies. . . . Return the papers immediately."[7]

Oliver Wolcott, Jr., of Connecticut, succeeded Alexander Hamilton as secretary of the treasury, taking office on February 1, 1795. Perhaps the most competent of Adams's original secretaries, he is now known to have been generally devoted to Hamilton. Yet he did support John Adams more frequently than either Pickering or McHenry, and on occasion acted in a very independent and sometimes honorable manner. For example, on July 16, 1799, Wolcott wrote to Trumbull refusing to join the "draft Washington, dump Adams" movement the latter had proposed. Wolcott declared, "It will be improper for me while I hold an office to exert any influence on the delicate subject to which you have hinted."[8] Yet at times Wolcott was as bitter and unscrupulous in his secret attacks on Adams as either McHenry or Pickering.

The fourth secretary inherited from Washington's cabinet was Charles Lee, the attorney general. Member of a distinguished Virginia family but usually described as a man of modest ability, Lee seems to have worked cooperatively with Adams and to have been loyal to him.

Less than twenty-four hours after he took the oath of office as president, John Adams had his first unpleasant confrontation with a cabinet member. He had discussed with Jefferson the idea of a bipartisan mission to negotiate America's differences with France. Jefferson had been receptive to the idea, though doubtful that James Madison, a Republican, would accept such an appointment. Then on March 5, perhaps by chance, Adams met Oliver Wolcott and broached the idea of such a bipartisan mission and of asking Madison to head it. Wolcott at once, presuming apparently to speak for the rest of the cabinet, expressed his disapproval of Madison for any such responsibility and offered (or threatened?) the resignation of the entire cabinet should President Adams pursue such intentions.

John Adams quickly dropped the idea. When the president met Jefferson that evening, the latter thought Adams seemed embarrassed to discuss the mission. Jefferson guessed the reason: Adams was unwilling to risk an open break with his cabinet at the very start of his administration. Adams's personal reaction to such blind partisanship and anti-French thinking as Wolcott's is shown by a letter he wrote to his wife a few days later. If "the Federalists go to playing pranks," the president wrote, "I will resign the office and let Jefferson lead them to peace, wealth and power if he will."[9] This was the first but certainly not the last time that a frustrated and momentarily disheartened John Adams would mention the possibility of resignation.

John Adams's actions during the summer and fall of 1797 tell much about both his conduct of executive business and his relationship with his cabinet. Every day the mail brought dispatches from the secretaries in Philadelphia to the farmhouse in Quincy. Adams spent long hours at his desk, reading, thinking, and responding to the reports, recommendations, and queries he received. In his frequent correspondence with the secretaries, Adams was attentive to the smallest details. In fact, an examination of his correspondence during the fall of 1797 reveals that three and four times a week the president wrote long letters to his secretary of state, usually on official State Department business. He also wrote to the other secretaries, but less often. He appears to have consistently treated his secretaries with courtesy and consideration and to have made an effort to give both praise and credit.

Even when the president and his advisers were all in the capital, Adams's consultation was usually by written query and response. Occasionally, in times of urgent decision or action, he would assemble the members of his cabinet, usually at his home.

The working relationship between a president and Congress is most important. Some presidents have been able to work cooperatively with the legislative branch, others have fought bitter political battles for supremacy. When strong differences exist between a president and Congress, or when, for a considerable period of time, the executive has been in the saddle, Congress may become stubborn and refuse to cooperate. How an executive gets along with Congress may depend upon factors beyond his control, like economic conditions, the record of his predecessor, or the prevailing political climate. Yet the success of any presidential administration must be written partly in terms of the executive's relationship with and ability to lead the Congress.

John Adams refused to attempt direct influence on the discussion or determinations of the legislative branch. At no time under either Washington or Adams was there a member of Congress recognized as the executive's spokesman (although during the first session of Congress, James Madison had often reflected Washington's opinions). As secretary of the treasury, Alexander Hamilton had exercised continuing influence in Congress, but none of Adams's secretaries commanded such a following.

The relationship between President Adams and Congress was influenced by several factors, over many of which John Adams had little or no control. He lacked George Washington's image and charisma. Many influential men in his party continued to look for leadership to Hamilton, who seemed determined that he and not the president would be the dominant figure in the administration.

From the first month of his presidency until almost the end of his term, Adams faced the threat of war, and the conduct of foreign relations demanded his continuous attention. He was determined to prevent the involvement of the United States in a war with France and he hoped to avoid alliance with Britain. He realized that most Federalists favored Britain and hated France and that the Jeffersonians feared England and were uncritical of France.

Thus in the direction of foreign affairs Adams knew he would often find himself at odds with a majority in his own party and unable to attract the support of the opposition party. Yet he believed the only way to avoid a war with France was to build a nationwide unity of purpose and a strong national defense. The Republicans, he feared, would not help with either. He must, therefore, avoid an open break with the Hamiltonians, or Arch Federalists.

Party lines were not as sharply drawn in 1797 as today. Most representatives and senators who met in special session in May 1797, however, considered themselves either Federalist or Republican, although some from both parties were stauncher in their loyalty than others. The Republicans were, in general, better organized than the Federalists. The latter were divided between the extremists or the Arch Federalists and the moderate or Adams Federalists. The Arch Federalists looked to Alexander Hamilton as their spokesman. The moderate Federalists looked to Adams and tended increasingly to distrust Hamilton.

In his inaugural address, given before the combined Senate and House on March 4, 1797, John Adams sought to tone down party differences. He spoke of his esteem for the French nation, based on his long residence in the country, and of the friendship between that country and his own. This address was well received by Republican leaders and newspapers. It appeared that John

Adams might get along smoothly with the opposition, and some Arch Federalists were alarmed at the prospect.

The adjournment of the special session of Congress, in the second week of July 1797, however, found both the president and the Arch Federalists disappointed. With a slight numerical majority, the Federalists had been unable to push through the president's program for coastal defenses, new ships for the navy, or the reorganization of the militia. Too many Federalists were cautious and a few were fearful of any attempt to stand up to France. Theodore Sedgwick complained that not a single essential measure had been passed, and William Hindman of Maryland reported that some Federalists had failed to support the party. The president must have been frustrated and disturbed at the unwillingness of Congress to act decisively.

There were additional frustrations. American commercial losses, suffered at the hands of French privateers and frigates, had accelerated the worsening economic conditions. (In the preceding year, under George Washington, over three hundred American vessels had been captured.) Business was stagnant. Land speculators were going into bankruptcy—even Robert Morris was reported to be in financial difficulty. The general public was pessimistic about the future.

The new president faced other problems beside the maligning of his character, the disloyalty of his cabinet and party members, and the unwillingness of Congress to take a stand against piracy and impressment. There was little monetary reward connected with the presidency in the last decade of the eighteenth century. Washington is said to have used $5,000 a year from the profits of his plantation. Jefferson went $20,000 in debt during his eight years in the White House. Adams's salary of $25,000 a year would meet expenses only with the most careful management.

At the start of his term of office Adams listed the rent on the house Washington had occupied as his official residence in Philadelphia, and which Adams would use, as $2,700 a year. Furthermore, Washington had bought his own furnishings and Adams would have to replace them. Prices were increasing. The President noted that good horses cost from three to five times as much as seven years before. Only Abigail's careful management and the use of meat, vegetables, and cider from the farm in Quincy helped Adams get through the four years without large debts.

There appears to have been no expense allowance for the chief executive, yet he had to have servants. John and Esther Briesler continued to serve the Adamses as they had for so many years. Polly Tailor came from Quincy to be Abigail's maid. Louisa Smith, Abigail's niece, helped manage the household; she was to continue to do this as long as John Adams lived. There was always a coachman and at least one cook. It was the latter with whom Abigail had the most difficulty; seven different women so served during the first eighteen months of Adams's vice-presidency. Abigail once complained that most cooks were either indolent or alcoholics. It has been said that she refused to engage in the common practice of hiring domestics from slave owners.

Perhaps most difficult for Adams to overcome was the absence of adequate secretarial help. Admittedly the national government was, when compared to the twentieth century, a tiny operation. There were apparently no more than two thousand civilian employees in the entire establishment in 1800; and when the offices were moved from Philadelphia to the new city of Washington that summer, it was said that the complete records of the executive branch were transported in seven packing cases. Yet, when it is remembered that the president was provided with no secretarial help, that he must personally read and answer the hundreds of addresses and letters of application for positions as well as the official reports and the communications from abroad, it is little wonder that presidents complained of the work load.

In the summer of 1798, at his own expense, John Adams employed Billy Shaw, Abigail's nephew who had lately graduated from Harvard, as his secretary. This young man continued to serve throughout the remainder of Adams's presidency. Besieged with applications for a variety of positions, often inundated with letters making one request or another, Adams personally read each letter, carefully considered the merits of applicants, and passed on to department heads those applications that seemed most meritorious. Billy Shaw could file papers, make copies of documents, write letters, and help the president in a variety of ways, but the president's work load remained staggering.

As a young man Adams was gregarious. His diary of the years before his marriage records dining, tea, or conversations with friends almost daily. Abigail enjoyed people and after their marriage they were a hospitable couple. The demands of the presidency, however, soon curtailed John's sociability.

It was Abigail who bore the brunt of social life in the capital.

Her days were full. Usually up at 5:00 A.M., she spent the next three hours in a variety of tasks and contemplations. She read her Bible and prayed; she wrote letters; she often watched the first rays of the sun finger their way over the window panes, and faced up to many of the problems of the coming day. It was she who, by means of letters written to her sister, Mary Cranch, and to her uncle, Dr. Cotton Tufts, cared for the farm and house at Quincy. A cow or horse must be sold, cider stored in the cellar for the next year's consumption, a roof must be fixed, a fence mended, some cheese purchased—there were always things that seemed to demand her attention.

At eight o'clock came breakfast. John, who might have been at his desk for an hour or two, would join her at the table; some days this was the only opportunity she had to talk with him. For the next two or three hours Abigail was the housewife: talking to servants, planning meals, making out purchase lists, ordering food. At eleven she made a careful toilet and dressed to receive company. Then came visiting, driving, or walking, and at night she frequently had a large dinner party—sometimes as many as thirty or forty guests. She entertained the entire Senate at one dinner.

Abigail held her first reception as First Lady in May 1797, with fifty or sixty guests. On the next July 4 she held a giant reception; members of Congress and the cabinet and their wives, and the foreign ministers, all attended. The Philadelphia Light Horse came in full uniform, drank their toasts, and fired salutes.

Even though dignified affairs, Martha Washington's receptions had been rather unpretentious, with simple refreshments. Abigail followed the same pattern, though it was remarked by contemporaries that she obviously loved to be with people and that her receptions often lasted later than had Mrs. Washington's. In March 1798, in a letter to her sister, Abigail described one unusual reception which seemed to please her very much:

> I had yesterday to visit me after the Presidents Levee, the Kings of 3 Indian Nations. One of them after sitting a little while rose and addrest me. He said he had been to visit his Father, and he thought his duty but in part fulfilld, untill he had visited allso his Mother, and he prayd the great spirit to keep and preserve them. They all came and shook me by the Hand, and then took some cake and wine with me. There were nine of them. One of them spoke English well. They then made their bow and withdrew, much more civil than the Beast of Vermont [referring to Matthew Lyon].[10]

34

When first in Philadelphia, during her husband's vice-presidency, Abigail had been very friendly with Martha Washington. Later she numbered among her close friends Mrs. Samuel Powel, aunt of the beautiful and wealthy Ann Bingham, and Mrs. John Allen, mother of lovely daughters known as "the three Graces."

In May and June of 1800, perhaps because the capital would soon move to the new city on the Potomac, greater numbers of people began attending Abigail's receptions. She was overwhelmed with social invitations and many ladies came to call.

It would seem that Abigail was especially drawn to the wife of Benjamin Stoddert, secretary of the navy. Mrs. Stoddert's letters are revealing in regard to the Adams family and social life in Philadelphia. In January 1800 a Stoddert daughter drew this charming picture of Abigail: "I must not omit to add, that though Mama has not been as yet to wait on Mrs. Adams, that good and handsome old lady [Abigail was then fifty-five years of age] called to see her this afternoon, with her daughter, Mrs. Smith, and brought more plum cake for the children than all of them could eat. You may be sure that after this she is a great favorite of the whole family."[11]

4

★★★★★

FACE TO FACE WITH DANGER

The closing months of Washington's second administration had been marked by internal division, extreme bitterness over the Jay Treaty, fear of France, and dissatisfaction with the new government. The glamor of independence was wearing thin. As president, Adams would have enjoyed promoting many of his interests: the improvement of agriculture, the development of the arts, the promotion of education. Interested in financial reform, he wished a limitation placed on the use of paper money. He distrusted some features of Hamilton's bank. Yet, even before his inauguration, he knew that the crisis in foreign affairs would demand his immediate attention. Few of our nation's chief executives have been subjected to such immediate and continuous threat of foreign war and national destruction, or to such constant need for decision making, as was John Adams.

In the 1790s France and Great Britain were engaged in bitter warfare, and both desired trade with and the economic assistance of the United States. War news from Europe frequently brought panic to the wharves of American seaports. England captured American ships and impressed American sailors. In one single twenty-four hour period marine insurance bounced up 10 percent. England neglected to honor her obligations under the Treaty of Paris of 1783; and this, coupled with impressment, had resulted in a real "war crisis" in 1794. President Washington had sent John Jay to London on a special peace mission. While the treaty he brought back was disappointing in many ways, it did forestall immediate war with England and it was accepted by Washington, albeit with some reluctance.

The French Directory considered the Jay Treaty to be a concession to Great Britain and unfriendly to France. John Adams was aware of the growing friction and misunderstanding between his country and its former ally. While vice-president he had distrusted the interest of both France and Spain in the affairs of the New World. He knew that James Monroe, while serving as minister to France, had been considered pro-French and had been well liked in that country. He had heard rumors that the French were incensed when Washington replaced Monroe with General Charles C. Pinckney of South Carolina.

Adams was disturbed by the "idolatrous worship" of France and the French Revolution by many of his countrymen and by the lack of understanding of the European situation that he saw all about him. "There is a curious Mass of Matter in ferment at this Time," he wrote Abigail on January 18, 1797. "The people of America must awake out of their golden dreams, consider where they are, and what they are about."[1] In a letter to Samuel Griffin, Adams expressed concern "that our citizens have been so little informed of the true temper and character of French policy toward this country." He expressed alarm that "For twenty years many important facts have been concealed from" the people, "lest they should conceive prejudices or entertain doubts of . . . [France's] disinterested friendship and the whole character of their government since the revolution has been tinged with false colours in the eyes of our people by French emissaries and disaffected Americans."[2]

Nine days after his inauguration, President Adams received a courtesy call from Pierre Adet. Having terminated his ministry to the United States, the French diplomat was about to return to his own country. France had the largest army in the western world. Her fleet, though not equal to Britain's, was powerful; her political leaders were skillful, ambitious, and often without scruple. The United States was a new nation, lacking wealth, without an army worthy of the name, and with the barest nucleus of a fleet. In the midst of perplexing internal problems, including the growing threat of civil conflict, her people were divided on political matters and there was no general agreement on foreign policy. Adams, face to face with Adet, recognized the delicate situation.

It must have been an interesting confrontation: the polished French diplomat and the stocky Yankee lawyer. Adams knew that

French agents were in the Mississippi Valley and that Adet had meddled in the recent presidential election, had tried by his machinations to secure the election of Adams's opponent, Thomas Jefferson. At the end of the preceding November, when the results of the election were still in doubt, John had written to Abigail, "At Hartford I Saw Mr. Adet's Note in Folio to our Secretary of State, and I find it an instrument well calculated to reconcile me to private life. . . . Although . . . I think the moment a dangerous one, I am not Scared. . . . I dread not a war, with France or England, if either forces it upon US, but [I] will make no Aggression upon either, with my free Will, without just & necessary Cause and Provocation."[3]

Adams had learned the demands of international protocol and courtesy in the courts of England and France, was extremely conscious of the dignity of his new office, and felt that he must handle the meeting with Adet tactfully. The president assured the retiring French diplomat that he desired peace with France, and Adet seems to have been convinced that Adams was sincere. Despite the underlying personal hostility, the meeting was conducted on a calm and courteous note.

John Adams was aware of his country's weaknesses. Presiding over the Senate during the previous session of Congress, he saw the Jeffersonians consistently chip away at the nation's defenses. Usually in the name of economy, and frequently under the skillful leadership of Albert Gallatin, they maintained that there was no need to spend additional money for arms, ships, and men; France, they insisted, posed no threat to the United States. They tried to prevent the completion of three frigates, already on the ways, and they attempted to reduce the four regiments (sixteen hundred men) of the standing army to three. In both cases their efforts were barely defeated.

While America's relations with France during these years were precarious, so were her dealings with Britain. If the United States were to remain truly independent and neutral, she must refrain from accepting a partnership with either country. Among the political leaders of both parties, only John Adams seems to have understood both the necessity and the demands of neutrality. He believed that he must lead the nation in the development of a policy of neutrality, that the people must understand and support such a policy and that this support must be broader than partisan lines. His position was reflected in his overtures to Jefferson and the mildness of his inaugural address, which was warmly received by the Republicans.

In the absence of any official news from Europe, therefore, the rumors that Pinckney would not be accepted as America's diplomatic representative to France were disturbing. Newspapers began discussing the need for a special mission to France.

The word that Pinckney had, indeed, been rejected by France, that he had been insulted and ordered to leave France, was probably received by President Adams on the evening of March 13, or very early the next forenoon. At the same time, news was received of the seizure of American merchantmen in the West Indies by French frigates. If Adams had received this information prior to the evening of the thirteenth, it seems unlikely that his interview with Adet would have been "calm and courteous."

Following Washington's policy of addressing written questions to his cabinet and asking for their written responses, Adams on the fourteenth sent numerous questions to his advisers. Dealing with the French crisis, these questions indicated that the president was wrestling with an urgent and serious situation and almost certainly meant he had received word of Pinckney's rejection by France.

Adams had several alternatives open to him. He could summon Congress and call for an immediate declaration of war. He could ask Congress to authorize the arming of American merchantmen and, thus protected, attempt to carry on commercial and maritime business as usual. He could impose economic sanctions and stop all trade with France, or even with both France and Britain. He could seek an alliance with Britain and thus use the British navy as a shield for American commerce. He could send another mission to France in the hope that it might arrange a temporary accommodation that would postpone the need for any of the above actions. He favored this last solution, but he asked his secretaries for their evaluation of the situation. Should the United States send a mission to France to attempt a resolution of the difficulties? Would such an attempt be "too great an humiliation of the American people in their own sense and that of the world?" Other questions dealt with such related matters as the strengthening of coastal defenses, the building of new frigates, and the sending forth of privateers.[4] For the next three and a half years John Adams was to be head of a nation at war in everything but name.

On March 25, climaxing several days of feverish activity, the president summoned Congress to meet in special session on May 15. Republicans at once exploded in opposition. The president, they declared, was leading the country into war against France. Why else, but for a declaration of war, would he summon Congress?

Before the Congress assembled in mid-May, John Adams faced several tasks. He must concentrate on the protection of his nation's commerce. Farmer though he was, he was also a son of maritime Massachusetts and the tides washed within sight and sound of his own acres. He knew commerce was essential to the economic health of his country, and the loss of American shipping to French frigates and privateers in the West Indies disturbed him deeply.

Adams was aware of the bitter gulf between the thinking of Federalist and Republican. Even more alarming to the president was the lack of agreement within his own party. A strong nation, John Adams firmly believed, must be built on common goals and values, a broad consensus rather than deep cleavages. His first task, then, was to unite the people behind a vigorous program of defense so that the United State would not tremble when either France or Britain roared.

The president made his own personal attitude toward European involvement clear in a letter to Henry Knox, written on March 30. Knox had evidently suggested a new mission to France, and John Adams indicated he was already at work on such a project. The very next day Adams wrote to his eldest son: "My entrance into office is marked by a misunderstanding with France, which I shall endeavor to reconcile, provided that no violation of faith, no stain upon honor, is exacted. But if infidelity, dishonor, or too much humiliation is demanded, France shall do as she pleases, and take her own course. America is not SCARED."[5]

At the beginning of his administration it appeared that John Adams would enjoy warm and friendly relations with his old friend the vice-president. In late February 1797, when Thomas Jefferson arrived in Philadelphia, he at once went to call on John Adams. The president returned the call within twenty-four hours. A few days later, shortly after the inauguration, they both dined with George Washington. After dinner they walked together for several blocks as they headed for their respective quarters. Their views on the foreign situation, on the need for peace and the desirability of a new mission to France, seemed in accord. Arch Federalists were alarmed lest the new president be "captured" by the Republicans; the latter were delighted at the prospect of a harmonious administration.

For a brief period after his inauguration John Adams may have hoped for a ready solution to the varied problems facing the new nation. John Quincy Adams, in his frequent letters from Europe, firmly maintained that while France wanted to dominate America she did not want war and that a united front on the part of his father's administration might cause the French to relax their pressure. Better relations with Britain seemed possible in the spring of 1797. The president's inaugural address had been well received by both political parties; Henry Knox had written that "the part relative to France" had pleased most Americans.[6] The Republican *Aurora*, so soon to take the lead in damning John Adams and demanding his resignation, praised his leadership.

Yet realistic John Adams must have seen the many ominous clouds on the horizon. He had been a witness to the scorching calumny that Jeffersonian editors directed at Washington; and he knew that if any of his future actions irritated the opposition, he would surely be treated less leniently.

Adams did not trust the French Directorate and he had little confidence in the French Revolution. Nor did he place great reliance on the friendship of Britain. Already he questioned the motives of some of his cabinet and the diplomatic understanding and judgment of his secretary of state. In this respect, however, Adams had one great advantage over a modern-day holder of the presidency. The State Department was small, the flow of information was relatively slight, and an energetic and concerned president could read the reports, see the memoranda, talk with the personnel involved. He could, in short, keep his finger on the pulse of foreign affairs and know all that went on. In the first weeks of Adams's presidency he also reaped the advantage that accrued from Hamilton's basic agreement with the president's policies, for at this time both advocated another mission to try to find an accommodation with France.

In early April, William Vans Murray, staunch Maryland Federalist, supporter of John Adams, and close friend of John Quincy Adams, was about to leave for his new diplomatic post at The Hague. Not willing to leave to Secretary of State Pickering the entire matter of instruction, the president invited Murray and his wife to dine with him. Over a leisurely meal Adams talked of his own experiences in Holland, nearly two decades earlier. He warned the young man to be short and sincere in dealing with the Dutch. Murray was to be careful when discussing foreign policy. He must make it clear that the United States desired peace, that his country would be willing to continue negotiations in Paris, and he must never,

41

under any provocation, become involved in any hot-tempered remarks about Adet's role in the previous election.

As requested by the president, Congress met in special session on May 15. The following day the president delivered a carefully prepared message. He reported the French rejection of Pinckney and contrasted this with the tribute the French had paid to Monroe, whom Washington had relieved of his post. Such contrast, the president asserted, "evinces a disposition to separate the people of the United States from the Government . . . and thus to produce divisions fatal to our peace. Such attempts," John Adams continued, "ought to be repelled with a decision which shall convince France and the world that we are not a degraded people, humiliated under a colonial spirit of fear and a sense of inferiority, fitted to be the miserable instruments of foreign influence, and regardless of national honor, character, and interest."[7] At the end of the month, when George Washington read Adams's message, he asserted that the new president "had spoken well."

This approach of the president, however, was especially disturbing to the Jeffersonians, who seemed unable to accept any criticism of France. So also was Adams's recommendation for the defense of the seacoast, the protection of commerce, the strengthening of the navy, and the reorganization of the militia. Indeed, May 16, 1797, marked the end of the honeymoon between John Adams and the Jeffersonians. Two days later the *Aurora*, leading Republican journal, attacked President Adams in a most savage manner, branding his speech a "war whoop," accusing him of base deceit, of being pro-British all along, and of desiring war against France. Some Jeffersonian newspapers went so far as to demand Adams's resignation.

Throughout the special session of Congress, the Republicans consistently opposed all defense measures. This was but a continuation of their attitude and policy as evinced in the preceding session, which had met in December 1796. Thus over a trying period of more than half a year the Republican party illustrated its almost total acceptance of French action and refused to recognize the French threat to the United States and its commerce.

While Jeffersonians resented the strong words directed at France by the president and misunderstood his motives, most Federalists, especially the Arch Federalists, approved. Six days after the address was delivered George Cabot wrote to Pickering, "We are all charmed with the speech of the President, and I am persuaded this part of the country will support the policy he indicates."

On the last day of the month Cabot wrote to Wolcott, "If it were doubtful whether the government could give a tone to the nation, I think the effect of the President's speech is a proof of its truth. *All* the Federalists, and *many others,* approve highly the style he has used, and swear to support him."[8]

For three months John Adams considered various courses of action. Henry Knox and Elbridge Gerry were two of the many who had written to advise that Jefferson be sent to negotiate with France. To Gerry, on April 6, Adams wrote that many had proposed this, that he had talked with Jefferson about such a mission as early as March 3, and that Jefferson had declined. Adams would not ask him again, for he felt the vice-president had been quite right to decline. After all, the president indicated, King George of England did not send the Prince of Wales on diplomatic missions.

On May 31 the president sent the names of Charles Coatesworth Pinckney, who had remained in Holland and awaited further instructions, Francis Dana of Massachusetts, and John Marshall of Virginia to the Senate. These nominees were to serve as "envoys extraordinary and ministers plenipotentiary to the French Republic." They were to "dissipate umbrages," "remove prejudices," "rectify errors," and "adjust all differences by a treaty between the two powers."[9] The nominees were confirmed two days later.

This commission represented a compromise on the part of John Adams. Since early March he had been thinking in terms of a bipartisan membership. His early dream of nominating Jefferson or, later, Madison from the political opposition had not been realized. Later he had proposed his old Massachusetts friend Elbridge Gerry, who had refused to sign the Constitution in 1787, yet had often voted as a Federalist in Congress and, as a presidential elector in 1796, had cast his vote for John Adams. He and Adams had been friends for many years and the president trusted him. Yet he was known as an admirer of Jefferson, and when Adams suggested his name Pickering and other Arch Federalists had recoiled in horror. Adams had yielded to their protests and had named Dana instead.

Dana, chief justice of the Massachusetts Supreme Court and a former protégé of John Adams, declined to serve because of ill health. Without consulting his cabinet, several of whom he knew were strongly opposed, John Adams then submitted to the Senate the name of Elbridge Gerry to join Pinckney and Marshall. This appointment shocked and alarmed the Arch Federalists.

Gerry was more volatile and perhaps less cautious than Dana.

Yet even with this substitution, the commission was an unusually able group. It represented a diverse spectrum of political views and an equally wide geographical range. Adams was well aware of the difficulties and dangers that might confront his mission, and he took all possible precautions to guarantee its success. For example, on July 8 he wrote to Gerry, "It is my sincere desire that an accommodation may take place; but our national faith, and the honor of our government, cannot be sacrificed. You have known enough of the unpleasant effects of disunion among ministers to convince you of the necessity of avoiding it, like a rock or quicksand. . . . It is probable there will be manoeuvres practised to excite jealousies among you, both by Americans, English, Dutch, and French; this should not produce too much irritation, but should press you closer together."[10]

In June 1797 Thomas Jefferson wrote to Peregrine Fitzhugh, a Republican leader in Maryland, charging that there had been no justification for calling Congress into special session and that the president was inclined to war rather than peace. General Uriah Forrest, a staunch Federalist, secured a summary of Jefferson's letter to Fitzhugh and forwarded it to Adams. In one of his own personal letters Adams hit back at his vice-president with the oft-quoted remark that Jefferson's letter was "evidence of a mind, soured, yet seeking for popularity."[11]

At the end of June 1797, while Congress was still locked in bitter debate over the question of our relations with France, James Monroe arrived in Philadelphia. The discredited diplomat, discharged from his responsibilities in Paris by President Washington the previous winter, was warmly welcomed by the Republicans. A huge banquet at Oeller's Hotel on Chestnut Street, almost within hearing distance of Congress, was arranged as a tribute and a "welcome home." Vice-President Jefferson and Pennsylvania's Governor Thomas McKean, as well as half a hundred members of Congress, toasted Monroe's services. No better example of the deep cleavage between Federalist and Republican could be found.

On July 13, 1797, President Adams commissioned Pinckney, Marshall, and Gerry and gave them their instructions. These were conciliatory in tone. On July 20, after a private dinner with John Adams, Marshall sailed from Philadelphia. Three days later Gerry left Boston. They would join General Pinckney in Holland and proceed to Paris. The president and his countrymen settled back for the long wait before news of the commission's reception and accomplishments could be learned.

In early July, by a vote of sixteen to thirteen, the Senate added twelve new frigates to the tiny navy. In another close struggle, this time by a margin of seven votes, the House of Representatives voted for stronger coastal fortifications. A bill to establish an army of fifteen thousand men, however, was defeated. The president wanted all merchant vessels to be armed, but Congress authorized this for only the East Indies and Mediterranean trade—not in the West Indies where conflict with the French would be most probable. The president was puzzled by this action, and Abigail in private correspondence referred to the "timidity" of Congress.

On July 19 the president and his wife left Philadelphia for Quincy. The summer months of 1797 marked the depth of John Adams's uncertainty about the French reaction to his attempt to maintain peace. He had been sure that another mission to France, another effort to remove misunderstandings and resolve differences, was the best course, perhaps the only course. Yet on July 17 he wrote to Gerry in regard to French policy, "I sincerely wish peace and friendship with the French; but, while they countenance none but enemies of our Constitution and administration, and vilify every friend of either, self-defence, as well as fidelity to the public, will compel me to have a care what appointments I make."[12]

For several weeks the president had been fearful lest France defeat the British. At the beginning of July he had written a friend that "the situation of the United States is uncommonly Critical. If a peace is made between France and England as it is already known to be made with the Roman Emperor, and France is not in a better temper, or Conducted by different Governors, this Country has before it one of the most alarming prospects it ever beheld."[13]

John Quincy Adams continued to send information regarding the European situation to his father, much of it rather pessimistic in nature. From London, on September 21, 1797, he wrote of the changes in the attitude of the French government toward the United States as a result of the coup d'état of September 4: "Everything that envy and malice, both against our country and against you personally, can suggest, they will attempt. I speak it now without hesitation, because I am convinced that all the preparation possible to meet such conduct on their part *must be made.*"[14]

The internal political situation in France also troubled Timothy Pickering, the secretary of state. He was concerned lest France and Britain make peace, and for a few months in the summer and fall of 1797 Pickering was inclined toward peace with France. This was not because of any friendship for France or admiration for the

French Revolution, but simply because he was fearful that the United States might be left to oppose France alone.

It is easy to emphasize the differences already existing between the president and his secretary of state. Whether personal, as in their attitude toward Gerry, or political, as in their feeling about Britain and France, these differences were significant. They would become increasingly troublesome as time went on.

Meanwhile John Adams, shrewdly assessing both the information available to Pickering and the personal messages he was receiving from his son in Berlin and from Murray at The Hague, concluded that France did not really want war with the United States but merely wanted to make the young republic subservient to French policy and interest.

Adams sensed that there was a division of opinion in the French Directory and that a majority of the French legislative branch were friendly to the United States. He correctly surmised that the Directory might turn to the army for support, and he realistically appraised the chances for the success of his mission in terms of the outcome of the struggle for power within France. That country would, John Adams concluded, benefit more from simulating anger and despoiling American commerce than from actual war.

By fall, John Adams's basic policy was established. Just as his goal was peace, so his policy was to build a strong defense, attempt to unify the popular will, and remain neutral. Although opposed by many in his own party as well as by the Jeffersonians, and despite his strong prejudice against the violence of the French Revolution, the president clung tenaciously to his plan to avoid war with that country. For the next three years, however, he strove to strengthen his nation's defenses lest his appraisal of the European situation prove incorrect and war become inevitable.

5

★★★★★

THE COUNTRY RALLIES
BEHIND ADAMS

Throughout the fall and early winter of 1797 there was no word from the three envoys Adams had dispatched to France. Americans knew only that Marshall and Gerry had arrived in Holland, probably in late September, and that they had met Charles Coatesworth Pinckney and proceeded to Paris in early October. In a personal letter, John Adams expressed considerable pessimism about the outcome of the mission to France. He suggested that the French would drag their heels while continuing to prey on American commerce. Possibly the way to bring them to a settlement, the president wrote, was to arm all American merchantmen and embargo all trade with France.

Thomas Jefferson, however, felt much relieved. Believing the administration had heard from the envoys, he decided that negotiations were going well and that peace with France would soon result. He was sure the president and his secretaries were suppressing the good news so the expectation of an approaching peace would not end the "war scare." Jefferson believed that France would soon invade and conquer Britain and establish world peace.

In the first days of the New Year (1798) the president learned that Austria had succumbed to Napoleon's forces and England stood alone against the French. John Adams realized negotiations with the Directory would now be even more difficult. But while Federalists worried, the Republicans rejoiced at news of French victories. The rift between the two parties deepened.

On January 20, 1798, Abigail wrote to her sister, Mary Cranch, concerning the European situation. "We have Letters from Mr. Murry [William Vans Murray, U.S. Minister to Holland]. A few lines from Mr. Marshall to him informs him: that the envoys were not received, and he did not believe they would be. They dare not write, knowing that every word would be inspected. They have not been permitted to hold any society or converse with any citizen. In short they have been in a mere Bastile. We are in daily expectation of their return."[1] Four days later, probably because of the communication from Murray with its relayed message from Marshall, John Adams submitted a list of questions to his cabinet: What should be done if the envoys were refused an audience? Should he recommend war or an embargo? Should the United States ally herself with England? (As usual, John Adams gave the secretaries a wide range of possibilities with no hint of what he himself believed.) None of the cabinet recommended an alliance with England, and only Attorney General Lee wanted a declaration of war.

The newspaper war continued. On February 16 the Boston *Chronicle* contained an article written by "Plain Truth" which claimed that John Adams had received dispatches from France "*a month ago*" and had been withholding them from the public. This was strongly denied in the *Columbian Centinel* the next day. Marshall's note to Murray was certainly not an official dispatch, but there had been "word" from the envoys, unofficial as it was. Were the Jeffersonians shooting in the dark? Or had someone leaked the information? Adams did not know.

Late in the evening of March 4, 1798, exactly a year after John Adams assumed the presidency, a bundle of mail from the envoys arrived at the office of Secretary of State Pickering. The secretary scanned the contents quickly and hurried with them to the president. One can imagine the hushed tension as the letters were opened. There were several long reports and messages, most of them in code and the most recent one dated January 8. It would take time to decode the longer messages, but it was quickly learned that the envoys had proceeded to Paris, arriving there on October 4. Four days later they met briefly with Tallyrand, who had refused to consider serious business at that time. Soon after, the envoys had been approached by secret agents, who had demanded a loan, a bribe, and an apology from President Adams for his remarks to Congress concerning France. Not until all of these demands were met would the American envoys be allowed to conduct negotiations with the French government.

The very next morning the president sent a message to both houses of Congress. "The first despatches from our envoys extraordinary since their arrival at Paris," he reported, "were received at the Secretary of State's office at a late hour last evening. They are all in a character which will require some days to be deciphered, except the last, which is dated the 8th of January, 1798. The contents of this letter are of so much importance to be immediately made known to Congress and to the public, especially to the mercantile part of our fellow-citizens, that I have thought it my duty to communicate them to both Houses without loss of time."[2] This letter of January 8, which Adams sent to Congress, declared the situation hopeless and the mission impossible. John Adams asked Congress to pass, at once, measures for the protection of American commerce.

Federalists were soon roaring for war with a new-found vigor. On the ninth of March, Robert Goodloe Harper wrote to his South Carolina constituents urging them to "rouse once more the spirit of '75," and three weeks later Jonathan Mason, Jr., suggested to Harrison Gray Otis, "We must reconcile our minds to a few moments of Warfare. It will not hurt us."[3]

As the documents were decoded and the whole sorry story of French intrigue and insult became clear, President Adams was both angry and alarmed. A release of the documents, disclosing all the details, might incense his countrymen and make war inevitable. The president still wished to avoid war if it could be done. Furthermore, John Adams did not know the whereabouts of Pinckney, Gerry, and Marshall. A violent American outcry, before our envoys were safely out of France, might even endanger their lives.

On March 13 the president again turned to his cabinet for advice. Should he "present immediately to Congress the whole of the communications . . . with the exception of the names of the persons employed by the minister Talleyrand . . . under an injunction of secrecy," the president queried. "Ought the President, then, to recommend, in his message, an immediate declaration of war?"[4]

Did John Adams, in March of 1798, want war with France? Or did he feel war was inevitable? These are key questions in any attempt to understand the significance and meaning of this period. Some historians have believed that John Adams wanted peace and feared war, that he thought war with France would of necessity throw his country into an alliance with Britain—and John Adams feared Britain and her power almost as much as he resented French arrogance. Others have believed that the report from the commissioners aroused John Adams's anger and that he saw no alternative to war. A few have suggested that he both expected and desired war.

In mid-March 1798 John Adams was angry and concerned about the French insult to American envoys. For a few days he was indecisive. But on March 19, exactly two weeks after his notification to Congress of the receipt of the messages, the president took positive action. In his message to Congress on that day, Adams did not reveal the exact contents of the dispatches received from the envoys, but he asserted that after the documents had been "examined and maturely considered," he felt it necessary to "declare that I perceive no ground of expectation that the objects of their mission can be accomplished on terms compatible with the safety, the honor, or the essential interests of the nation." The president called again for measures of defense and this time asserted that Congress must authorize the arming of merchant vessels. As evidence of the aggressive manner in which John Adams took charge of the situation, he announced that he had revoked his former order to port collectors to prohibit the sailing of armed merchant vessels.[5]

The Republicans at once attacked. Newspapers called the president's message a declaration of war; Thomas Jefferson termed it "insane." Madison denounced the message, claiming that history showed the executive to be the branch of government most interested in war and that Adams was trying to trick the nation into war with France. The following day Abigail commented on the issues in a long letter to her sister,

> It is a very painfull thing to him [the president] that he cannot communicate to the publick dispatches in which they are so much interested, but we have not any assurance that the Envoys have left Paris and who can say that in this critical state of things their dispatches ought to be publick? . . . I expect the President will be represented as declaring War, by taking off the restriction which prevented Merchantmen from Arming. It was always doubtfull in his mind, whether he had a Right to prevent them, but the former President had issued such a prohibition, and he thought it best at that time to continue it.[6]

On March 23 the president sent new instructions to the three envoys. Unless they had been officially received and were engaged in serious negotiations, they were to return home at once. Before these instructions were received, Pinckney and Marshall had left Paris—the former to seek a warmer climate and the latter to return home to report to the president and Congress. Elbridge Gerry yielded to the pleas of Talleyrand and remained in Paris. Today it is easy to understand that Talleyrand begged him to stay because he did not wish war with the United States; to many Americans in 1798 it seemed that he wished Gerry to remain because he hoped to divide the Americans and influence the "Jacobin" faction in this country to yield to French demands.

As seems natural in view of the element of secretiveness about the dispatches and the high degree of partisan tension that existed, it was but a short time before Republicans in Congress, and in the newspaper press, began demanding to see all of the dispatches that had been received. A few moderate Federalists joined the Republicans in these demands. On March 14 and again on April 3 the *Aurora* blasted John Adams for his failure to submit all the papers and reports to Congress. On March 27 Carey's *United States Recorder*, a Philadelphia newspaper, labeled the entire affair a dishonest trick aimed at helping the Federalists win the April elections. The same day the Republicans in Congress held a caucus and prepared three resolutions designed to embarrass the Federalists and prevent measures for an effective defense. The first resolution opposed the idea of a war against France, the second attacked the legality of arming merchantmen, and the third was obliquely aimed against Great Britain. Inability to pass such resolutions did not prevent Gallatin and his associates from continuing their efforts.

On Friday, March 30, Representative William B. Giles, a Jeffersonian from Virginia, introduced a resolution calling on John Adams to send to the House of Representatives all dispatches received from the envoys, and on Monday, April 2, by an overwhelming vote of sixty-five to twenty-seven, the House voted to demand both the reports and the original instructions. The Arch Federalists, knowing the publication of all the documents would arouse national indignation and be damaging to the pro-French Republicans, were delighted. Too late, Giles and the usually careful Albert Gallatin realized the trap into which the Republicans had fallen.

Meanwhile the president had come to the conclusion that the envoys were out of France and that, in order to get the support of Congress for the defense measures he felt essential to the nation's safety, he must release the complete dispatches. On the day after the House demanded the papers, therefore, John Adams sent all the messages and the original instructions given to the envoys to both

51

the House and the Senate, withholding none but substituting the names X, Y, and Z for the names of the French intermediaries. The president requested "That they may be considered in confidence until the members of Congress are fully possessed of their contents and shall have had opportunity to deliberate on the consequences of their publication . . . ."[7] In the House of Representatives the galleries were cleared, all doors secured, and guards posted outside, and in a tense, hushed silence, the documents were read, one by one.

Perhaps no contemporary description of the confusion and dismay these documents caused in the Jeffersonian ranks is equal to the brief comment Abigail sent to her sister the very next day: "The Jacobins in Senate & House were struck dumb, and opend not their mouths . . . ."[8] The dispatches revealed the insulting French demands. Federalists were enraged; Jeffersonians were astounded and confused; independents and fence sitters hurried into the Federalist camp. Three days after receiving the documents the Senate voted to release them to the newspapers.

The next months were to mark the height of Federalist popularity. Newspapers soon reprinted portions of the documents that the president had released. The tale of French duplicity and intrigue, the insults to the American commissioners and to the nation, spread from state to state and city to city. Almost overnight the temper of the nation changed. Some Republican representatives left Congress and returned to their homes; some members of Congress who had been undecided as to their political loyalty now joined the Federalists; the general public endorsed President Adams and drank toasts to Pinckney and Marshall—there were already rumors that Gerry had been less firm than his colleagues.

For the time being, even the Arch Federalists were full of praise for the president. While Republicans cowered or changed sides, Federalists rushed forth to condemn France and defend their administration. Dozens of letters addressed to Rufus King, the American minister to England, during the spring and early summer of 1798 attest to the enthusiastic endorsement of the president by those who would soon be crying for his scalp. Early in April, Theodore Sedgwick wrote:

> The President, under circumstances the most trying, and discouraging, has acted, *from* the time of his inauguration speech, a noble part. No instances of impatience, no whining croaking complaints, regardless of the infamous attacks that have been made on his character, he has exhibited a manly fortitude & dignified composure. His

conduct has, indeed, increased the confidence of the friends of the government, and I am very much mistaken if it has not commanded the respect of his adversaries.[9]

Newspapers, political orators, clergymen, even housewives and artisans, were quoting Pinckney's "No! No! Not a sixpence!" though usually in the more colorful form of "Millions for defense, but not one cent for tribute." Resolutions of support literally poured in on the president and the Congress.

On April 8 Samuel Sewall introduced into the House the defense measures that John Adams was officially proposing. These measures called for improved harbor and coastal defenses, an expanded navy, the arming of all merchantmen, and the establishment of a provisional army. National sentiment seemed ready for such measures.

Alexander Hamilton had anticipated the possible failure of the mission to France. As early as January he had been at work on a series of proposals for national defense. In March and April he set forth his program in a series of essays signed "Titus Manlius." In these widely published exhortations he enunciated the need for a strong nation and set forth a program the cornerstone of which was a greatly expanded national army. He suggested that the need for a large army was so obvious that only traitors would oppose its establishment. On March 17, two days before President Adams's second and still general announcement of the XYZ affair, Hamilton wrote to Pickering, enlarging upon his previous proposals and suggesting eight actions that he felt Congress should take at once. These were: authorize the arming of merchant ships, rush the completion of the frigates then building, authorize the president to build ten more ships of the line in the event of war, provide for an army of 20,000 plus a provisional army of 30,000, fortify all major seaports, provide new taxes, license privateers, and suspend all treaties with France. These proposals went much further than the president's request to Congress, and it was soon apparent that the Arch Federalists would not be satisfied with the milder requests of John Adams.

Readers of the April 12 issue of the *New York Gazette* were told that "To be lukewarm after reading the horrid scenes [revealed in the XYZ papers] is to be criminal—and the man who does not warmly reprobate the conduct of the French must have a soul black enough to be *fit* for *treasons strategems* and *spoils*."[10] Even in rural sections that had been strongly pro-Jeffersonian, anti-French sentiment grew rapidly. Western Pennsylvania farmers hurried to de-

nounce the French, and in New Hampshire the young chaplain of
the state legislature was dismissed for praying for the success of the
French arms against England.

On April 14 Secretary of State Pickering wrote to George
Washington. Commenting on the consternation in Jeffersonian
ranks, he noted the disappearance of their obstructionism in Congress. Henrietta Liston, wife of the British minister to the United
States, wrote to her uncle on May 3:

> The President went to the Play last night for the first
> time. He is a Presbiterian and goes seldomer into publick
> than Washington did—Mr. Liston's Box was oposite to
> him . . . . Nothing could equal the noise and uproar, the
> President's March was played, & called for over & over
> again, it was sung & danced to, some poor Fellen [fellow?]
> in the Gallery calling for sa ira [*Ca ira*, one of the march-
> ing songs of the French Revolution] was threatened to
> be thrown over . . . . at this moment the British are extolled
> as the first People, (next to themselves I mean) for having
> so long resisted the Tyrants of France, an alien bill is to be
> brought into the Senate immediately, a secretary of the
> Navy is appointed, Frigates are fitting out . . . & every
> Man speaking with a degree of violence at which I often
> stare with astonishment.[11]

In his definitive study of the newspapers of this period, Donald
Stewart noted evidence of the changing sentiment; the *South Carolina Gazette*, for one instance, began to attack the French Directory
and to support the administration. At the end of April, Jefferson
feared that Bache's *Aurora*, the largest and strongest of the anti-
Federalist papers, would be forced into bankruptcy as both sub-
scriptions and advertising were falling off dangerously.

New popular songs such as "Adams and Liberty" and "Hail
Columbia" were being sung throughout the nation. Up in Boston,
Fisher Ames noted, "The Jacobins were confounded, and the
trimmers dropt off from the party like windfalls from an apple tree
in September, the worst of the fruit—vapid in cider and soon
vinegar."[12] Support for the president and his policies was widespread. In Philadelphia, Abigail wrote to her sister:

> The Young Men of the city . . . to the amount of near
> Eleven Hundred came at 12 oclock in procession two and
> two. There were assembled upon the occasion it is said
> ten thousand Persons. This street as wide or wider than
> State Street in Boston, was full as far as we could see up &

down. One might have walkd upon their Heads, besides the houses window & even tops of Houses. In great order & decorum the Young Men with each a black cockade marchd through the Multitude and all of them enterd the House preceeded by their committee. When a Young Gentleman by the Name of Hare, a Nephew of Mrs. Binghams, read the address, the President received them in his Levee Room drest in his uniform, and as usual upon such occasions, read his answer to them, after which they all retired. The Multitude gave three Cheers, & followd them to the State House Yard, where the answer to the address was again read by the Chairman of the committe, with acclamations.[13]

In May 1798, largely as a result of John Adams's predilection for "wooden walls" as a means of national defense, a Navy Department was created. Benjamin Stoddert of Maryland became the first secretary of the navy. He began work a month later, and before the end of June, Congress had passed an act to strengthen the navy. Efficient and diligent, Stoddert was to be Adams's most faithful and effective ally in the executive department.

Born in 1751, of a prominent Maryland family and the son of a militia officer, Stoddert enlisted as a captain in a regiment of Continental Cavalry. He was severely wounded and incapacitated at the Battle of Brandywine, and in 1779 became secretary of the Board of War.

After the Revolution, Stoddert engaged in commerce and became a successful and prosperous merchant. He yielded, with some reluctance, to Adams's plea to become the first navy secretary. In the following months he proved an unusually efficient organizer as he expanded and strengthened the fledgling navy. Ships were built, others were redesigned, officers were chosen, articles of government for the navy were drawn—articles that were not revised for more than a century. An excellent administrator, Stoddert not only worked diligently and effectively to develop the new navy that John Adams relied on to counter the diplomatic and political moves of France, but he also proved a loyal and insightful adviser to the president.

John Adams sent other documents concerning the dispute with France to Congress on June 5, 18, and 21. As late as the next January the president sent the seventh and last installment of these papers to Congress. It was he, rather than the secretary of state, who decided when and what to submit. That he kept the entire affair under his own control seems evidence that he distrusted

Pickering and his hostility toward France, and may be taken as further evidence that despite the popular demand John Adams wanted peace and not war.

At the end of May, Henrietta Liston wrote, "This Country still breathes War," and in mid-June she declared, "This Country is preparing for War; it is a circumstance worthy a Philosopher's observation, how suddenly a whole Nation can change its sentiments with its politicks. . . . In truth the insolence of the French has done its work."[14]

Federalists during these weeks anticipated war with France; some with relish and some with a degree of caution. Stephen Higginson wrote to Oliver Wolcott, "Nothing but an open war can save us, and the more inveterate and deadly it shall be, the better will be our chance for security in the future."[15] John Jay, on the other hand, seems not to have desired war but to have determined to be ready for the war he felt was inevitable: "Being of the number of those who expect a severe war with France, the moment she makes peace with Britain," he wrote to Timothy Pickering on July 18, "I feel great anxiety that nothing may be omitted to prepare for it."[16] Some of the Arch Federalists saw the "XYZ frenzy" primarily as a means to destroy the Republican opposition.

In mid-June 1798 Vice-President Jefferson left Philadelphia and returned to Monticello without waiting for the adjournment of Congress, and from this time on the Federalists were really in the saddle. Arch Federalists vied with each other to praise John Adams. Bills against aliens and penalizing sedition passed Congress, as did appropriations for naval and military defense.

Hamilton was jubilant at the turn of affairs. Throughout the first two and a half years of Adams's presidency, he sought to continue his former influence over executive decisions, often through his allies in the cabinet. In March of 1798 he wrote secretly to Pickering, spelling out in detail the kind of a message he wanted the president to send to Congress. "In my opinion," he wrote, "bold language and bold measures are indispensable. The attitude of *calm defiance* suits us. It is vain to talk of peace with a power with which we are actually in hostility. The election is between a tame surrender of our rights or a state of mitigated hostility."[17]

Hamilton frequently obtained possession of secret information that was supposedly restricted to top government officials. On March 25, 1798, Pickering sent him information from John Marshall's report, just received, and asked Hamilton how much of the

Marshall report should be forwarded to the British government. It is safe to assume that John Adams knew nothing of this.

By the summer of 1799 Hamilton, now desperately anxious to form an alliance with Britain and develop the army that he would move into the Southwest against Spain—and perhaps equally eager to use that army against the Jeffersonians at home—was encouraging a "palace revolt" against Adams. On June 27 he advised James McHenry, "It is a pity, my dear sir, and a reproach, that our administration have no general plan. . . . If the chief is too desultory, his ministry ought to be more united and steady, and well-settled in some reasonable system of measures. . . . Break this subject to our friend Pickering. His views are sound and energetic. Try together to bring the other gentlemen to a consultation. If there is everywhere a proper temper, and it is wished, send for me, and I will come."[18]

On June 16, 1798, without any advance notice, John Marshall arrived in New York from France. Two days later he reached Philadelphia, and as he approached that city he was met by hundreds of men on horseback, dozens of carriages, and a large body of cavalry in full uniform. Everywhere he was greeted as a returning hero. On the evening of the eighteenth the Federalist members of Congress gave him a testimonial dinner at Oeller's, where Monroe had been feted a year earlier. Cabinet members and Supreme Court justices joined with a hundred congressmen and friends to praise Marshall's "patriotic firmness." "Millions for defense, but not one cent for tribute" received the loudest applause of all the sixteen toasts that were offered to the returned diplomat. While Marshall's public utterances were in tune with the then current nationalistic tempo, in private speech he was much less bellicose. Although he could report publicly only failure of the mission, he later indicated a private belief that France wished to bully and control the United States but did not desire all-out war.

On June 21, 1798, John Adams sent a special message to Congress. It consisted of only four sentences, yet there have been few presidential messages more important. The first three sentences summarized the status of America's relations with France, the fourth promised "I will never send another minister to France without assurances that he will be received, respected, and honored as the representative of a great, free, powerful, and independent nation."[19] Apparently many of the Arch Federalists considered this sentence the equivalent of a declaration of war, or at least of an intention to make war. Certainly Adams was stern and adamant, yet he stated his position without completely closing the door to a resumption of negotiations.

On July 1 a Federalist congressional caucus failed to obtain support for the hoped-for declaration of war against France. The next day Henrietta Liston wrote, "The Congress have carried every measure against the French except the Declaration of *War*, which it was found the feder[alist] Members were not steadily enough united to though it was very much the wish of Many."[20] On July 7 John Adams signed into law an act of Congress abrogating all existing treaties with France. Two days later Congress authorized the seizure of French ships, anywhere, if they endangered American commerce—the "undeclared war" was on in earnest.

Yet such legislation was not passed without some difficulty. Republicans were often in strenuous opposition, and moderate Federalists like John Williams of New York complained about the cost of defense and the new taxes being levied. Williams suggested, during congressional debate, that the agrarian interests of the country were being sacrificed to those of the commercial classes, but the Arch Federalists usually had their way. Williams's position is especially interesting because he represented a district in the upper Hudson Valley that was not only agrarian but was in process of becoming Republican. Williams himself became a Jeffersonian in later years.

John Adams wanted a stout defense to prevent war. The Arch Federalists desired military strength primarily to make war with France, which they anticipated and often desired. On June 30 and again on July 2, 1798, the House voted on two measures that were crucial. Both were introduced by Peleg Sprague of New Hampshire and the passage of either would have meant a vote for war. The first would have legalized the attack on and capture of unarmed French ships. It was defeated thirty-two to forty-one. The second balloting, three days later, was on a similar motion and was defeated by a wider margin, thirty-one to fifty-two—perhaps some Republicans had returned to Congress. At any rate, the moderate Federalists, perhaps unwittingly, helped save the president's program and prevented war.

News traveled slowly and important pieces of information often passed each other unknowingly in mid-Atlantic. On July 31 the French Directory passed decrees more friendly to the United States and even sought to restrain French privateers who had been preying on American commerce in the West Indies. These actions, however, would not be known in America for several months.

The role of John Adams in this mounting foreign tension cannot be understood without some discussion of French opinion, French policy, and French actions toward the United States. It is apparent that many people in France believed that both George Washington and John Adams were unfriendly to France and to their revolution. Many of those in positions of power in France, moreover, believed that Washington and Adams represented a minority position and that the majority of Americans were friendly to France and would support her against both Britain and the Federalists. Furthermore, French leaders after 1794 held that the Jay Treaty with England was a violation of the Franco-American treaties of 1778 and that its acceptance by the United States represented a surrender to the pro-English minority. Favoring the spread of international revolution, fearing the economic and naval power of England, and convinced that Gouveneur Morris, while United States minister to France, had acted secretly to aid England, the French Directory through Adet and others had sought the overthrow of the Federalists and the establishment of a pro-French government in the United States.

In July 1796, nearly six months before Adams's election to the presidency was assured, the French government had issued two decrees regarding neutral commerce. Basically, these indicated that the French would treat the vessels of neutrals, as to confiscation, search, or capture, in the same manner that a given neutral allowed her merchant ships to be treated by the English. Thus before that summer was over French privateers were capturing and condemning American ships in the West Indies. By the decree of October 31 the Directory banned all goods either manufactured in Britain or handled by British merchants or shipowners from any territory of the French Republic.

Two days before John Adams was inaugurated, the French government moved once more against neutral commerce. According to her decrees of March 2, 1797, any neutral ship that carried even a single item of an enemy's property could be captured and condemned. Any enemy property in neutral possession could be confiscated. Furthermore the decrees modified several of the agreements of the Franco-American treaties of 1778. Most important, any American ship that did not carefully list its crew in an approved fashion could be confiscated. The treaties of 1778 had referred to such records of ships' crews but there had never been any effort to enforce such a listing. The French knew that such lists were seldom available. Thus for many months nearly every American merchantman afloat would be liable to capture and confiscation.

In the month in which John Adams assumed the presidency, elections were held in France for members of their legislative bodies—the Council of Five Hundred and the Council of Elders. As a result of these elections the government became more friendly to the United States; there is evidence that many people in France were opposed to military involvement with the United States and in favor of peace. The political situation changed suddenly on September 4, however, when three members of the Directorate used the army to effect a coup d'état. They ousted the two directors who had been friendly to the United States and declared some two hundred of the seats in the legislative bodies to be vacant. When, late in 1797, the United States mission reached Paris, John Marshall declared, "All power is now in the undivided possession of those who have directed against us those hostile measures of which we so justly complain."[21]

Among the French officials who played dominant roles in the Franco-American negotiations, none was so important as Talleyrand. He had succeeded Delacroix as minister of foreign affairs in July 1797. He had been an emigre in the United States in the mid-1790s and reportedly had been well received and well treated. It was expected by John Adams and others that he would, therefore, be friendly to America. Talleyrand, however, was wily, unscrupulous, and deeply dedicated to the interests of both Talleyrand and France. While he would not hesitate to use the United States for his own or his nation's advantage, he preferred a half-war. He hoped to regain the Louisiana territory for France, but he did not wish to fight an open war that might drive the United States into the arms of Britain.

In the spring and early summer of 1798 a combination of factors caused Talleyrand to do an about-face and become most anxious to reestablish friendly relations with America. The wave of nationalism that swept over the United States upon publication of the XYZ papers; the stiffened United States resistance, led by the strengthened navy; the fear that Arch Federalists might turn to an alliance with Britain; Talleyrand's realization that he had been misinformed concerning the strength of the pro-French sentiment in the United States; and the visit of Quaker George Logan to France in an attempt to promote peace—all changed Talleyrand's attitude. Perhaps most important was the role played by Victor Du Pont de Nemours. He had been sent to the United States to replace Consul General Letombe. Acting on the recommendation of Rufus King, the American minister to Britain, who had concluded that the French Directory was in reality sending another political agent to spy on the United States, the U.S. government had refused him an exequatur and he had returned to France. Prior to his return, however, he had conversed with many Americans and had had a long interview with his old friend Thomas Jefferson, on May 31, 1798. Du Pont arrived in Bordeaux on July 3 and sent Talleyrand a written report that stressed the military preparations in the United States, the rising tide of anti-French sentiment, the desire of some for an alliance with Britain, and the growing resentment at French interference with American commerce, especially in the West Indies.

Talleyrand now acted rapidly and forcefully. On July 27 he appealed to the Directory to adopt a policy of reconciliation with the United States. On July 31 a decree was passed to limit the role played by French privateers in the West Indies. Shortly thereafter Talleyrand ordered the return to France of all West Indies judges suspected of illegal practices in the confiscation of American shipping.

It is apparent now that a major reason for Talleyrand's pressure on Gerry to remain in Paris when Pinckney and Marshall left (in late March 1798) was connected with his efforts to avert war. On July 15, 1798, Talleyrand sent word to Gerry that France wanted reconciliation. Just a week later he wrote Gerry again, urging the resumption of negotiations in Paris and insisting that there need be no American loan and no apology from the president. He informed Gerry of the actions being taken to curb French excesses against American commerce in the West Indies. Gerry left Paris for Le Havre on July 26. On the third of the next month Talleyrand wrote to him there, enclosing a copy of the decree of July 31 restraining French privateers in the West Indies. Gerry sailed for home on August 8 fully convinced that France wanted peace and that the United States could secure an honorable settlement of existing disputes without war.

The astute Talleyrand hoped Gerry would persuade the president that France wanted peace, but he did not rely exclusively on this effort. As will be discussed below, he had sent an agent named Pichon to The Hague with instructions to improve relations with the United States. On August 15 Talleyrand wrote Pichon, "Continue unostentatiously to see Mr. Murray [William Vans Murray, U.S. Minister to Holland], and endeavor to learn the views of his own government as well as to convince him of the good disposition of the French government. It is important to make some impression on the men devoted to the administration of Mr. Adams and to make them doubt at least the justice of the measures he continues to enact in the Legislative Body of the United States."[22]

Word traveled so slowly in the 1790s that it would be two or three months before John Adams knew of the changing French attitude reflected in the actions of June and July 1798. On June 25 Secretary of State Pickering ordered Gerry to return home at once, and on the same day Congress authorized the arming of merchant ships and legalized their defense against French vessels. Two days later Congress passed an act to strengthen the navy. On July 11 a marine corps was established. A new tax bill, levying a direct tax on houses and slaves and designed to raise two million dollars for defense, became law. Satisfied that the United States could defend herself in case of war, in late July, perhaps on the twenty-fifth, the president left for Quincy.

6

★★★★★

JOHN ADAMS AND THE MILITARY

An emerging nation, without economic stability or military might, caught in the web of European warfare and diplomacy, faced many difficulties. Could it remain neutral or must it seek alliances? How imperative was the creation of a navy or the expansion of the army? How aggressive, both in defense and offense, could such a nation afford to be?

In the late spring of 1798, when most Federalists and even independents were wroth with anger over the French insult to American diplomats in the XYZ affair, and when pro-French Republicans tended to retire to their own fireside rather than the public forum, increasing numbers of Americans became concerned with matters of defense. The Arch Federalists pushed for legislation to provide for a larger army. President Adams, however, favored a larger navy.

Alexander Hamilton placed high priority on the building of an army. In mid-May 1798 he wrote to George Washington emphasizing the crisis in our relations with France and suggested that war was imminent. Washington replied on May 27 that although he would be reluctant to return to duty as army commander, if war was actually declared he would feel it his duty to serve. He did not, however, believe that France would resort to open war. Congress was less optimistic. The very next day it legislated an increase of 10,000 troops, but it waited nearly a month to authorize the commissioning of the necessary officers for the new army.

On June 2 Hamilton replied to Washington's letter of May 27, expressing his pleasure that Washington was willing to return to military service, if needed, and indicating he would like to serve under him as "Inspector General with a command in the line."[1]

On June 6, after Hamilton had received Washington's letter of May 27, Secretary of State Pickering wrote the first of a series of letters to the former president. These were designed to cast doubt on Adams's ability to prepare the nation for its defense, to promote the candidacy of Hamilton for a position of authority in the new army, and to convince Washington that all Federalists were demanding that Hamilton be placed second in command. "From the conversation that I and others have had with the President," Pickering wrote in this June 6 letter, "there appears to us to be a disinclination to place Colo. Hamilton in what we think is his proper station, and that alone in which we suppose he will serve: the *Second* to You; and *Chief* in your absence. . . . If any considerations should prevent your taking the command of the army, I deceive myself extremely, if you will not think it should be conferred on Colo. Hamilton: And in this case, it may be equally important as in the former, that you should intimate your opinion to the President."[2]

Unaware of Hamilton's correspondence with the former president, Adams wrestled with the problem of army command and wrote directly to George Washington. Admitting his own inexperience in military affairs, he suggested, "If the Constitution and your Convenience would admit of my Changing Places with you, or of my taking my old station as your Lieutenant civil, I should have no doubts of the ultimate Prosperity and Glory of the Country." But, said the president, "in forming an Army, whenever I must come to that Extremity, I am at an immense Loss whether to call out all the old Generals, or to appoint a young Sett. . . . I must tax you, Sometimes for Advice. We must have your Name, if you, in any case will permit us to use it. There will be more efficacy in it, than in many an Army."[3]

On July 2, although he had not received a reply from his predecessor, John Adams submitted to the Senate the nomination of George Washington as lieutenant general and commander in chief of the new army. Possibly this was a move to head off support for Hamilton, as Adams knew that few Federalists, even those favoring Hamilton, would object to Washington's appointment. The president also recognized the prestige the name of Washington would add to the defense efforts.

The Senate, by a unanimous vote, quickly approved the nomination of Washington, and Adams signed the appointment on July 4. On that same day Washington replied to Adams's letter. It was a cordial response. Washington would accept a call to command the army if there were war, and he stressed the need for complete harmony between the commander in chief and his principal subordinates.

On July 5 Washington wrote to Secretary of War McHenry. Adams had, the day before, signed Washington's appointment to be commander in chief, but Washington did not yet know this. The letter to the secretary of war, who had served in the same capacity under Washington, is very revealing when read in terms of the bitter controversy over staff appointments that would develop in the coming weeks. Washington wrote in part as follows:

> The Presidents letter to me, though not so expressed in terms, is, nevertheless strongly indicative of a wish that I should take charge of the Military force of this Country; and if I take his meaning right, to aid also in the Selection of the General officers. The appointment of these are *important*; but those of the General Staff, are *all important*: insomuch that if I am looked at as the Commander in Chief, I must be allowed to chuse such as will be agreeable to me.[4]

On the morning of July 9 Secretary of War McHenry, who had not yet received Washington's letter of the fifth, left for Mount Vernon. He carried with him a letter from the president, dated July 7. It explained that the pressure of time (Congress was nearly ready to adjourn) had forced the president to make the nomination without first obtaining Washington's permission and expressed the warm desire of the president that Washington would accept the appointment. McHenry also carried—and this was unknown to the president—a letter from Hamilton. The latter had arrived in Philadelphia and learned, to his surprise, that John Adams had nominated Washington and that the Senate had approved. He at once sat down and wrote a letter to Washington and gave it to McHenry to deliver. His letter was certainly aimed both at undermining Washington's confidence in John Adams and promoting Hamilton's own interests. "The arrangement of the army may demand your particular attention," Hamilton wrote. "The President has no relative ideas, and his prepossessions on military subjects in reference to such a point are of the wrong sort. . . . If you accept, it will be conceived that the arrangement is yours, and you will be responsible for it in reputation . . . you should, in one mode or another, see efficaciously that the arrangement is such as you would approve."⁵

James McHenry arrived at Mount Vernon on the evening of July 11. On that same day, but prior to McHenry's arrival, George Washington sat down to answer the letter Pickering had addressed to him on the sixth. Washington wrote, "Of the abilities and fitness of the Gentleman you have named for a high command in the *Provisional Army*, I think as you do, and that his Services ought to be secured at *almost* any price. What the difficulties are that present themselves to the mind of the President in opposition to this measure, I am entirely ignorant. . . ."⁶ Washington then went on to suggest that he believed any French attack would come in the South, that Charles C. Pinckney would probably refuse to serve beneath one so junior as Hamilton, and that Pinckney's services would be essential in a southern campaign. "What arrangements the Secretary of War is empowered, by the President to make with me, I know not," Washington wrote. "In the letter of the former to me, he has not touched upon them. He is not yet arrived. . . . I regret however, that he [McHenry] should have left Philadelphia before a Letter which I had written to him [see Washington's letter to McHenry of July 5, above], could have reached that place."

Thus it seems clear that at least as late as mid-day, July 11, Washington felt preference for Alexander Hamilton, but a practical need for C. C. Pinckney as his second-in-command. McHenry arrived that evening, and spent two and a half days at Washington's home. It is probable that much of that time was spent in private consultation with Washington. McHenry seems to have made effective use of this opportunity to advance his prejudice for Hamilton and his contempt for Adams's handling of the army. Certainly he delivered the letter written by Hamilton, and would seem to have convinced Washington that there was a strong popular demand to raise Hamilton to a position next to the commander himself.

While McHenry was at his home, Washington wrote two important letters. It seems probable that both were given to McHenry to carry north. To John Adams, on July 13, Washington wrote of the French Directory's

> disregard of solemn treaties and the laws of Nations; their war upon our defenceless Commerce; their treatment of our Minister of Peace, and their demands amounting to tribute, could not fail to excite in me corresponding sentiments with those my countrymen have so generally ex-

pressed in their affectionate Addresses to you. Believe me, Sir, no one can more cordially approve of the wise and prudent measures of your Administration. They ought to inspire universal confidence, and will no doubt, combined with the state of things, call from Congress such laws and means as will enable you to meet the full force and extent of the Crisis.

Satisfied therefore, that you have sincerely wished and endeavoured to avert war, and exhausted to the last drop, the cup of reconciliation, we can with pure hearts appeal to Heaven for the justice of our cause. . . .

Thinking in this manner . . . I have finally determined to accept the Commission of Commander in Chief of the Armies of the United States, with the reserve only, that I shall not be called into the field until the Army is in a situation to require my presence, or it becomes indispensable by the urgency of circumstances.[7]

The next day Washington answered the letter from Hamilton. He stated that he had consented to serve with but two reservations: first, the chief officers must be men in whom he had confidence, and second, he would not be called to active duty until his presence became indispensable.[8] Washington expressed his conviction that any French land attack would come in the southern states. He indicated his personal preference for Hamilton as second in command but explained that Charles C. Pinckney of South Carolina, with his knowledge of the terrain and his local popularity, would be indispensable. Part of that letter follows:

If these premises are just, the inference is obvious, that the services and influence of General Pinckney in the Southern States would be of the highest, and most interesting importance. Will he serve then, under one whom he will consider a junr Officer? and what would be the consequence if he should refuse, and his numerous, and powerful connections and acquaintances in those parts, get disgusted? You have no doubt heard that his Military reputation stands high in the Southern States; that he is viewed as a brave, intelligent and enterprising Officer; and, if report be true, that no officer in the late American Army made Tactics, and the art of War so much his Study. To this account of him, may be added, that his character has received much celebrity by his conduct as Minister and Envoy at Paris.

Under this view of the subject, my wish to put you first, and my fear of loosing him, are not a little embarrassing. But why? for after all it rests with the President to use his pleasure.[9]

On July 29 Hamilton replied to Washington. It was a curious letter. Hamilton went all out to justify a superior rank for himself, insisting that his experience and ability, his sacrifice (giving up his lucrative law practice), and the popular demand all indicated he should rank next to Washington. Then he suggested that if the national interest demanded, he would accept less than he deserved. His comments can be, and have been, subject to different interpretations. Was he being truly unselfish and patriotic? Or was he shrewdly playing on Washington's regard for him by seeming to emulate the general's own civic pride and unselfishness?

When James McHenry returned from Mount Vernon he brought with him not only the letters mentioned above but a list of officers that Washington had approved. Originally John Adams had suggested several names. It seems evident that he hoped to develop a bipartisan approach to the defense problem by granting responsible positions to moderate Republicans. The list approved by Washington, however, included only staunch Federalists.

George Washington wrote to Major General Henry Knox on July 16, explaining why he felt it necessary to name Hamilton and Pinckney ahead of him, and assuring Knox of his deep personal regard. Surprised and hurt, Knox replied on July 29 that he would not accept a position inferior to that of one so young and inexperienced as Hamilton. Knox appealed to President Adams, who had left Philadelphia for Quincy. Soon Arch Federalists were protesting that Knox and General Lincoln (both in Boston) were using their proximity to try to influence Adams in Knox's behalf. Weeks went by and the order of army command was not resolved.

Washington was disturbed by the refusal of Knox to serve under Hamilton, and the new commander in chief became apprehensive lest Pinckney make a similar refusal. General Pinckney and his wife had been in the south of France, following his difficulties in the XYZ affair. They sailed for the United States on August 7, 1798, arriving about two months later. As soon as Pinckney received word of his appointment he indicated his willingness to serve under Hamilton, and Washington was greatly relieved.

President Adams continued to insist that the rank Knox, Pinckney, and Hamilton had held in the Revolution should determine their relative seniority in the new army. He proclaimed this opinion numerous times, once in a letter to Secretary McHenry on August 14. McHenry had stressed the need for developing the new army and had requested permission to call Hamilton and Knox to active duty. The president replied that if ranking the three new major generals in the order of Knox, Pinckney, and Hamilton was agreeable to all, McHenry could call Hamilton to active duty at once. This was not the answer McHenry wished.

More of the Arch Federalists were being drawn into the controversy. On September 20 Pickering wrote to George Cabot of Massachusetts, begging him to write to the president in support of Hamilton for the number two spot under Washington. To strengthen his request, Pickering quoted from a private letter from Knox to the president. On September 29 Cabot wrote such a letter to John Adams, a long and urgent appeal to place Hamilton above Knox. John Adams kept the letter but marked it "not to be answered."

During September 1798 both Secretary Wolcott and Secretary McHenry wrote long letters in support of Hamilton. Adams felt the pressure to appoint Hamilton and on September 24 he drafted (but did not send) a careful reply to Wolcott. He minimized the importance of popular criticism of his appointments and made it clear he would follow his own judgment. Adams's papers also contain a second draft of a possible reply to Wolcott, but both are clearly marked "not sent." The president closed one draft with a patent attempt to demonstrate flexibility. "I have given so much attention to your representation," he wrote, "that I have dated the commissions to Knox, Pinckney and Hamilton all on the same day, in hopes that under the auspices of General Washington the gentlemen may come to some amicable settlement of the dispute."[10]

On September 25, 1798, George Washington sat down at his desk in Mount Vernon and brought the matter of the rank of generals to a head. He reminded the president that he had had no opportunity to stipulate the conditions under which he would serve "*before* I was brought to public view," and that he had not listed these conditions in his letter of acceptance because he assumed, correctly, that the letter would be released to the press. Washington also reported that he had listed several conditions to Secretary McHenry with the request that they be relayed to the president. Then Washington, in effect, demanded that he be given his choice of officers or he would resign. "I have addressed you, sir," wrote Washington, "with openness & candour—and I hope with respect; requesting to be informed whether your determination to reverse the order of the three Major Generals is final—and whether you mean to appoint another Adjutant General without my concurrence."[11]

It took two weeks for Washington's September 25 letter to reach the Adams farm in Quincy. When it was received, on October 8, John Adams realized that the resignation of General Washington would be a serious blow to the country's defense as well as a loss of both prestige and popularity for the administration. Determined to maintain a strong front toward France, hopeful that such a stance would bring peace, John Adams replied to Washington the very next day. While he reiterated the authority of the president, he pledged his support of Washington's choices. Washington acknowledged receipt of this letter on the twenty-first, in a cordial and friendly message. The controversy over the generals had been resolved. Adams had delayed as long as he could against the pressures of the Arch Federalists. Finally he had accepted Hamilton's appointment as second to Washington.

The entire controversy seems to have rested on three important facts. The first is that George Washington left it to McHenry to explain to John Adams that he would accept the appointment as commander in chief only on condition that he, Washington, select his major subordinates. Throughout the weeks of controversy Washington seems to have assumed that McHenry had done this, but Adams seems never to have known, or at least understood, this condition until he received Washington's September 25 letter. The second fact reveals Washington's agreement with Adams on the authority of the president. In his letter to Hamilton on July 14, when Washington was discussing the rank of generals, he stated that "after all it rests with the President to use his pleasure." In the third place, it seems apparent that Hamilton and his friends used every possible pressure to persuade Washington to oppose Adams's preference for Knox, and to secure high rank for Hamilton.

It was not until three days after he had sent his ultimatum to Adams that Washington learned that McHenry had shown the president Washington's July 14, 1798, letter to Hamilton upholding presidential authority. Perhaps Washington may then have realized how the pressure from the Hamiltonians had changed his position in regard to the president's authority to appoint officers of the army. Certainly Adams must have realized the change in Washington's attitude and he quickly responded to it. In a letter to McHenry the president had written, "When I dated the commissions of the major Generals on the same day I had made up my mind that if an acquiescence by amicable agreement in the opinion of Gen. Washington should not take place I would confirm his judgment whatever it might be."[12] Adams then did so.

It is quite possible that one of John Adams's chief motives in carrying on the controversy over the rank of generals, even stronger than his distrust of Hamilton, was his desire to delay recruitment and organization of the new and enlarged army. He felt it was unneeded and too costly. On October 22, for example, the president wrote to Secretary McHenry, "Regiments are costly Articles, everywhere and more so in this Country than any other under the sun. If this Nation sees a great Army to maintain without an Enemy to fight, there may arise an enthusiasm that seems to be little foreseen—at present there is no more prospect of seeing a french army here than there is in Heaven."[13]

Certainly the controversy over Hamilton's rank became a major deterrent to the early organization of the army. Ultimately the president was forced to accept Hamilton's appointment as second in command, but the new army was not organized until after the XYZ hysteria had died down, and it became little more than a paper structure.

When, toward the end of Washington's presidency, France became more aggressive toward the United States, America had had no navy to protect her commerce. She had a handful of tiny revenue cutters, each manned by a crew of six men, and the brig *Sophia*, a dispatch boat attached to the State Department. There was not a single warship to protect her shipping. The result was that French privateers swarmed out of the West Indies, attacked America's lucrative trade with those islands, and, aware of her helplessness, at times even patroled the Atlantic coast as far north as Long Island.

The construction of six frigates, four of forty-four guns and two of thirty-six, had been authorized on March 27, 1794, during Washington's presidency when there was the threat of trouble with the "pirates" of the North African coast. Henry Knox, then secretary of war, decreed that the new ships should be speedier and more powerful than the frigates of France and Britain. Peace with Algiers, however, had stopped the work on these vessels.

In the closing weeks of Washington's administration, the lame-duck session of Congress witnessed some activity in naval matters. William Smith of South Carolina, a strong navy man, was chairman of the Ways and Means Committee in the House of Representatives. In the winter of 1797 he persuaded the House to provide the money to complete three frigates that had been started two years before: the *Constellation* with thirty-six guns, and the *Constitution* and the *United States*, each with forty-four guns. The forty-fours were 175 feet long, weighed 1,576 tons, and carried a crew of 400 men. The thirty-sixes were eleven feet shorter, some 300 tons lighter, and their crews numbered 340. The *United States* was launched at Philadelphia on May 10, 1797, the *Constellation* at Baltimore on September 9, and the *Constitution* at Boston on October 21.

From the opening of his administration, John Adams was concerned about his country's naval power. In his message to the special session of Congress on May 16, 1797, he stated that the French Executive Directory had passed laws harmful to American commerce and of danger to her citizens. He then went on to speak of the commerce and fisheries that occupied many citizens, and emphasized naval power as America's essential defense.

Adams had been president but a few months when the inadequacy of American naval strength was further evidenced by increases in insurance rates. At one time the cost of insuring a ship from New York or New England bound for Jamaica skyrocketed to 40 percent of the value of both ship and cargo. The president believed it imperative to build a strong navy for two reasons: (1) it was needed to protect America's commerce from both France and England; and (2) naval strength would allow the United States to function independently of the British navy and thus maintain her position as a neutral country.

In a reply to an address of the Boston Marine Society in September 1798, Adams insisted that "Floating Batteries and Wooden Walls have been my favorite System of Warfare and Defense . . . for three and twenty years."[14] Often quoted, this is a clear statement of Adams's fundamental belief in the primacy of naval strength.

On November 23, 1797, some eight and a half months after he had assumed the presidency, Adams addressed the first regular session of the Fifth Congress. He reemphasized the need for defensive naval strength, which he had pointed out the preceding May. Continuing depredations by French corsairs, he asserted, increased the need for naval strength. Regardless of the outcome of the current negotiations with France, and even if a general peace were to be established in Europe, Adams believed that "tranquillity and order will not soon be obtained. The state of society has so long been disturbed, the sense of moral and religious obligations so much weakened, public faith and national honor have been so impaired, respect to treaties has been so diminished, and the law of nations has lost so much of its force . . . [that] there remains no reasonable ground on which to raise an expectation that a commerce without protection or defense will not be plundered." In this address to Congress, the president also declared:

> The commerce of the United States is essential, if not to their existence, at least to their comfort, their growth, prosperity, and happiness. The genius, character, and habits of the people are highly commercial. Their cities have been formed and exist upon commerce. Our agriculture, fisheries, arts, and manufactures are connected with and depend upon it. In short, commerce has made this country what it is, and it cannot be destroyed or neglected without involving the people in poverty and distress. . . . Under this view of our affairs, I should hold myself guilty of a neglect of duty if I forebore to recommend that we should make every exertion to protect our commerce and to place our country in a suitable posture of defense as the only sure means of preserving both.[15]

A few Arch Federalists, notably Theodore Sedgwick of Massachusetts, supported the naval interests of the president, but in general they favored either cooperation or actual alliance with Britain as the means of protecting commerce. Yet the president persevered in his demands for naval strength.

When Congress finally heeded the requests of the president and created a Department of the Navy, in April 1798, Arch Federalist George Cabot refused to become its first secretary (a fortunate refusal for the president in view of Cabot's later antagonism and support of Hamilton). After first declining, Benjamin Stoddert yielded to the president's pleas and, in the last week of June, began work as the secretary of the navy. Meanwhile, on April 27, 1798, Congress authorized the president to secure a dozen ships of not more than twenty-two guns each. On May 4 Congress made provision for the procurement of cannon and ammunition. On May 27 an act to legalize naval action against French privateers and French warships "found hovering on America's seacoast with the intent of attacking American shipping" passed the House of Representatives by a vote of fifty to forty.

French privateers were striking in the Caribbean and as far north as Long Island. "Inbound merchantmen brought reports of sightings, seizures and 'chaces' with almost every tide."[16] Thoroughly aroused, the small but busy commercial city of Newburyport, in Massachusetts, voted to build a twenty-gun ship and loan it to the federal government. Not to be outdone, both New York and Philadelphia took similar action. "We shall have a navy spring up like the gourd of Jonah," Abigail wrote to her eldest son.[17] At the end of May 1798 the forty-four-gun frigate *United States* put out to sea in defense of American ships and cargoes. Soon two smaller warships, the *Delaware* and the *Ganges*, were out searching for the annoying and destructive French privateers.

Merchant ships were often purchased and converted for service against the smaller French privateers. By the summer of 1798 American shipping was receiving increasingly effective protection. United States merchantmen were now allowed to arm themselves and to repel efforts of French ships to search them. U.S. naval vessels were authorized to seize armed French ships whether or not the latter had been harassing our commerce. When the British minister, Robert Liston, made an informal offer of naval cooperation, the president felt the United States Navy was strong enough so he could ignore the proffered assistance.

In late August 1798 the president, secure in the knowledge of growing naval strength, addressed a note to Stoddert: ". . . 60 or 80 [French] privateers out of Guadalupe must be generally very small & trifling I should think. We shall be very indiscreet if we depend on the English to protect our commerce or destroy French privateers. Whether their ships [the French] in the West Indies have been sickly or whatever has been the cause of their inactivity it has been very remarkable. We must depend on God and our right as well as the English."[18]

By the winter of 1798–99, the United States had fourteen men of war and eight large, converted merchantmen. All were well armed, well manned, and competently officered. By that time French privateers were rarely encountered along the Atlantic coast and the American navy was basing its operations in the West Indies. In December the Navy Department proclaimed that U.S. forces in the West Indies would be superior to the French by the coming winter.

One of the most dramatic moments in America's undeclared naval war with France occurred on February 9, 1799. Off the island of Nevis, Thomas Truxton, a seadog who had seen service in the Revolution as skipper of a privateer, commanding the *Constellation*, captured the French *L'Insurgente*. This French frigate had been especially annoying to American commerce and had seized many American merchant ships. In the same month Truxton fought the larger French *La Vengeance* to a draw. Such news must have been heart-warming to the president.

Emphasis on the navy brought other far-reaching legislation. For example, the need to acquire timber lands to supply the expanding navy resulted, on February 25, 1799, in the first federal legislation concerning forests.

Evidence of John Adams's confidence in the growing strength of his young navy is seen in a letter he addressed to Stoddert in May of 1799:

> . . . I think with you that some of our fast sailing vessels might be employed to advantage in a cruise on the coasts of Spain and France during the hurricane season in the West Indies. Nor do I think we ought to wait a moment to know whether the French mean to give us any proofs of their desire to conciliate with us. I am for pursuing all the measure of defence which the laws authorize us to adopt, especially at sea, with as much zeal and to as great an extent as if we knew the first vessels would bring a declaration of war against us from Paris.[19]

While John Adams's correspondence with Secretary of War McHenry was carefully considered but fitful, a sense of urgency is apparent in his letters to Secretary of the Navy Stoddert. Especially in the spring and summer of 1799, letter follows letter, sometimes two or three in one day. The secretary of the navy was faced with many problems, not the least of which was the dread yellow fever. Ship construction was held up; Stoddert's office had to be moved. Yet there was always presidential pressure to complete new warships, commission officers, recruit crews or procure supplies. In July the president noted that the *Constitution* "employs my thoughts by day and my dreams by night."[20]

In September 1799 Secretary of the Navy Stoddert informed the president that three new squadrons were ready for sea duty. Each squadron would consist of a frigate and five brigs. On September 9 Stoddert gave the three squadron commanders, Silas Talbot, Daniel McNeill, and Richard Morris, their sailing orders. Each squadron had its own destination in the West Indies, but all three were to rendezvous on October 10.

Nearly a year and a half before John Adams left the White House, his "floating batteries and wooden walls" were strong enough to challenge the navy of France and to give the United States the security to remain neutral in the European controversy. At its peak strength, the navy had more than fifty war vessels in service.

Adams's new mission to France would deal from strength rather than from weakness. Furthermore, the nation's expanding and protected commerce paid the cost of building and maintaining the navy. It has been suggested that American citizens saved more than eight million dollars in insurance rates after the navy was enlarged, a sum more than twice the total naval expenditures between 1794 and 1798.

Seven years after he left the presidency, Adams was to write to his friend Adrian Van Der Kemp, "I have always cried, Ships! Ships! Hamilton's hobby horse was Troops! Troops! With all the vanity and timidity of Cicero, all the debauchery of Marc Anthony and all the ambition of Julius Caesar, his object was the command of fifty thousand men. My object was the defense of my country, and that alone, which I knew could be affected only by a navy."[21]

7

★★★★★

ADAMS DEALS WITH THE
SPECTER OF FOREIGN WAR

During the summer and fall of 1798 John Adams was at Quincy, continually beset with personal fears, with animosities and cleavages within his administration, as well as by uncertainties in foreign affairs. It was no easy matter to follow the revered George Washington. The second president possessed neither his prestige, his commanding appearance, nor his wealth.

Adams's personal fears were perhaps the most difficult to withstand. In many respects a dauntless man; a man who had stood firm against George III, the most powerful monarch in Europe; a man who had always dared to make the unpopular choice when he thought it right, he was now ridden by fear. Abigail, his wife of more than thirty years, who had stood by his side in both victory and defeat, lay critically ill.

Never strong, Abigail is said to have had rheumatic fever and she suffered most of her life from rheumatism and what she called "intermitting fever." She may also have been diabetic. Three days before the thirty-fourth anniversary of their marriage, the president wrote to James McHenry, "Mrs. Adams's health is so low, and her life so precarious, that it will be impossible for me to force myself away from her till the last moment."[1]

The hostility and divisions within both his administration and his political party were increasingly apparent to John Adams. He was aware of the intrigue that surrounded the choice of generals for the new army. He knew of the manner in which Pickering had gone to the Senate to prevent appointment of Adams's son-in-law, Colonel Smith, to a responsible command. While Adams had never really trusted Hamilton, he now became convinced that Hamilton was not only ambitious but at times quite unscrupulous in his quest for power.

Over and above all the president's worries, frustrations, and uncertainties loomed the question of France and the possibility of war. He knew that the first obligation of a country's chief executive was to prepare his nation to face any emergency, especially a threat from a foreign country. Yet Adams felt that he must pursue every avenue toward peace that would not divide the country or dissipate the strength that would be needed if war suddenly erupted.

So through the hot days of July and August 1798 John Adams stayed on his farm at Quincy, weighing the proper course for his administration to follow. Could he continue to work with Pickering, McHenry, and Wolcott, his cabinet members who gave their first loyalty to Hamilton? Should he risk dividing his party in order to form a cabinet he could trust? As with most of the president's major decisions, the question of the retention of his cabinet was related to the international situation. The adequate defense of his country required the legislative support of all Federalists, as few Republicans would take any action that might be interpreted by France as unfriendly. To replace the Hamilton-led clique in his cabinet would surely antagonize many of the most influential members of the Federalist party and jeopardize Adams's plans for building a strong navy and presenting a united front to France. John Adams searched the dispatches from Europe, reread the long letters from John Quincy in Berlin, watched the newspapers for their reports of military and naval engagements between France and her opponents.

The president placed little credence on a land attack against the United States by the French. Yet he knew how devastating were her raids on American shipping; and his correspondence with Benjamin Stoddert, the newly appointed navy secretary, occupied much of his time. On hot, still August evenings, with scarce a breeze around the Quincy house and barns, with Abigail ill in the adjoining room, John Adams labored over his state papers and constantly kept track of his emerging navy. He knew that most of the Federalist leaders in Congress were more intent on building an army than a navy, yet he dared not oppose them at this crucial time when unity was so important.

How the Arch Federalists, especially Hamilton as the army's

second-in-command, planned to use this army also caused John Adams anxiety. He thought about it as he read state papers, perused letters of application, worked in his fields, or climbed Penn's Hill to look out over the ocean.

The president was not the only person who was confronting problems and making decisions in the summer of 1798. At his home in Mount Vernon, Adams's predecessor was becoming ever more prejudiced against revolutionary France and increasingly pessimistic about the chances for peace. In August, Attorney General Lee expressed his opinion that the United States and France were actually at war. Across the Atlantic, although John Adams would not learn of this for many weeks, the French Directory was alarmed and concerned about the possible reaction of the French people to the disclosure of corruption in their government. Faced with many domestic problems, the Directory did not wish a full-scale war with the United States, and approached Joel Barlow, an American poet residing in Paris, with expressions of friendship for America. Barlow would eventually play an important role in Adams's plans for peace.

There were other encouraging signs on the European front, signs that did not escape the president's attention. The Irish rebellion was a failure; Turkey had declared war on France; and on August 1, 1798, the French fleet was overwhelmed by the British at the Battle of the Nile. But the picture was not all bright. From his law office in New York City, Alexander Hamilton had been aggressively seeking to dominate U.S. foreign policy. In seven essays titled "The Stand," essays first appearing in the *New York Commercial Advertiser* in the spring of 1798 and then widely republished in succeeding weeks, Hamilton surveyed the record of Franco-American relations and sought to mold an anti-French public opinion.

August, September, and October of 1798 were busy months for the president in Quincy. Every day brought letters, special messages, or government papers. Even as Adams gave in to the ultimatum of Washington and allowed Alexander Hamilton to become the ranking major general in the newly forming army, he also made several decisions that infuriated the Arch Federalists. Adams turned a cold shoulder to the proposal of Miranda that the U.S. intervene in South America, evaded the advances of Britain searching for an Anglo-American alliance, and encouraged the revolt of Toussaint L'Ouverture in Saint Domingue.

John Adams gave attention to the role that the smaller European neutrals might play in any expanded military action between France and his own country. One of the tasks of John Quincy Adams in Berlin had been to secure new treaties with Prussia and Sweden. On October 16 the president wrote to his son asking him to sound out the attitude of the small European neutrals in the event of war between France and the United States. He warned John Quincy that, if the European neutrals would not join the United States in any war with France, she would not allow them to carry French goods under their neutral flags.

By August and September, although he did not know of the changed attitude of the Directory, Adams was hopeful that his policy and the legislation on defense might convince France that they could not easily bluff the United States into a state of vassalage. His shrewd handling of the British offers of cooperation had left many Americans who favored France fearful lest the president accept an agreement of naval cooperation, if not an outright alliance with Britain. Adams knew that either action would alarm the Directory. Talleyrand had no desire to drive the U.S. into the arms of Britain.

The controversy that raged over Gerry is important to an understanding of the tensions and animosities that divided Americans in the summer and fall of 1798. On June 13, 1798, Abigail wrote to her sister regarding a letter received by the president from William Vans Murray at The Hague. Murray had reported, "I learn that France will treat with Mr. Gerry *alone*. The other two will *be ordered* away." "Can it be possible," Abigail reflected to her sister, ". . . that Talleyrand has thus deluded and facinated Mr. Gerry, that he should dare to take upon him such a responsibility? I cannot credit it, yet I know the sin which most easily besets him is obstinacy, and, a mistaken policy. [Abigail may be referring here to Gerry's attachment to France.] You may easily suppose how distrest the President is at this conduct, and the more so, because he thought Gerry would certainly not go wrong, and he *acted* his own judgment, *against his counsellors* . . . . Gerry means the Good of his Country, he means the Peace of it, but he should consider, it must not be purchased by national disgrace & dishonour."[2]

By April, at least, William Vans Murray at The Hague and John Quincy Adams in Berlin knew of this schism among the three commissioners. Rumors that Gerry had remained in Paris circulated in Philadelphia that summer and John Adams probably knew by June. The president was thoroughly dismayed and many of the

Federalists were furious. Gerry was branded as a fool, a traitor, or both. It is now known, however, that Gerry was always careful to protect his country's honor and that he made it clear to Talleyrand that he was remaining in an unofficial capacity. By the end of May, Talleyrand had promised that he would send an emissary to the United States, that France would assume all debts due American citizens for the confiscation of ships and would withdraw the request for a loan.

On May 27, 1798, the Paris newspapers carried a story about the publication, in America, of the XYZ papers and of the great anger that this had aroused. Talleyrand, according to Gerry, then decided that negotiations at that time would be impossible and withdrew his promise to send an emissary to America. On June 25 Secretary Pickering wrote to Gerry, censuring his behavior and demanding his prompt return.

As his anger over the entire XYZ incident cooled, Adams became sure that his old friend Gerry would not be disloyal. Gerry might make mistakes, might be impetuous, Adams admitted, but he would never play the traitor. On August 4 Adams wrote to Pickering, supporting the payment of Gerry's salary and expenses— a sum that Pickering had refused to honor. Pickering had even gone so far as to issue a public denunciation of Gerry in which he branded him as "a man steeped in duplicity and treachery" who should be impeached.

Letters written by Arch Federalists in the fall of 1798 reveal the depth of the distrust and bitterness with which many Federalists viewed the actions of Gerry. In September, Stephen Higginson wrote to Oliver Wolcott that he feared "by the accounts we have from Europe, that we shall be cursed with the intrigues of a new French agent, under the patronage of Mr. Gerry, who seems to have been under the influence of an evil spirit ever since he arrived in Europe. Those of us who knew him, regretted his appointment, and expected mischief from it; but he has conducted worse than we had anticipated."[3]

Elbridge Gerry arrived home from France on the first day of October 1798. Even before his ship reached its wharf, when it first touched land at Nantasket Road, Gerry dispatched a letter to the president at Quincy. He assured Adams that France wanted peace, not war, with the United States. He also mailed a report to Secretary of State Pickering. In this report he repeated Talleyrand's assurances and indicated his own belief that an honorable peace with France was obtainable. It is not difficult to imagine how Timothy Pickering, eager for war against France, anxious for an alliance with Britain, and suspicious of Gerry, reacted to the receipt of such a report.

As soon as possible, Gerry made his way to Quincy and had a long conversation with his old friend the president. It must have been a dramatic meeting. John Adams listened attentively as the returned envoy spelled out in detail the reasons for his decision to remain in Paris when Pinckney and Marshall left, and, later, his conviction that war with France was not inevitable and that a just and honorable peace could be obtained.

Two decades later John Adams was to write, "Mr. Gerry's letter to the Secretary of State . . . confirmed these assurances [that he had been receiving from many sources to the effect that France did not intend to make war on the United States] beyond all doubt, in my mind, and his conversations with me at my own house, in Quincy, if anything further had been wanting, would have corroborated the whole."[4]

The Arch Federalists in Boston, eager for war against France and distrustful of Gerry, were both incensed and alarmed at the reports of Gerry's visit to Quincy. Stephen Higginson declared, "Gerry should have been pushed into the shade with a strong arm immediately on his arrival," but instead he had been warmly welcomed to the president's own fireside. George Cabot wrote to Rufus King that John Adams's intention to "cover the follies & improprieties of his friend" would surely result in "new & mischievous schisms" among the Federalists.[5] Harrison Gray Otis was chosen as the Federalist least likely to arouse the president's anger or suspicion and was sent to Quincy to try to persuade Adams to denounce, or at least to ignore, Gerry. John Adams, however, was not persuaded to turn against Gerry. He was courteous to Otis, whom he had always liked, but he left him with the clear impression that his visit and its purpose were presumptuous, that John Adams could choose his own friends and make his own judgments.

Timothy Pickering continued his public and private harassment of Gerry. On October 20, 1798, Gerry wrote a long letter to John Adams, protesting Pickering's published criticism of Gerry's conduct while he was in France and answering Pickering's charges. On October 26 John Adams forwarded the criticism to Pickering, asking him to "have it inserted in a public print. It will satisfy him [Gerry] and do no harm to anyone."[6] On November 5 Pickering replied to the president, refusing the latter's request to send Gerry's defense to the newspapers. Pickering said that if he did he would be forced to attach to it his further criticism of Gerry with the charge that the latter was dishonest and disloyal.

A pamphlet war between Gerry and Pickering was certainly imminent. John Adams was striving for national unity in order to impress France that she could neither bully nor frighten the United States. He had worked hard to develop a spirit of national loyalty and optimism. He did not want that spirit to be destroyed by unnecessary partisan warfare. The stubborn, intractable Pickering would make no concessions. John Adams, therefore, turned to Gerry, assured him that the president respected and believed him but asked that Gerry ignore Pickering's charges for the time being. The president pointed out that he and Gerry wanted the same thing, peace and neutrality. Gerry agreed. The voluminous files of John Adams's correspondence reveal, however, that while Gerry was willing to refrain from a public debate at the president's request, he could not refrain from a continuing bombardment of the president with the proofs of his loyalty and wise conduct.

On October 3, 1798, John Quincy Adams was in the embassy in Berlin, reading a letter just received from William Vans Murray, American minister at The Hague. Murray told of his conversations with Pichon, Talleyrand's personal envoy to negotiate with Murray, and reported Pichon's apparently sincere insistence that France wanted peace.

The ninth of October marked John Adams's receipt of two communications from Murray. They were in cipher, but their general content was evident. One was the letter that Murray sent on July 17, containing Talleyrand's letter of July 9 and a summary of many conversations Murray had had with Pichon. This information was very important to the president and lessened his fears of war.

President Adams at once forwarded the letters to Pickering in Philadelphia with orders to have them completely deciphered and returned. He also instructed Pickering to "keep them within his bosom," which Pickering did not do. The completely deciphered messages, together with a letter from Pickering dated October 18, were in Quincy perhaps as early as the twenty-second and most certainly by the end of the month. John Adams learned in detail of the Dutch offer to mediate between France and the United States, as well as all the circumstances of the meetings and conversations Murray had had with Pichon.

On October 20, probably before the deciphered messages from

Murray had arrived back in Quincy, John Adams took a step that further infuriated and alarmed the Arch Federalists. He wrote to Pickering and mentioned the forthcoming session of Congress and the president's need to prepare his message for the opening session. Adams asked Pickering to obtain the advice of the other cabinet members on two questions: first, should the president recommend a declaration of war against France; second, should there be renewed efforts to negotiate with France, perhaps even sending a new commissioner to treat with that nation? If the latter were to be attempted, Adams queried, whom should he recommend for the task?

There is no indication that Pickering ever responded directly to the above queries, but it seems quite possible that his alarm over the suggestion of a renewal of negotiations with France was a factor in his meeting with Hamilton, and later with Washington and Pinckney, and the preparation of a "form of words for his [Adams's] adoption at the opening session [of Congress], as should leave him no loop hole for retreat."[7] This statement, prepared for Adams's inclusion in his message, declared that "the United States could negotiate only if France sent an envoy to assure the President of its sincere intentions first."

When, in the following February, John Adams decided on a new mission to France, another attempt at reconciliation, Secretary of State Pickering seemed both alarmed and surprised. The first emotion may have been completely genuine; it is difficult to see how he could have been surprised. In addition to Adams's letter to Pickering of October 20, noted above, John Adams had sent another letter on October 29, which should have made his desire for peace perfectly clear to Pickering. "The two letters [obviously the letters from Murray that Pickering had originally forwarded on October 18] returned in yours are important," the president wrote. "The first has made a great Impression on me."[8]

A month earlier Rufus King had written to Hamilton, indicating the change in French policy and his conviction that France wished to avoid further confrontation with the United States. "You will have no war!" King had exclaimed.[9] It seems probable that Hamilton would have received that letter from King by late December 1798, but there is no sign that the thrust of Hamilton's ambition and actions was in any way changed.

Through the month of October and well into November other bits of information were being assimilated by the president. He had probably learned of Nelson's August 1 victory at the Nile. Certainly we know that the president paid careful attention to the political and military events in Europe and was always quick to assess their relation to the demands on his own nation.

Late on October 28, well after dusk, Harrison Gray Otis came to the Quincy farmhouse. He brought with him a letter he had recently received from Richard Codman. Codman, who was a Bostonian and a "sound Federalist," was then conducting a mercantile business in Paris. In this letter he assured Otis that Talleyrand wanted peace with the United States. Codman gave much credit to George Logan, who had declared to the French minister that there was no party in the United States that would side with France in the event of war and that all Americans would stand together against any French aggression.

"I hope to God," Codman's letter fervently expressed, "that on the arrival of the dispatches which Mr. Skipwith sends, by the Vessel that carries this, no declaration of War will have taken place or alliance with Great Britain, if not & the desire for Peace still continues with our Government I think they may count on an equal desire on the part of France, & a reconciliation yet be brought about, which ought to be desired by all true friends to both countries."[10]

October 1798 was a time of decision for the president. On October 16 he wrote to his eldest son in Berlin that he must assume war with France was still a possibility. Yet in the following two weeks the president saw many signs that pointed to the effectiveness of his efforts toward peace: Codman's letter, the decoded letters from Murray, the frequent and increasingly optimistic letters from John Quincy. These strengthened John Adams's conviction that Gerry had not been wrong to remain in Paris and his belief that Gerry had not been duped by Talleyrand as the Arch Federalists insisted.

On October 22 John Adams wrote to McHenry, lamenting the excessive cost of the new army and indicating his sensitivity to the rising tide of opposition to the higher taxes. News of Nelson's victory at Aboukir Bay probably reached Philadelphia at the start of November. Two weeks later Noah Webster, Federalist though he was, attacked the new army in the pages of his *Minerva* as expensive and unnecessary.

In the second week of November 1798 George Logan came back to Philadelphia. Logan's unofficial trip to France had provoked bitter denunciation from the Arch Federalists. The Philadelphia Quaker had been convinced that peace with France was possible, and he felt impelled to try to obtain it. On his return, Logan went to see the secretary of state and tried to convince him that France sincerely sought peace with the United States. Pickering, well aware of Hamilton's plan to seize Louisiana as soon as war broke out with France, had no desire for peace. His reception of Logan was frigid. In the coming session, Congress would pass an act that made it a crime for a private citizen to "meddle" in the nation's foreign affairs.

When Logan called on George Washington, in Philadelphia for military conferences with his two major generals, Hamilton and Pinckney, he was given a reluctant hearing and was dismissed curtly. On November 26, the very day after John Adams's return to the capital, Logan visited him. Logan insisted that Talleyrand wanted peace. The president received Logan courteously, listened attentively, served him tea, and thanked him for coming.

Through the summer of 1798 events of importance had been taking place in France. It has been mentioned above that President Adams, alerted by Rufus King in London, refused to accept Victor Du Pont as French consul general. Du Pont's pessimistic report of the anti-French feeling in America may well have been an important factor in changing Talleyrand's attitude toward the United States. It certainly did not initiate the new policy, however, as Talleyrand had dispatched Pichon to The Hague before Du Pont had returned to France. So secret was Pichon's mission that even his superior at The Hague knew nothing of Talleyrand's intent. Pichon's instructions were to cultivate acquaintance with William Vans Murray, American minister there, and to attempt to convince Murray that France desired peace.

Louis André Pichon was only twenty-eight years old in June of 1798 when Talleyrand sent him to The Hague. He had spent several years in the United States, having served as secretary to both Genêt and Fauchet. He may have made the acquaintance of Murray during this period.

When Pichon first contacted Murray in June 1798, the latter was suspicious of French intentions. Murray, however, came to believe that Pichon was sincere and that France was anxious to avoid war. By June 26 the two were deep in conversation about Franco-American policy. During the next fortnight the two emissaries met often.

Murray always insisted to the Frenchman that he had no authority to negotiate, and that while he hoped for peace he could make no official promises and was acting as a private citizen. He also kept both his close friend in Berlin, John Quincy Adams, and the president fully informed. Furthermore, he was always alert to the threat of Pickering's Francophobia and was most discreet in his correspondence with the secretary of state.

Through the late summer and fall of 1798 Talleyrand may well have been perplexed about American policy. Du Pont had reported the Adams administration was eager for war against France. Talleyrand had made every effort to convey his desire for peace through Gerry. He had even sent to Gerry, just prior to the latter's departure for home, a copy of the July 31 decree regulating French privateers. Yet he had had no response to his peace feelers.

One of the major difficulties during this tense period was the slowness of communication. Some of William Vans Murray's most important letters were received by the president only after delays of four or even five months. On August 20, for example, Murray wrote to the president enclosing a copy of a letter from Talleyrand to the Dutch Government indicating his interest in the offer of the Dutch to mediate between France and the United States. John Adams did not receive this until January 21, 1799.

Perhaps the most important letter in the entire series that Murray sent to John Adams regarding his conversations with Pichon was written on October 7, 1798. Murray described his insistence to Pichon that the president must have assurances of a desire for peace directly from Talleyrand. Pichon had then gone to Paris to relay this message to Talleyrand, and had mailed back to Murray the letter Talleyrand had written on September 28. John Adams did not received this until the first of February. Then the president was able to read Talleyrand's assertion that any "plenipotentiary whom the government of the United States might send to France, in order to terminate the existing differences between the two countries . . . would be undoubtedly received with the respect due to the representative of a free, independent, & powerful nation."[11]

William Vans Murray was in close touch with John Quincy Adams during these weeks of summer and early fall. The two had been good friends for several years. Murray not only trusted the loyalty and intelligence of the president's eldest son, but he knew that the president gave much weight to his son's opinions. On September 28, in a letter received by John Quincy Adams on October 3, Murray wrote about his continuing discussions with Pichon. It was a long letter and it indicated Murray's belief that France was now ready to accept an envoy on the president's terms.

Murray was a cautious young man. He realized that he might endanger his own political and professional position by holding secret conversations with Pichon. He knew of Pickering's hatred of the French and of the Arch Federalist attack on Gerry because he had continued secret negotiations with Talleyrand. Perhaps Murray thought that the president might not approve of his efforts. Thus it may have been partly out of a desire for self-protection that Murray kept the younger Adams informed about all of his dealings with Pichon. He sent John Quincy copies of messages and memos he received from the French agent and, at least once, a copy of one of the letters Talleyrand wrote to Pichon. Murray also encouraged John Quincy to write freely to his father about the conversations with Pichon.

Early in October 1798 John Quincy Adams sent a dispatch (number 137 in his series) to the secretary of state. A copy sent to the president may have reached Adams before his youngest son, Thomas Boyleston, arrived home with letters and messages from his older brother. The dispatch is not to be found in the State Department archives, which suggests, but does not prove, that Pickering destroyed it. The copy in John Quincy Adams's Letterbook reveals that he strongly recommended authorizing Murray to enter into negotiations with a representative of the French government. In view of Pickering's bias, it seems possible that he might not refer such a message to the president.

As noted above, John Adams arrived back in Philadelphia on November 25, 1798. He met with his cabinet and at once brought up for discussion the two questions he had addressed to them on October 20, and to which they had never made formal reply. Should war be declared? Or should another mission be sent to France to seek a resolution of the difficulties between the two nations?

It was Wolcott's suggestion that proved the key to the discussion between John Adams and his cabinet, and it dealt with the second of the president's questions: should there be another mission to France? Jefferson believed at the time, and since then numerous historians have come to an identical conclusion, that Wolcott's statement in answer to this question was prepared in consultation with Hamilton and perhaps with the approval of generals Washington and Pinckney. The most significant sentence in Wolcott's draft declared that appointing a commission to negotiate with France "would be an act of humiliation to which the United States ought not to submit without extreme necessity." Such a necessity, Wolcott indicated, did not exist. In short, negotiations must not be pursued until France sent a minister to the United States to apologize and to assure that negotiations would be conducted honorably. There seemed little possibility that France, at this time, would take such action.

President Adams may have revealed to his cabinet that he was more ready to seek a reconciliation than they were. On October 20 he had certainly implied such a possibility. There exists among the Adams papers an undated memo that may have been a draft the president had prepared for consideration by his cabinet. In it he declared his hope for another mission to France as soon as he received assurances that it would be received respectfully by the French. Pickering may have been aware of this draft.

There must have been many pressures on John Adams. On December 6, 1798, two days before he addressed Congress, an anonymous "Friend to our Happy Government" pledged his support to the president and pleaded with him to be vigilant and to thwart the "old Tories" who would throw the United States into the arms of Britain. This anonymous writer urged neutrality and begged Adams to stay clear of both Britain and France.[12] In this same letter the writer reported hearing Hamilton remark with insolence that John Adams was "a mere old woman and unfit for a President."

The climate of the country was not conducive to calm and dispassionate thinking. Arch Federalists were still demanding a declaration of war; Republicans were pleading for peace. The newspapers, perhaps the best indicator we have of the general public climate, were filled with violent and abusive essays. Each political faction denounced the other in unrestrained language.

Yet there is contemporary evidence that some Republican leaders were aware of the changing policy of the French government and felt the Federalist president could make peace. On December 7 the Republican Albert Gallatin wrote to his wife, "As to politics, you know [of] the destruction of the French fleet in Egypt. The news of peace being made by them at Radstat with the Empire and Emperor is generally believed. That they have found it [to] their interest to change their measures with all neutrals, and that an honorable accommodation is in the power of our Administration is, in my opinion, a certain fact."[13]

In the waning days of 1798 President Adams was more confident that war could be avoided, an honorable peace realized. While the country was still divided, Adams's perseverance and the labor of men like Murray, Gerry, John Quincy Adams, Pichon, and even Talleyrand were beginning to open up new possibilities for peace.

8

★★★★★

ADAMS STANDS ADAMANT
FOR PEACE

On December 8, 1798, both houses of Congress had a quorum
and President Adams appeared before a joint session. It must have
been a dramatic moment. John Adams, no doubt a bit nervous and
much aware of the importance of the occasion, occupied the center
of the platform. On one hand were the three generals of the army:
George Washington, Alexander Hamilton, and Charles C. Pinckney;
on the other, the British and Portuguese ministers. Men of widely
varied opinions—Arch Federalists like Pickering and Sedgwick, Republicans like Gallatin and Jefferson, moderates like Stoddert—
listened intently as the president stood to deliver his address.[1]

John Adams began on a low key by lamenting the yellow-fever
epidemic of the preceding summer and calling on Congress to
"examine the expediency of establishing suitable regulations in aid
of the health laws of the respective States." (The U.S. Public Health
Service had been established the previous July.) Then, noting the
"manly sense of national honor, dignity, and independence" that
had lately arisen, he declared that those attributes would make it
possible for the United States "to view undismayed the enterprises
of any foreign power and become the sure foundation of national
prosperity and glory."

Asserting that "nothing is discoverable in the conduct of France
which ought to change or relax" the national measures of defense,
the president declared that "to extend and invigorate . . . [measures
of national defense] is our true policy. We have no reason to regret

90

that these measures have been thus far adopted and pursued, and in proportion as we enlarge our view of the portentous and incalculable situation of Europe we shall discover new and cogent motives for the full development of our energies and resources."

The president proclaimed, "in demonstrating by our conduct that we do not fear war in the necessary protection of our rights and honor we shall give no room to infer that we abandon the desire for peace. An efficient preparation for war can alone insure peace. It is peace that we have uniformly and perseveringly cultivated, and harmony between us and France may be restored at her option." Next came John Adams's adaptation of the Wolcott statement: ". . . to send another minister [to France] without more determinate assurances that he would be received would be an act of humiliation to which the United States ought not to submit." With hardly more than a quick breath the president appended, "It must therefore be left with France . . . to take the requisite steps." The presidential address was concluded with a plea for naval reinforcement and attention to boundary problems with both Britain and Spain.

Arch Federalists were furious, declaring that the president had gone soft on France, that he was willing to make peace at the cost of honor. The same address infuriated some Republicans. Madison and Jefferson were among those who maintained that the president was under Hamilton's influence and that he would deviously conceal evidence of France's peaceful intention until he obtained a declaration of war.

After a lapse of 175 years, it is difficult to understand how the president's contemporaries could so misread his attitude in this address of Adams's to Congress. Hamilton, Pickering, and other Arch Federalists wanted war with France and no conciliation; Jefferson and Madison wanted an unquestioning acceptance of the good intentions of France. John Adams hoped to pursue a middle course that would maintain peace and alienate as few Federalists and Republicans as possible.

There were, of course, some who recognized this and knew that Adams was leaving the door open for Talleyrand if he chose to enter. In view of the uproar that was to greet the president's nomination of Murray as minister to France, on the following February 18, it is interesting to note that at least one of the Arch Federalists interpreted Adams's December speech to Congress as an indication that the president would soon name a new mission to France. Yet very few contemporaries, regardless of their political persuasion, seem to have understood John Adams's thinking or recognized his goals. On December 14, for example, Gallatin wrote to his wife that John Adams had changed his attitude toward France because he had been unable to obtain a defensive-offensive treaty with Britain.

Congress began its sessions, in mid-December 1798, torn by factionalism, by mistrust and misunderstanding. President Adams still had no guarantee that peace with France could be obtained, yet he felt more confident of such a possibility. He hoped his address, which revealed his country's strengths, would mark a turning point in the relations between France and the United States.

The first two months of 1799 witnessed growing animosity between Hamiltonians and Republicans. The latter were sure that the Arch Federalists desired war against France, and some of them certainly did. Friction between John Adams and some of his cabinet members increased. The president's knowledge and understanding of international affairs grew as he received information about the political and military situation in Europe and the French Directory's changing attitude toward the United States.

The president was encouraged by the increasing evidence that France did not wish war with the United States. One of the most important letters received by Adams during these weeks came from his youngest son, Thomas. Written at the end of October, the letter told of the destruction of Napoleon's transports at the Battle of the Nile, and said that a French squadron, about to land troops in Ireland, had been routed and nearly destroyed. Such information about French losses added credence to the evidence that the Directory was less intransigent.

Through January the *Aurora*, most influential of all the Republican newssheets, printed news items, letters, and releases concerning the French government that often indicated a changing position toward war with the United States. On February 1 that newspaper published statistics released by the Insurance Company of North America. These showed that loss of American shipping to British vessels during the preceding six months had totaling $280,000, a loss that was $20,000 greater than that caused by French privateers. Such realistic assessments of English and French damage to American commerce tended to lessen the demands for war against France. George Cabot wrote to Pickering that many merchants who profited from the French West Indies trade would oppose a war against France.

92

On Friday evening, January 11, 1799, the president's youngest son disembarked at New York. Thomas had been in Europe for four years and had been both secretary and confidant to his brother in Berlin. He brought with him confidential letters and dispatches, and immediately forwarded these to his father in Philadelphia. A twenty-four-hour stage trip brought Thomas to the capital late on Tuesday, the fifteenth, and he went directly to his father's house. With Abigail ill in Quincy, the lonely president must have eagerly awaited his son's arrival.

Father and son had many things to talk about: Abigail and her health; John Quincy and his work; the daughter-in-law (Mrs. John Quincy) whom the president had never seen; prospects for new trade treaties with Sweden and Prussia; political events throughout Europe. Above all, they would have discussed the changing attitude of France and the possibility of reconciling her differences with the United States. The previous October, John Quincy had written his mother that he withheld no confidences or information from his brother. We can be sure that Thomas knew as much about Murray, Pichon, and the correspondence with Talleyrand as did his older brother.

John Adams had become increasingly confident that an honorable peace was possible ever since he had learned of the British victories at Aboukir on August 11 and at Camperdown on October 11. He had devoured with increasing optimism the messages from Murray and the long letters from John Quincy. Talking face to face with his son, he relived the thoughts, expectations, and hopes of the past weeks.

Earlier that same day, after the receipt of the packet of letters and dispatches that Thomas had mailed to his father from New York, John Adams had sent a memorandum to his secretary of state, asking that Pickering prepare the draft of a treaty and consular convention "such as in his opinion might at this day be acceded to by the United States, if proposed by France."[2] The president asked Pickering to consult with and obtain the advice of the other cabinet members in preparing such a draft, to prepare it as soon as possible, and to keep the matter in "inviolable confidence."

President Adams and Secretary Pickering continued their dispute over the role that Gerry had played in France the preceding spring and summer. On Friday, January 18, the president sent Gerry's official report to Congress. On Saturday he and Pickering argued heatedly over the rebuttal to Gerry's report that Pickering had prepared. John Adams stoutly defended his old friend's motives and actions and would not accept Pickering's criticism of Gerry's conduct. He did agree, however, that Pickering was entitled to send his criticism of Gerry to Congress for their consideration.

Late in January, James Madison wrote to Jefferson that he had "long been anxious to know the real complexion of Gerry's report. Several symptoms concur with your information that it does not favor the position which our Government wishes to take. . . . If truth shall be found to have been suppressed in order to trick the public into a war or an army, it will be one of the most daring experiments that has been made on the apathy of the people."[3] John Adams would not have known of this letter when, on February 2, he released the Gerry papers for publication. Yet the publication of these, including the notes Gerry had made of his conversations with Talleyrand, was certainly a part of the president's carefully laid plan to prepare the public for news of yet another attempt at reconciliation with France.

Early February brought information that strengthened the president's growing conviction that he had succeeded in laying the groundwork for peace. In a letter written on October 7 Murray described his insistence to Pichon that any reconciliation between France and the United States must be on the terms John Adams had set forth in his message to Congress the preceding June. Pichon had relayed this information to Talleyrand, and on September 28 the latter promised a cordial reception to an American envoy. Pichon had given Talleyrand's letter to Murray and the latter forwarded it to the president with his October 7 letter.

On the last day of January 1799 George Washington received an important letter from Europe. It was from Joel Barlow, an American residing in Paris, and it set forth in emphatic terms the thesis that France wanted peace with the United States. "The point that I wish to establish in your mind," Barlow wrote the former president, "is that the French Directory is at present sincerely desirous of restoring harmony between their country & the United States, on terms honorable and advantageous to both parties." On February 1 Washington forwarded Barlow's letter to John Adams, together with his covering letter. This letter from Washington had great influence on Adams and was a strong link in the chain that led to the Convention of Môrtefontaine and peace with France. "From the known abilities . . . [of Barlow]," Washington wrote to Adams, "such a letter could not be the result of ignorance *in him*—nor, from the implications which are to be found in it, has it been written without the *privity* of the French Directory." George Washington went on to indicate he would gladly accept any honorable peace that John Adams could arrange. Such a peace, Washington believed, was "the ardent desire of all the friends of this rising Empire."[4]

This statement from Washington must have lifted Adams's spirits, for Washington was, in effect, promising his moral support for any presidential effort to establish an honorable peace with France. Now John Adams could be sure that if an attempted settlement with France led to a break with the Arch Federalists, these extremists could not count on the support of Washington.

At this very time (February 2, 1799) Timothy Pickering was complaining to George Cabot. Pickering insisted that he was, in spite of his high office, virtually powerless to influence the president. The cabinet members, he stated, were all unhappy about Adams's December 8 address to Congress. They had been unanimous, Pickering dishonestly asserted, in the belief that the president should give an ironclad promise that he would not send another ambassador to France.

Historian Robert Palmer has concluded that although there were indications that France wanted peace, "the war spirit of the Hamiltonians . . . was running very high."[5] They believed, Palmer is convinced, that the "French Revolution was at last over, that the Bourbons would be restored, that Britain was about to triumph and that the moment was therefore opportune for an Anglo-American liberation of Spanish-America." Expressing an opposite and more realistic view, John Adams proclaimed that "the French Revolution would go on for years."

In late January, Alexander Hamilton wrote to Harrison Gray Otis urging Congress to authorize a declaration of war against France. Hamilton wished it specified that if negotiations with France were not under way by the next August, or if differences were not satisfactorily settled by then, the president must declare a state of war and use both the army and the navy against France. The same letter advocated the detachment of South America from Spain and the more rapid "advancement" of the army.

It was in an atmosphere of mutual distrust, in the midst of strong demands for war from the Arch Federalists, that John Adams made the most decisive move of his presidency. On February 15, 1799, he received word that France had retracted some of the more humiliating and infuriating maritime decrees. Three days later the president sent his fateful message to the Senate. One can imagine the surprise of Vice-President Jefferson as he interrupted the business of that body to read the short message that had just arrived from the president: "Always disposed and ready to embrace every plausible appearance of probability of preserving or restoring tranquillity, I nominate William Vans Murray, our minister resident at The Hague, to be minister plenipotentiary of the United States to the French Republic." Jefferson read on:

> If the Senate shall advise and consent to his appointment, effectual care shall be taken in his instructions that he shall not go to France without direct and unequivocal assurances from the French Government, signified by their minister of foreign relations, that he shall be received in character, shall enjoy the privileges attached to his character by the law of nations, and that a minister of equal rank, title, and powers shall be appointed to treat with him, to discuss and conclude all controversies between the two Republics by a new treaty.[6]

Adams's message was truly the culmination of months of deliberate assembling and weighing of information. Long conversations with Gerry, the many letters to and from William Vans Murray and John Quincy Adams, the messages from Talleyrand and Pichon that had been forwarded by Murray, the letters of Codman and Barlow, the efforts of Logan, the long talk with his son Thomas, the assurances of George Washington—all played a role in John Adams's decision to make another effort to secure peace, despite the opposition of some of his own cabinet and the most powerful leaders in his party.

The surprise and anger in the Senate chamber was exceeded only by the dramatic receipt of the news in the House of Representatives. In a report he sent to Talleyrand the next day, Létombe, the French consul general at Philadelphia, described the manner in which the House learned of Murray's nomination:

> The debate at this moment was very brisk. The Whigs and Tories [Republicans and Federalists] were highly animated. They were discussing a bill giving the President eventual authority to increase the army by 24 regiments of infantry . . . . The motion for the second reading of this bill had just been defeated by 45 votes against 37, and Mr. Otis was renewing discussion of a bill concerning the capture of French privateers by vessels freighted or belonging to citizens of the United States, when one of the members, informed by a Senator, of what had just happened, notified the House that there was no more reason to

work for this bill, since the President had just nominated a minister to the French Republic! The majority acted as if struck by a thunderbolt. The orator Otis, the friend and confidant of Adams, showed embarrassment, grew pale. The House adjourned, and is still adjourned today.[7]

The next day, perhaps early in the morning as was his wont, the president sat down to write George Washington of his nomination of Murray. It had been Washington's letter, accompanying the one forwarded from Barlow, that had convinced the president that Washington, too, felt peace was desirable. His letter had seemed proof that the former president would not lend his name and influence to any Arch-Federalist attack on Adams for seeking a reconciliation with France. But John Adams, astute tactician that he was, left nothing to chance. "I yesterday determined to nominate Mr. Murray," Adams wrote, "to be minister plenipotentiary to the French republic. This I ventured to do upon the strength of a letter from Talleyrand himself, giving declarations, in the name of his government, that any minister plenipotentiary from the United States shall be received according to the condition at the close of my message to Congress, of the 21st of June last. As there may be some reserves for chicane, however, Murray is not to remove from his station at the Hague until he shall have received formal assurances that he shall be received and treated in character."[8]

That John Adams was astute to inform George Washington at once is shown by the fact that Timothy Pickering sent a letter to Mount Vernon on the twenty-first. Pickering's letter to the ex-president was carefully written to convince the latter that President Adams had been both unwise in his decision and improper in his methods. Pickering fairly exploded that the "*honor* of the Country is prostrated in the dust—God grant that its *safety* may not be in jeopardy." It is not known when these two letters arrived at Mount Vernon, but on March 3 Washington replied to the president. He thanked John Adams for the latter's courtesy in keeping him informed and expressed the hope that war might be avoided. It was a cordial, friendly letter.

Thomas Jefferson, the presiding officer of the Senate, seems to have failed completely to sense the position or the goal of John Adams. This is not surprising, for we have seen that ever since the special session of Congress in May 1797 Jefferson had misunderstood John Adams's aims and actions and had been unable or unwilling to understand the political climate in which Adams had to function.

If Jefferson and the Republicans were surprised and suspicious,

97

the Arch Federalists seemed equally surprised and were furious. Appraising the situation today, aware of Adams's information and his moves since October 20, we may well wonder at the sincerity of their surprise. There is, however, no doubt about their anger. The day following the nomination of Murray, Senator Theodore Sedgwick sought Hamilton's advice, declaring that if "the foulest heart and the ablest head in the world had been permitted to select the most embarrassing and ruinous measure, perhaps it would have been precisely the one which had been adopted."[9]

That evening Sedgwick and the president met in an angry confrontation. John Adams belittled the senator's expressed fears of civil war and he accused Sedgwick and his friends of attempting to weaken the executive's position as commander in chief of the armed forces. Sedgwick became very angry but in effect admitted the truth of the president's accusation.

Peter Porcupine, one of the leading Federalist editors, now turned against the president and used the pages of his press to denounce the nomination of Murray. Three days later Secretary Pickering wrote to George Cabot: "Dear Sir,—You will be shocked, as we all were, by the President's nomination of Mr. Murray minister plenipotentiary to negotiate a treaty with the French republic. I beg you to believe that it is the sole act of the President."[10]

Yet for several months Rufus King had been writing from England that France wanted peace. Several days before the nomination of Murray was sent to the Senate, Robert Goodloe Harper, Arch Federalist from South Carolina, had sent a letter to his constituents in which he indicated his belief that the French were making overtures to Murray and that peace with France would surely be the result. Therefore the Federalist attack on John Adams after the nomination of Murray may have been designed to create a false impression of Federalist surprise at the unexpectedness of Adams's move.

Not all Federalists, of course, condemned the president. The nomination of Murray was destined to reveal the deep divisions that existed within the Federalist party. Both Stoddert and Lee, in the president's cabinet, supported his action (proof of the duplicity of Pickering and McHenry, who had claimed unanimous cabinet opposition). John Marshall wrote at once to the president, applauding his decision. Henry Knox, from Boston, commended the president and pledged his support.

On February 22, 1799, John Adams wrote to Abigail and discussed the developing controversy. He said that he had been advised to nominate John Quincy Adams and Rufus King to go to Paris with Murray, but that he felt "the nomination of either . . . would probably defeat the whole measure. Rivalries have been irritated to madness," he told his wife, "and Federalists have merited the Sedition Law and Cobbett the Alien Bill—But I will not take Revenge. I don't remember that I was ever vindictive in my life, though I have often been very wrath. I am not very angry now, nor much vexed or fretted. The Mission came across the Views of many and Stirred the Passions of some. This I knew was unavoidable. The Reasons which determined me are too long to be written."[11] The president continued that some people in Philadelphia were saying that if Abigail had been there she would not have allowed the president to make such an appointment. "That ought to gratify your vanity enough to cure you," he wrote.

Thomas heard the same idea suggested in Boston and reported to his mother that some "wished the old woman had been there; they did not believe it would have taken place." Abigail relished this story and wrote her husband on the twenty-seventh, "This was pretty saucy, but the old woman can tell them they are mistaken, for she considers the measure a master stroke of policy." Again on March 3, Abigail wrote to John regarding his message to Congress on the eighteenth of the preceding month:

> I yesterday received yours of Febry 22d. There has not been any measure of the Government since you have been placed at the Head of it, which has so universally electrified the public: as the appointment of Mr. Murray to France, not the man, but the appointment, it came so sudden, was a measure so unexpected, that the whole community were like a flock of frightened pigeons: nobody had their story ready; Some called it a hasty measure; others condemned it as an inconsistent one; some swore Some cussed, and as you observe, the Federalist[s] deserved the Sedition Bill . . . .[12]

The Arch Federalists in the Senate soon took action to appoint a committee of five to consider the matter of Murray's nomination. Theodore Sedgwick was appointed chairman of this committee. Writing to Hamilton on the twenty-second, Sedgwick, who now detested Adams, groaned, "It is one of the misfortunes to which we are subjected by the wild and irregular starts of a vain, jealous, and half frantic mind, that we are obliged to practise an infraction of correct principles, a direct communication between the President and Senate. I am this morning to wait on him and solicit an interview between him and the committee upon his nomination. The objections are to induce him to alter it, as it respects the person; and instead of an individual, to propose a commission . . . ."[13]

When John Adams received the request of the Sedgwick Committee for an interview he was, if we can trust his memory a decade later, "distressed" because he thought such an interview unconstitutional. Specifying that any meeting should not become a part of the report and that it should not be considered to establish a precedent, the president agreed to the consultation. This was held on Saturday evening, February 23. We have two accounts of that meeting, and they differ substantially. Sedgwick described it in a letter he wrote to Hamilton the next Monday and John Adams described it a decade later.

It seems probable that the conference began amicably enough, with Sedgwick asking the president to appoint a committee of three. During the resultant discussion Sedgwick may have lost his temper, charged that Elbridge Gerry was at the bottom of the president's nomination, and asserted the Senate would never accept Murray. Adams may have threatened to resign and allow Jefferson to assume the presidency before he would alter his decision.

The next evening, Sunday the twenty-fourth, Arch Federalists in the Senate held an informal caucus at Senator Bingham's home. Who was there is not known, but the decision seems to have been that the committee of five should recommend to the Senate the rejection of the president's nomination of Murray. The president may have learned of this decision. At any rate, early Monday morning he sent a messenger to Senator Sedgwick to inform him that Adams was preparing a second message to the Senate regarding his nomination and to ask that the committee of five make no report until his message had been read to the Senate. Soon after noon the president's new message reached the Senate. He withdrew his nomination of William Vans Murray as minister plenipotentiary to the French Republic, and substituted the proposal of a commission of three: Oliver Ellsworth, chief justice of the Supreme Court and a staunch Connecticut Federalist, and Patrick Henry of Virginia were to join Murray as envoys to France. Later, after Patrick Henry had declined, the president substituted Governor Davie of North Carolina. The Senate quickly ratified this proposal for a commission of three.

One may well wonder why John Adams, apparently so inflexible about Murray on Saturday evening, should have recommended a commission of three on Monday. Yet there is probably no great mystery involved. On Saturday evening John Adams was angered and stubborn as a result of the demands, and possibly the language, of the senators. By Monday morning he had not only had time to cool off, but he seems to have learned that the committee would recommend that the Senate reject Murray's appointment. In order to make one more attempt at peace, Adams was willing to compromise on the number of commissioners.

Congress adjourned on March 4, 1799, but the president summoned the cabinet to meet at his house at 5:00 P.M. on Saturday, March 10, and the chief subject of discussion was Pickering's proposed terms for a treaty. With surprisingly little disagreement they decided three points: (1) France must agreed to indemnify United States citizens for all spoliations during the undeclared naval war; (2) all American ships seized and condemned because they had lacked a *rôle d'équipage* (proper listing of the crew) should be returned or compensated for without any question except as to their value; and (3) the United States was not to guarantee any protection of French territory in the Western Hemisphere, as she had been obligated to do by the Treaty of 1778. The next Monday, March 12, the president left for Quincy.

Writing confidentially to Charles Lee, at the end of March, the president revealed both his knowledge of the Arch-Federalist hope to prevent peace and the fact that he was willing to go as far as resignation, if need be, to prevent such an action.

Pickering and his followers came to believe that they had effectively scuttled the plan for sending a commission to Paris, since the president revealed no urgency about the mission's departure. Moderate Federalists, many of them ardently desiring peace, were discouraged by the president's lack of action. Murray, at The Hague, chafed at the delay. It is necessary to investigate the president's actions, appraise his motives, and check his information in order to understand his seeming lack of interest in peace with France.

John Adams's sincerity in seeking peace and his belief that France might be ready to begin serious negotiations seem established. Yet he was not completely sure of France's basic motives. Adams may have feared that France was offering peace feelers only to further divide American sentiment and weaken her ability to effect a united action. He was certainly conscious of the insulting reception accorded his last mission to that country. He believed it probable that France would accept a new mission and negotiate a peace; yet he was aware that he might be wrong, that the French might reject the mission or refuse to negotiate as they had done in 1797–1798. If this should happen there seemed no alternative to all-out war. The president, therefore, wanted to be as prepared as possible for war before his envoys actually sailed.

There is overwhelming evidence that John Adams was in no hurry for his new mission to get under way. His message to Congress on February 18 had specified that William Vans Murray was not to leave for Paris until the president had additional assurances that he would be well received. Adams's letter to Washington had emphasized the same fact. The nomination of Patrick Henry for the mission to France cannot be overlooked. It would seem that Adams had every reason to expect that Henry would decline, even as he had recently declined two other appointments, because of his age. The president must have realized that offering the nomination to Henry, and then waiting for his decision, would take several weeks. This nomination, therefore, seems to provide additional evidence that Adams was in no hurry to get the mission to France under way.

John Adams's early departure for Quincy and his stay there for seven months also seems indicative of his unwillingness to hurry the mission, despite repeated warnings that his absence from the capital endangered its prospects. He was aware of the disloyalty in his cabinet and must have realized that Pickering would do all in his power to delay or frustrate the mission. Yet all through the summer and into the fall, Adams did nothing to speed the departure of the envoys.

It seems probable, then, that both John Adams and Timothy Pickering hoped to benefit from delay in sending the new mission to France. The day after John Adams left for Quincy, Pickering wrote to Rufus King: "Of one thing . . . I am happy to inform you—before his departure after serious consultation with all of us, it was concluded unanimously that certain terms should be demanded of France, without which no Treaty should be made. These terms are what we have a clear right to, and our interest and honor oblige us to insist on. Yet I very much doubt whether France will yield them. I am morally sure she will not; and this has put us all much at our ease."[14] History proved Pickering wrong, but the important point to note is that Pickering felt that delay decreased the possibility of peace.

John Adams accepted and even encouraged delay so that the naval vessels then being built might be completed and ready for action before any final show-down with France. It was these vessels, he believed, that would give the United States, not France, the preponderance of power in the Caribbean. With the new American vessels completed and ready for active duty, the United States would no longer fear the French privateers operating in the West Indies area. Nelson's defeat and virtual destruction of the French fleet meant that France could not, even if she wished, transport an army to the New World. Adams felt that time was on his side and the position of the United States would become stronger as he waited.

In April, William Vans Murray had written from Holland to Secretary Pickering, optimistically suggesting that the prospects for peace were bright. This letter seems to have arrived in Philadelphia in late June or early July. On July 10 Pickering replied. Bristling with contempt for his president and antagonism for France, Pickering asserted that "every man whom you knew and respected, every *real patriot*, every man who has steadily and faithfully supported . . . [Adams's] and his predecessor's administration was thunderstruck" by the announcement of a new mission to France.[15]

In the summer of 1799 the usual rumors were floating about Philadelphia. One was to the effect that Talleyrand had been removed, others indicated that the French monarchy might soon be restored. Arch Federalists were greatly encouraged by these rumors and felt that it might be possible to delay the mission until the Revolution collapsed and a monarchy was again estabished in France. Hamilton and others actively tried to persuade Chief Justice Ellsworth that the mission should not go forward, regardless of what Adams might decree. Ellsworth began to vacillate, to look for excuses to desert the president. Hamilton contacted the British minister, Robert Liston, declaring, truthfully, that he had tried to discourage Lafayette from coming to the United States as a goodwill representative of France.

The Arch Federalists seem to have been, with few exceptions, humorless men. Nearly two centuries later it is still amusing to read a letter Fisher Ames of Massachusetts wrote to Pickering in the early fall of 1799. He reported that the Arch Federalists had seen the governor's Thanksgiving proclamation before it was released and had managed to delete the governor's invocation of God's blessing on the mission to France.

On the twenty-third Florial (May 13) Talleyrand wrote to President Adams. This letter came to Philadelphia, was read by Pickering, and was forwarded to the president at Quincy on July 31. Pickering interpreted the letter as an insult to the United States, since Talleyrand suggested that the U.S. was wasting time in getting new negotiations under way. Just a week later, having received and read both Talleyrand's letter and Pickering's cover-note, John Adams replied:

> It is far below the dignity of the president of the United States to take any notice of Talleyrand's impertinent regrets & insinuations of superfluidities. . . . I will say to you, however, that I consider this letter as the most authentic intelligence yet received in America of the success of the coalition [opponents of France in Europe]. That the design is insidious and hostile at heart, I will not say. Time will tell the truth. Meantime I dread no longer their diplomatic skill. I have seen it & felt it & been the victim of it, these twenty one years. But the charm is dissolved, their magick is at [an] end in America—Still they shall find as long as I am in office, candor integrity & as far as there can be any confidence or safety, a pacifick & friendly disposition. If the spirit of exterminating vengeance ever arises, it shall be conjured up by them, not me. In this spirit I shall pursue the negotiation, & I expect the cooperation of the heads of departments—Our operations & preparations by sea & land are not to be relaxed in the smallest degree. On the contrary, I wish them to be animated with fresh energy.

In this same letter the president indicated his eagerness to move forward with the mission to France in view of Talleyrand's new assurances. "I pray you to lose no time," the president instructed his secretary of state, "in conveying to Governor Davie his commission, and to the Chief Justice and his Excellency, copies of these letters from Mr. Murray and Talleyrand, with a request that, laying aside all other employments, they may make immediate preparations for embarking."[16]

Some of his friends were distressed by Adams's long absence from Philadelphia and his apparent reliance on his secretaries to carry out his directions. As early as the end of April 1799 Uriah Forest urged that Adams return to the capital. Two weeks later John Adams replied,

> I received on Saturday your friendly letter of 28 April, and I thank you for it, and should be very happy if it were in my power to comply with your advice . . . . "The people elected me to administer the government," it is true,

and I do administer it here at Quincy, as really as I could do at Philadelphia. The Secretaries of State, Treasury, War, Navy, and the Attorney-General, transmit me daily by the post all the business of consequence, and nothing is done without my advice and direction, when I am here, more than when I am in the same city with them. The post goes very rapidly, and I answer by the return of it, so that nothing suffers or is lost.[17]

The president continued with the words, "Mrs. Adams, it is true, is better; but she is still in a state so delicate" that she could not travel.

Secretary of the Navy Stoddert, a loyal supporter of Adams, was concerned about the president's absence from the capital. Because yellow fever raged in Philadelphia, the cabinet moved to Trenton, New Jersey. From there, on August 29, Secretary Stoddert urged Adams to return:

> The officers are now all at this place & not badly accommodated. Will you, sir, pardon the liberty I take, not in my official, but private Character, in expressing a wish that it may not be inconvenient for you to join them here, before our Ministers depart for France.
>
> It may happen, that a knowledge of recent events in Europe, may be acquired just before the sailing of the Ministers, which would make some alteration in their Instructions necessary—and possibly these events might be of a nature to require the suspension for a time of the mission.
>
> I would urge both Public considerations & those which relate more immediately to yourself, to Justify the wish I have ventured to express—but I will only say that I have the most perfect conviction that your presence here before the Departure of the Ministers would afford great satisfaction to the best disposed & best informed men, in that part of the Country with which I am best acquainted: and I believe, to the great mass of good men all over the United States.
>
> I will only add that I write this letter without communication with any person: that if I err, the error is all my own—in my motives I cannot be mistaken.[18]

Stoddert was quite aware of Hamilton's maneuvers and the troubles within the cabinet. It is perhaps revealing of their relationship that he wrote another letter to the president that same day, dealing only with matters of business.

Adams replied to Stoddert on September 4, indicating that he would come to Trenton at once if it were a "public necessity." He seemed completely sure, however, that the suggestions for a treaty of peace with France would present no problems. "The terms of accommodation with France were so minutely considered and discussed by us all, before I took leave of you at Philadelphia," the President wrote, "that I suppose there will be no difference of sentiments among us. The draught will soon be laid before you." He was "well aware of the possibility of events which . . . [might] render a suspension, for a time, of the mission, very proper." The letter included two sentences that must be the key to any real understanding of the president's position at that time: "If any considerable difference should unexpectedly arise between the heads of department, I will come at all events. Otherwise I see no necessity for taking a step, that will give more eclat to the business, than I think it deserves." The president went on to appraise the political changes in France, and again indicated his willingness to suspend the mission if that seemed desirable. Then he closed the letter with this important note: "Upon this subject I solicit your confidential communications by every post."[19]

John Adams was now convinced that the completion of the three new frigates would give the United States such a preponderance of naval strength in the Caribbean that he need not fear French duplicity. Thus he felt little pressure to reach a quick solution to the misunderstandings with France.

By September, John Adams was receiving disturbing communications from Pickering. On the tenth, after what appears to have been lengthy and perhaps heated discussions between members of the cabinet, Pickering mailed to the president the completed instructions for carrying out the negotiation with France. John Adams received these late in the evening of September 14. On September 11 Pickering addressed a long, four-page letter to the president.

The letter of the tenth, with the instructions, has been noted by nearly all historians of this period, many of whom, however, have ignored the follow-up letter that Pickering wrote twenty-four hours later. In this second letter, after explaining at length the only deviation the cabinet had proposed from "the three leading points which were fixed" before the president's departure for Quincy the previous March, Pickering asked the president's blanket approval for any changes that might result from Chief Justice Ellsworth's reaction to the instructions. Such changes would be made, Pickering explained, only if there should be no time to solicit the presi-

dent's reaction. Discussing the news from France, Pickering also
proposed the suspension of the mission, indicating that the cabinet
unanimously endorsed such a suspension. He wrote: ". . . a state of
things [in France], and that final result [the restoration of the
monarchy] which you long since foresaw and predicted, appear to
be rapidly advancing. Such a suspension would seem to us to place
the U. States in a more commanding situation, and enable the
President to give such a turn to the mission as the impending
changes should in his opinion demand."[20]

On September 16, in reply to the letter of the tenth, and probably after the letter of the eleventh had been received, the president
replied: "The revolution in the Directory, and the revival of the
clubs and private societies in France [both of which had been
stressed in Pickering's letter of the eleventh], and the strong appearances of another reign of democratic fury and sanguinary anarchy approaching, seem to justify a relaxation of our zeal for the
sudden and hasty departure of our envoys." The Arch Federalists
may have been so pleased with the above that they ignored or
forgot the president's next sentence: "If they [the envoys] remain
in America till all apprehensions of the autumnal equinoctial gales
are passed, it will be so much the more agreeable for them, and not
less safe for the public."[21]

Chief Justice Oliver Ellsworth was a Yankee Federalist from
Connecticut. Reluctantly, in the preceding winter, he had accepted
appointment to the mission seeking peace with France. His an-
tipathy toward that country and his reluctance in accepting the
appointment must have been generally known. It is not strange,
therefore, that the Arch Federalists chose him as the weakest link
in the president's hope for peace. It has been suggested that as
early as the summer of 1799 Pickering and probably Hamilton
were trying to persuade Ellsworth to resign from the mission.

On September 18 Ellsworth wrote to Adams. Discussing "the
present convulsions in France," he raised the question of a possible
postponement of the mission. It would be interesting to know John
Adams's reactions when he received this letter. He must have felt
that Pickering and others were trying to discourage Ellsworth from
keeping his word to serve on the mission. Robert Liston in Trenton
was aware of Pickering's efforts to dissuade Ellsworth from making
the trip to France, and perhaps word had also reached Quincy.
Arriving at about the time of Stoddert's second warning, Ellsworth's
letter may have reinforced the president's determination to return
to Trenton and expedite the sailing of the mission to France. Four

days later Adams replied to Ellsworth, indicating that he was watching European developments very closely, that he was not averse to a temporary postponement of the mission, but implying the commissioners should leave no later than November 1.

On September 19 the president again wrote to Timothy Pickering. The general tenor of this letter was agreement with Pickering's assertion regarding the uncertainty of political conditions in France. The president deplored the prospect of "another reign of terror" and seemed reluctant to think of the departure of his mission. Within forty-eight hours, however, the president received a second and even more urgent warning from Stoddert. Requesting the president to hasten to Trenton, this letter endorsed Adams's desire for peace with both England and France. Stoddert wrote of "artful designing men" and hinted at plots to prevent peace with France and lessen the president's chances of reelection.[22]

The president replied to Stoddert at once. One paragraph of Adams's letter has direct bearing on the degree of his concern for his political future. Stoddert had hinted that a delay in coming to Trenton might have a damaging effect on the president's chance for reelection. Adams wrote, "I have only one favor to beg, and that is that a certain election may be wholly laid out of this question and all others."[23]

On September 24 Pickering again wrote to Adams, stressing the instability of the French government and suggesting that the mission should be suspended, thus obviating the need for the president to make the long trip to Trenton. Meanwhile, John Adams was paying careful attention to the instructions Pickering had sent him on the tenth. Among Adams's papers is a memo, dated merely "September 1799," showing that the president was rewriting the instructions. The simplest change in style merited his careful attention. At the same time he was alert to the need for flexibility and for giving the envoys the maximum amount of discretion. For example, one change he proposed read, "if you should be unanimously of [the] opinion, that an extension of seven to fourteen days or of twenty to forty is necessary or expedient, you are at liberty to make that extension."

John Adams knew the importance of secrecy if he were to maintain his freedom of action. He wanted peace, he expected the mission to depart, but he knew the power of the opposition and he was not sure of the best time for the mission to sail. Thus he would keep his own counsel and bide his time. On September 16 Stephen Higginson wrote to Oliver Wolcott that people in Boston were perplexed because both the president and his wife seemed to have lost interest in the mission to France.

On September 21 the president wrote to Pickering, "Sometime between the 10th & 15th of October I shall join you at Trenton, & will suspend till that time, the ultimate determination concerning the instructions [to the commissioners]."[24] On September 26 the president wrote to Wolcott, "I hope to salute you not long after the 10th [of] Oct." The same day the president sent a note to Elbridge Gerry in reply to a message just received from him. This note closed with three short sentences: "I shall not have the pleasure of seeing you again probably till next summer. Imperious necessity or absolute duty compel me to Trenton. This however I pray you to keep a secret till you hear I am gone."[25]

And keep his departure a secret John Adams did! On October 6 George Cabot wrote to Rufus King, noting that "Last Monday the President set off for Trenton, his departure was unexpected & was scarcely known until he had performed half his journey."[26] That close communication existed between the Arch Federalists is indicated by Cabot's speculation that the president's hurried departure was due to a communication from the secretaries opposing the mission to France.

While the president's final decision regarding the mission was a well-kept secret and his schedule for departing for Trenton caught some of his opponents unaware, the attitude of the Arch Federalists was no secret. On the very day that Adams left for Trenton, September 30, 1799, Robert Liston was writing to Grenville, his superior in London. Liston indicated that it was well known in the capital that Pickering and Wolcott, especially the former, were strongly opposed to the mission to France. Liston also reported that the secretaries were attempting to persuade Ellsworth to refuse to participate.

The end of September had found the Adams farm in Quincy bustling with activity: apples were being picked for the cider mill, potatoes were being hooked out of their hills, and carpenters were at work on a barn and a new cider house. The departure of John Adams and his secretary, Billy Shaw, had been set for Monday, September 30. Faced with a long journey, John Adams would have started early in the morning. The two men stopped at East Chester to see John's daughter and her children. The wife and children of his son Charles were also there, and for the first time the president learned the extent of Charles's degradation. He had become a hopeless alcoholic, deeply in debt. John Adams poured out his heartbreak in a letter to Abigail. Burdened by personal sorrow, the president moved on toward the temporary capital and the problem of the mission to France.

At this time Adams did not know that important changes were taking place in France. The political position of the Directory was weakened as French armies suffered defeats. Four of the directors were thrown out of office, including Merlin, the president. The armed forces of Great Britain were preparing another major attack on the French bastions on the Continent. A young officer named Bonaparte was coming rapidly to the fore. Persistent rumors forecast a return of the Bourbons and a reestablishment of the monarchy.

Sometime on Thursday, October 10, the president and his secretary arrived in Trenton. The small town had been hard put to it to provide shelter and office space for the influx of officials from Philadelphia, but the president was fortunate enough to find a bedroom and small sitting-room in a house owned by two maiden sisters named Barnes. Proud and somewhat flustered to find themselves hosting the president of the United States, they scurried about in an urgent effort to make him comfortable. Along the way from Quincy the president had caught a severe cold. He was ill, tired, and somewhat discouraged. The Misses Barnes were equal to the emergency. They located a down comforter to keep Adams warm and dosed him with their homemade remedies until he recovered.

Several messages and pieces of information were awaiting the president. News of Federalist defeats in the recently held Pennsylvania elections must have concerned him. A letter from Charles Lee, the attorney general, written in Winchester, Virginia, on October 6, strongly urged that the mission not be suspended, pointing out that the general public had been gratified by the original appointment and that a loss of confidence must surely follow any suspension. Furthermore, Lee maintained, even the reestablishment of the monarchy, if such occurred, need not invalidate the mission; surely the United States would find a king no less willing to negotiate than the Directory. Adams would have been even more disturbed if he had known that Alexander Hamilton was continuing his attempts to persuade Oliver Ellsworth to refuse to go on the mission, a step the chief justice was reluctant to take.

John Adams must also have been concerned when he discovered that both General Hamilton and General Wilkinson had reached Trenton before him. Gibbs would later declare their arrival there was "by an accident," but the president could surely smell a conspiracy, especially as Robert Liston, the British minister, was also there. To cap it all, Alexander Hamilton soon called on the president and attempted to persuade the latter to suspend the mission. The present turmoil in France, Hamilton argued, must certainly lead to the restoration of the monarchy. Such an event, he declared, would make the mission useless. Therefore, he persisted, it should be at least suspended.

The conversation between Hamilton and the president was later described by Abigail in a letter to her sister. Hamilton, Abigail asserted, "was perfectly sanguine in the opinion that . . . Louis the 18th" would soon regain the throne of France. To this John Adams replied, "I should as soon expect . . . that the sun, moon & stars will fall from their orbits, as events of that kind take place in any such period . . . ."[27] Considering the stubborn determination of both these men, their instinctive dislike for each other, and the depth of Adams's desire for peace, which was certainly no stronger than Hamilton's wish for war, there must have been a vigorous exchange of opinions.

On the evening of Tuesday, October 15, the members of the cabinet were summoned to meet with the president. The subject of their discussion was the set of instructions for the envoys. Originally agreed upon, at least in principle, before Adams's departure from Philadelphia the previous spring, then reworked by the cabinet in August and early September, and restructured by the president before he left Quincy, they were now given additional scrutiny. The session was a long one, lasting till nearly midnight. It was agreed that there should be no formal alliance with France and no guarantee to defend French territories in the Western Hemisphere. The claims of individual U.S. citizens against France, for damage to American property, should be established by a board of commissioners, and the American envoys were to be empowered to make concessions regarding national claims comparable to any granted by the French commissioners.

It is probable that the president did not mention a definite departure date for the envoys, and the Hamiltonians in the cabinet seem to have left the session with the expectation that the mission would be suspended, at least until political conditions in France were stabilized. They did not realize that Adams had been marking time in part, at least, to await the organization of the three new squadrons of the Caribbean fleet. Nor did they sense that he was aware of the role of General Wilkinson, commander of armed forces in the Southwest, or that he also knew of Hamilton's plans for an alliance with England and for intrigue with Miranda, looking toward seizure of Spanish territory.

John Adams always rose early. On the morning of October 16, 1799, he was up in time to write a note that was delivered to the secretary of state before the latter had his breakfast. Adams instructed Pickering to prepare, at once, the necessary papers and instructions for Davie and Ellsworth, who were to sail no later than November 1.

The die was cast. There would be one more attempt to prevent war with France. John Adams was willing to risk the disintegration of his political party in order to guarantee peace for his country. There would be no excuse for Hamilton to increase the army. There would be no military alliance with Britain. These situations are apparent today. They may have been apparent to those most intimately involved in 1799. Pickering, McHenry, and Wolcott must have been startled, and Hamilton infuriated.

On October 21, 1799, in what appears to be the last letter he ever wrote to George Washington, Alexander Hamilton lamented, "The President has resolved to send the commissioners to France, notwithstanding the change of affairs there. He is not understood to have consulted either of his ministers . . . . All my calculations lead me to regret the measure. I hope that it may not in its consequences involve the United States in a war on the side of France with her enemies."[28]

Even before the envoys sailed, Pickering had vented both his disappointment and his anger. On October 24 he complained to Cabot that "the great question of the mission has been finally decided by *the President alone*."[29] The next day Pickering wrote to William Vans Murray, a member of the commission, a letter as filled with venom toward the president as it was indiscreet. Could it be that Pickering was unaware of the close ties between Murray and John Quincy Adams? Was he completely ignorant of the fact that Murray had been in frequent and direct contact with the president for many months? Or was he so angry and frustrated that he had lost all sense of discretion? At any rate, the secretary of state wrote:

> In the bitterness of my indignation, chagrin and distress on the appointment of new envoys to the execrable government of France, I have vented my feelings in some private letters to you: for I thought it important that you should know truly the sensations which the measure has produced: and be assured that mine rise no higher than

those of the other members of the administration, and of men whom I am sure you remember with respect, esteem and affection—among them I need mention only General Hamilton, Mr. Cabot and Mr. Ames. The rumor of a *suspension*, gave them some relief; but the late positive orders of the President that the mission should proceed, has excited anew our deep regrets and will overwhelm them with the most poignant sorrow. Mr. Ellsworth I know is absolutely averse to the mission: but he goes for the same reason that he at first yielded to the nomination—to prevent something worse.[30]

Pickering then went on to declare that the president consulted with no one, took no advice, made the entire decision himself. He also included references to critical remarks the president had made about Murray, such as "that young man will ruin me."

The departure of the envoys, however, did not bring to an end the criticism and protest of the Arch Federalists. A group of the latter, including Ames and Cabot and several congressmen, met at the Boston home of Jonathan Mason, senator from Massachusetts, to discuss ways of frustrating the president's efforts to establish peace with France. Less than a week after the envoys sailed, Jedidiah Morse wrote to Wolcott that "the situation of our country since the nomination [of the mission to France], has filled me with deep concern," and "my solicitude has not been a little increased by the departure of our envoys. When the President left Quincy we expected that the mission would first be *delayed*, and then *relinquished*, and our former position, as far as possible, be resumed."[31] Morse continued his letter by quizzing Wolcott on the attitude of both the cabinet and the envoys on the president's decision to send them to France at that time. Fisher Ames addressed several letters to Secretary of State Pickering during these fall weeks, each criticizing the mission to France. Bitterly attacking the president's action, Ames advised Pickering to try to arouse public opposition to the mission and any treaty that it might draft.

Adams had finally pressed through the commission to establish peace with France, but it had cost him the enmity of influential men in his cabinet and in the ranks of the Federalist party. It might cost him his reelection. This Adams realized full well.

9

★★★★★

THE THREAT OF CIVIL WAR

John Adams was alert to the possibility of war at home as well as with France or England. Retired on his farm at Quincy, he often asserted that, as president, he had wrestled with the threat of civil war and the splitting of the Union. Such a possibility of internal strife was apparent at least as early as the bitter wrangling in Congress over the Jay Treaty. Between 1796 and 1800 the United States teetered on the brink of an internal revolution that, regardless of its ultimate outcome, would certainly have changed the political structure of the nation and might have dissolved the union that had been forged by the War of Independence.

With the Treaty of Paris in 1783, and the Revolution over, there had been no external enemy for the new nation to unite against. Small frustrations and petty needs disturbed the lives of the people, and bitterness grew as easy solutions to economic and political problems evaded the new nation. In the early 1790s there sometimes seemed to be as much difference between Federalist and Republican as there had been between Patriot and Tory. Smelser is one of several historians who have commented on the depth of bitterness and distrust that developed within the United States during these years. He has remarked on "the vast body of evidence" that marks the 1790s as an "Age of Passion," replete with "nightmarish fears" that from time to time "clouded the minds" of "practically all" political leaders and "influenced their judgments and their collective policies."[1]

Economic and geographic differences as well as political concerns often caused bitter disagreement. John Adams, from his vantage point as the Senate's presiding officer, was one of those who sensed the buildup of animosity and suspicion. On March 12, 1796, almost a year before he would assume the presidency and when it was by no means certain that he would ever achieve that office, he wrote to Abigail that much "apprehension [is] expressed for the Union in conversation. Some think and say it cannot last. Such is the repugnance between the east and the west." Two weeks later he again wrote his wife concerning the climate in Congress, saying "There is such rancor of party that the prospect of a change in administration quite cures me of all desire to have a share in it," while in another three weeks he reported, "The sensations of 19th April, 1775, and those of this morning, have some resemblance to each other. A prospect of foreign war and civil war in conjunction, is not very pleasant. . . . If the House refuses to make the appropriations [necessary to carry out the many provisions of the Jay Treaty], it is difficult to see how we can avoid war, and it is not easier to find out how we can preserve this government from dissolution."[2]

At the time of John Adams's inauguration as second president of the United States, on March 4, 1797, there was a brief lull in the sectional and political strife. The report that France had refused to accept General Pinckney and had ordered him to leave the country under the threat of arrest, however, opened wide the floodgates of bitter partisanship and led to increasing animosity between Federalist and Jeffersonian. Arch Federalists like Theodore Sedgwick were soon advocating a new army, even a "force of 90,000 militia," and the fortification of harbors. The atmosphere of violence increased, rumors of secession and of civil war were heard. At the end of June 1797 Jefferson wrote to Edward Rutledge, ". . . the passions are too high at present, to be cooled in our day. You and I have formerly seen warm debates and high political passions. But gentlemen of different politics would then speak to each other, and separate the business of the Senate from that of society. It is not so now. Men who have been intimate all their lives, cross the street to avoid meeting, and turn their heads another way, lest they should be obliged to touch their hats."[3]

The adjournment of Congress on July 8, 1797, eliminated one forum but in no sense silenced the partisan clamor. The press became more and more virulent. On his sixty-sixth birthday, in 1798, George Washington wrote to Alexander Martin, ". . . much to be regretted indeed it is, that in a crisis like the present, when all hearts should be united and at their Post, ready to rejoice at the good, or repel the evil which await us, that nothing but internal dissentions and political hostilities are to be found in the Councils of our common Country."[4]

It was on January 30, 1798, that Representative Mathew Lyon of Vermont, during a political argument in Congress, spat in the face of Roger Griswold of Connecticut. On the fifteenth of the next month, while old General Dan Morgan of Revolutionary War fame prevented several Jeffersonians from going to Lyon's aid, Griswold attacked him with a hickory stick. By May there were riots in Philadelphia. Deborah Logan, wife of the prominent Quaker-Republican, wrote to a friend describing the terror in the streets and "a state of society destructive of the ties which in ordinary times bind one class of citizens to another." She noted that "friendships were dissolved, tradesmen dismissed, and custom withdrawn from the Republican party . . . . Many gentlemen went armed."[5]

Writing to George Washington on May 17, 1798, Hamilton argued that war with France was inevitable and that the Jeffersonians were even more dangerous to America's future than the French. He insisted that the Republicans intended to change the Constitution, make an offensive and defensive alliance with France, grant her special trade concessions and, in effect if not in name, make the United States but a province of that country. In one of his less cautious moments Hamilton wrote that the Republicans were "ready in the gratification of ambition, vanity, or revenge, or in compliance with the wages of corruption, to immolate the independence and welfare of their country at the shrine of France."[6] Many Arch Federalists agreed with him. On August 10, 1799, some four months before his death, George Washington wrote angrily to Charles C. Pinckney of South Carolina. He lashed out at the Republican press, accusing them of attempting to destroy discipline in the army and provoke anarchy. He feared an explosion that might divide the nation.

Other Federalists, in addition to Hamilton, saw war with France as desirable since it would force an alliance with Britain and give them, at the same time, an excuse to crush the Jeffersonians. Stephen Higginson was among the Arch Federalists who "wanted a headlong plunge into the European political system and a British alliance as the only sure way to crush the American 'Jacobins.' "[7] Theodore Sedgwick welcomed war with France as a means of arousing the patriotic spirit of the nation and thus making the Alien and Sedition Laws unnecessary. "Without them," Sedgwick wrote to King on January 20, 1799, "we might [in a war] have hanged traitors and exported Frenchmen."[8]

Writing to an unnamed correspondent on February 18, 1799, Sedgwick mentioned the bill passed by Congress on the same day, a bill that not only extended the authorization for a provisional army but gave to the president the power to use the volunteers in either of two ways: to repel invasion or to "suppress insurrection."[9] Sedgwick asserted emphatically, "No act of Congress has ever struck the Jacobins with more horror; and I believe they have at last thought of force against the government as a possible event."

It is obvious from a reading of the private correspondence of the Arch Federalists during 1798 and 1799 that they not only thought in terms of retaining their control of the national government, but that at least some of them wished to strengthen that government at the expense of the states. It is likewise apparent that they saw the political strength of Virginia, the state with the largest number of electoral votes, as an impediment to Federalist control. Some hoped to decrease the political power of this Jeffersonian stronghold through the use of military force.

Thus on February 7, 1799, Theodore Sedgwick wrote to Hamilton, pleading for a speed-up in enlistments. The regiments authorized, he believed, were scarcely large enough to quell internal disorders. Some historians have argued that Federalist extremists wanted involvement in the European power struggle not only to strike at France and to "expand the nation's frontiers" but to increase the power of the central government, unite the people under Federalist leadership, and allow Alexander Hamilton to "reap the military glory befitting a conquering general."[10]

Robert Palmer has suggested, "There was ground also to suppose that Hamilton, whose dislike of Virginia was well known, and who had shown his taste for using martial methods to teach respect for government in the Whiskey Rebellion, might employ his new army against the agrarian Republicans in the south, or even to bring in what he would consider a more workable constitution."[11]

An examination of Alexander Hamilton's correspondence, during 1798 and 1799, casts a good deal of light on his desire for strong central power, on his attitude toward war, the Republican opposition, internal revolt, and possible uses of the army. On February 2, 1799, he had written to Theodore Sedgwick, urging more attention to recruiting the army.

> In times like the present, not a moment ought to have
> been lost to secure the government so powerful an auxil-

lary. Whenever the experiment shall be made to subdue a refractory and powerful State by militia, the event will shame the advocates of their sufficiency. . . . When a clever force has been collected, let them be drawn toward Virginia, for which there is an obvious pretext, then let measures be taken to act upon the laws and put Virginia to the test of resistance. This plan will give time for the fervor of the moment to subside, for reason to resume the reins, and, by dividing its enemies, will enable the government to triumph with ease.[12]

Three and a half months later, as mentioned above, Alexander Hamilton was asserting to Washington that the Jeffersonians would support France in case of an invasion and that they wanted to make this country a part of France. At the end of the year, in a letter to Harrison Gray Otis, Hamilton argued against any troop reduction. The possibility of civil war, Hamilton asserted, made the present army none too large. Citing his experiences with a modest citizen-army during the Whiskey Rebellion, Hamilton shuddered at what might have happened had the militia met with serious resistance.

In a letter to Jonathan Dayton, Speaker of the House of Representatives, probably written very early in 1799, Hamilton made what seems to have been his most direct attack on the motives and plans of the Virginians as well as his recommendations for dealing with them. He asserted that the Virginians were gathering arsenals of weapons and levying new taxes to meet the cost of arming their citizens. He strongly suggested that the Virginians hoped to destroy the national government. The letter also contained a long list of suggestions to strengthen the central government, including a more vigorous enforcement of the Alien and Sedition Laws.

Perhaps no historian has assayed the different motivations that influenced Federalists during this period with as much clarity and insight as the British historian Esmond Wright. He wrote:

The year 1798 saw the emergence of a group of High Federalists, of which Hamilton was the undisputed leader and policy maker. They included his aides in the Cabinet, Fisher Ames and Theodore Sedgwick of Massachusetts, Uriah Tracy of Connecticut, Robert Goodloe Harper of South Carolina, Rufus King and George Cabot, both in London. The essence of High Federalist policy was war with France; partly because, like Ames, they shuddered at the prospect of anarchy on the frontier; partly because, like old General Schuyler or Senator Sedgwick, they wanted to destroy the Jeffersonians; partly because, like Hamilton himself, they believed that order and stability in government were essential and that these could only be guaranteed by a standing army. As Gouveneur Morris put it after Hamilton's death, "Our poor friend Hamilton bestrode his hobby to the great annoyance of his friends, and not without injury to himself. . . . He well knew that his favorite form [of government] was inadmissable, unless as the result of civil war; and I suspect that his belief in that which he called 'an approaching crisis' arose from a conviction that the kind of government most suitable in his opinion, to this extensive country, could be established in no other way."[13]

By the end of the year 1798 many Republicans, especially those from the southern states, had become convinced that war with France was not imminent, that the French Directory would make reasonable concessions, and that an army was not needed. They felt, therefore, that Federalist insistence that the army be not only maintained but actually increased could be explained only in terms of their desire to use the army against their domestic opponents.

Jeffersonians, as well as Federalists, were motivated more by passion than by reason. For example, on the evening of Friday, December 7, 1798, Albert Gallatin, an important Jeffersonian in the House, sat in his room in Philadelphia writing a long letter to his wife. Presumably Gallatin was expressing his true feelings about Adams when he wrote, "We are to have the speech [President Adams's to Congress] only tomorrow (Saturday). I expect it will be extremely violent against an insidious enemy and a domestic faction. They . . . avow a design of keeping up a standing army for *domestic* purposes, for since the French fleet is destroyed they cannot even affect to believe that there is any danger of French invasion."[14] In another part of the same letter to his wife, Gallatin quoted Hamilton as having said at Governor Mifflin's table and in the presence of Washington and Pinckney that "the aspect of Virginia was threatening" and that violent insurrection was building up in western Pennsylvania.

Republicans in Virginia reacted in at least two ways to the threat of the Arch Federalists. The state made plans to purchase five thousand "stand of arms," and raised taxes by 25 percent. It also voted to establish three arsenals, each with ten thousand stand of arms, as well as to erect a plant for manufacturing arms in Richmond. Even more important as an indication of the seriousness with which Republican leaders viewed the possibility of military action against them were three letters written by Thomas Jefferson on January 30, 1799. Addressed to James Madison, T. M. Randolph, and Nicholas Lewis, the letters from Jefferson stressed the urgency of restraining Virginia Republicans from any action or proclamation that would provide the Federalists with an excuse for moving the army into Virginia.

On January 5, 1800, Alexander Hamilton wrote a long letter to Rufus King in London, revealing that Hamilton was still fearing or expecting civil war. The letter included long and bitter comments about the president and one paragraph that expressed a continued concern with revolution: "The spirit of faction is abated nowhere. In Virginia it is more violent than ever. It seems demonstrated that the leaders there, who possess completely all the powers of the local government, are resolved to possess those of the national, by the most dangerous combinations; and, if they cannot affect this, to resort to the employment of physical force."[15]

Just a week later, up in Dedham, Massachusetts, one of the Arch Federalists, Fisher Ames, was writing to Oliver Wolcott, the secretary of the treasury. Ames urged that well-officered, regular troops be always on the alert to move against Jefferson's supporters, in numbers sufficient to guarantee that the "cause of law and order" should at once seize the upper hand.

The question of civil violence was tied inextricably to the question of foreign conflict. Beginning in 1799, President Adams attempted to reduce the war fever and to persuade his countrymen that national honor was not dependent upon war. Adams also attempted to reduce the tempest of nationalistic fervor and dispel the thoughts of internal revolution that had been sweeping over the country since the XYZ crisis developed. He replied to an address from "The Inhabitants of part of the County of Edgecomb" with the following pronouncement: "I perceive no disposition, in the American People to go to war with each other: and no foreign Hostilities that can be apprehended, no just and necessary cause, have any terrors for you, or me."[16]

Ten years later, from the comparative quiet and isolation of his Quincy farm, John Adams dismissed the Arch Federalists with these words: "Let me repeat to you once more, Sir, the faction was dizzy. Their brains turned round. They knew not, they saw not the precipice on which they stood. . . . To despatch all in a few words, a civil war was expected." In our own time, Robert Palmer has written, "It was Hamilton and the High Federalists who, under pressure, were tempted by the thought of scrapping the constitution altogether."[17]

It seems quite possible that all-out war with France at this time would have become either the cause or the excuse for civil war. Possessed of a strong army, Hamilton and many of his supporters would have been anxious to weaken the position of the Jeffersonians and perhaps to change the political structure of the nation.

The bitter and emotion-clogged political atmosphere was never more strongly evidenced than in the debates, in Congress and in the press, over the Alien and Sedition Acts. These acts, actually four separate pieces of legislation, developed out of the XYZ frenzy.

On April 26, 1798, Thomas Jefferson wrote: "One of the war party [Federalists], in a fit of unguarded passion, declared sometime ago they would pass a citizen bill, an alien bill & a sedition bill . . . ." That same day the Senate appointed an all-Federalist committee to draft an alien bill. Later the vice-president wrote Madison, denouncing Adams's statements to the public and noting his own uncertainty about congressional action: "What new law they will propose . . . has not yet leaked out. The citizen bill sleeps. The alien bill, proposed by the Senate, has not yet been brought in. That proposed by the H of R has been so moderated, that it will not answer the passionate purposes of the war gentlemen."[18]

The Senate's committee reported on May 4, recommending an alien bill of thirteen parts. The president would be authorized to deport aliens when they were considered dangerous "to the peace and safety" of the nation. Such aliens, moreover, would be denied a jury trial, and the president would not have to explain or justify his decisions.

This committee report was widely discussed and after many weeks developed into four separate pieces of legislation. A Naturalization Act became law on June 18; an Act Concerning Aliens (sometimes known as the Alien Friends Act) was signed by the president on June 25, 1798; a third act, the Act Respecting Alien Enemies, passed Congress on July 6. The fourth and most widely discussed was the Sedition Act, known officially as the Act for the Punishment of Certain Crimes; it was designed to silence criticism of public officials and their actions. This was passed by the Senate on July 4.

Many of the Federalists felt that their failure to obtain a declaration of war against France necessitated the Sedition Act. Senator Lloyd, one of the bill's chief sponsors, wrote to George

Washington: "I fear Congress will close the session without a declaration of War, which I look upon as necessary to enable us to lay our hands on traitors, and as the best means that can be resorted to, to destroy the effect of the skill of the Directory in their transactions with Mr. Gerry."[19] A week later, on July 11, the House passed the Sedition Bill by a close vote of forty-four to forty-one. Signed by the president, it became law on July 14.

The Naturalization Act lengthened to fourteen years the period of residence required prior to obtaining citizenship. This act reflected the nativistic fear of immigrant influence as well as the political fact that the majority of the new citizens were joining the Jeffersonian party. The Federalists had been critical of the increasing immigration into the United States for several years. As early as May of 1797 they had tried to place a twenty dollar tax on naturalization. The frenzy over the XYZ affair provided an emotional climate in which Federalists in Congress could lash out at both new immigrants and Republican opponents.

The first of the alien bills, officially titled An Act Concerning Aliens, but usually referred to as the Alien Friends Act, was to expire in 1800. It empowered the president to deport any alien he considered dangerous to the public peace. The Alien Enemies Act allowed the president to deport citizens of any country with which the United States was at war. It was a bipartisan measure supported by many Republicans and was designed to be permanent.

The Sedition Act was most controversial and has been much criticized. It grew out of a variety of circumstances and conditions. Some have attributed it to the XYZ affair, but that excitement probably provided the occasion rather than the cause of its passage. It provided prison sentences for criticizing the president or Congress.

Senator Bingham wrote to Rufus King on September 30, "The Friends of the Government have improved the Opportunity of cloathing the Executive with additional Energies."[20] Certainly the desire to strike out at political opposition was one of the major causes of the alien and sedition legislation. Many Federalists were alarmed at the growth of Jeffersonian strength and fearful that their party would lose its dominant position. This attitude was compounded of two parts: selfish fear of losing power and sincere concern for the nation, which would certainly suffer, they felt, from being subjected to a different political philosophy.

In order to understand and properly appraise the Sedition Act, certain facts must be accepted. In the first place, English common law provided for the punishment of seditious speech or press. During congressional debate on the sedition bill, it was actually argued, and fairly so, that the legislation being proposed was more lenient than the common law. The act as it was finally passed by the House required the prosecution to prove "malice and intent," a safeguard never provided by common law. Furthermore, the Sedition Act as passed was more lenient than the common-law doctrine on libels.

In the second place, it must be remembered that the first prosecution of libelous editors took place before the Sedition Act was passed. Bache was arrested June 26, nineteen days before the Sedition Act became law. Furthermore, there is evidence that the debate over this act brought into the open a disagreement about the role of the federal judiciary that had existed between Federalists and Republicans for some time. At least as early as 1796, Chief Justice Francis Dana of the Massachusetts Supreme Court, in his address at the opening of a session of that court, had criticized the slanderous treatment accorded those in public office. In the spring of 1797 Supreme Court Justice Iredell, presiding over the circuit bench in Virginia, condemned the "unsettling tendencies" of some members of the House of Representatives.

It should also be noted, in appraising the Sedition Act, that there were rather recent English precedents for this type of legislation, and that the Republican opposition was very largely based on their objection to an extension of the power of the central government. There is little indication that the Republicans were fighting for a free press; they merely wanted the supervision of the press to be in the hands of the state courts. Such a position was no doubt compounded out of equal parts of political philosophy and of fear of Federalist dominance of the judiciary.

As finally passed into law, the Sedition Act consisted of two sections. The first set a maximum fine of five thousand dollars and a maximum sentence of five years for "conspiracies and combinations to impede the operation of federal laws." The second section set a possible two thousand dollar fine and a two-year sentence for "false, scandalous and malicious" accusations against the president, the Congress, or the government. The law imposed on the prosecution the necessity of proving "intent to defame" or "to bring them into contempt or disrepute, or to excite against them the hatred" of the American people.[21]

While a good number of Republicans supported the Alien Enemies Act, the other pieces of legislation were truly partisan acts, introduced, defended, and passed by Federalists, and signed into law by a Federalist president. Why this nearly unanimous support for the alien and sedition legislation by the Federalists? It is easy for us today, reading their private letters as well as the public pronouncements, to argue that the motivation for this legislation was compounded out of hatred for France and the desire to destroy the political power of the Jeffersonians. Yet there must have been many Federalists who were sincerely fearful lest what they thought of as an ideal society be destroyed. England had become alarmed by the influence of the French Revolution, and had passed legislation restricting both aliens and "dangerous" political doctrines. Federalists may have felt that such legislation was what had saved England. Robert Goodloe Harper, militant Federalist representative from South Carolina, in debate on June 19, 1798, pontificated that "Unless we follow their [the European nations which had escaped French dominance] example and crush the viper in our breast, we shall not, like them, escape the scourge which awaits us."[22]

It is always difficult to sense the true feelings of the average man or woman. Perhaps Billy Shaw, nephew of Abigail and secretary to John Adams, expressed the feelings of middle-class Federalists when he wrote his aunt, on January 2, 1799, that he had decided the Alien and Sedition Acts were absolutely necessary because a licentious press would destroy the social order.

John Adams has been condemned, or at least criticized, by most historians for his role in the passage of this legislation. That he neither drafted the legislation nor asked Congress, even in general terms, for such acts, is of course admitted by everyone. His involvement or responsibility would seem to consist of these elements: the president never opposed the passage of this legislation, and he did not kill the acts with a veto as he might have tried to do. Furthermore, almost every historian writing in this period has concluded that by his replies to addresses, especially in the late spring and summer of 1798, John Adams played a major role in whipping up fervent nationalism, and that this spirit, in turn, was in considerable part responsible for the repressive legislation then passed.

Historians have disagreed about John Adams's personal attitude toward the legislation at the time it was discussed and passed. Those historians who have argued that John Adams personally favored the acts are not convincing, although it is true that he did not oppose the acts nor veto the bills when they were passed. It is known that Adams was disturbed by the slanderous nature of the opposition press. Beyond that there seems no certainty of his position.

Pertinent to an evaluation of Adams's part in the laws, however, is the matter of its enforcement. A decade and a half after the passage of this legislation, John Adams wrote to Thomas Jefferson that "he had not applied the alien law in a single instance," and the historian Frank Malloy Anderson believed he "was at least technically correct." The same historian wrote, "There is no evidence to show that President Adams ever personally interested himself in the enforcement of either law."[23] There is evidence that many Federalists, especially Timothy Pickering, wanted to use the alien laws to deport large numbers of noncitizens. There is also proof that John Adams resisted this pressure—he refused to deport French consuls already stationed in this country, and he several times rejected Pickering's appeal that he sign blank warrants to be used at Pickering's discretion. There is evidence that Pickering was continually trying to persuade the president to move more energetically under these laws.

The Alien Acts were not without effect. Many aliens, especially recent French émigrés, hurriedly left the country, fearing the provisions of the Alien Acts would be turned against them. Enemy agents may well have reduced their activity for fear of reprisals. President Adams did sign warrants for the deportation of three aliens, but they had left the country before they could be apprehended.

It was the Sedition Act, however, that caused most of the anger and dispute, as it has attracted most of the attention of the historians of the period. That both John and Abigail were seriously nettled by the malign accusations and attacks of the Jeffersonian press is readily admitted. At the end of March 1798 for example, a Charleston, South Carolina, newspaper demanded the resignation of the president and his entire cabinet, accusing them of being the source of all the trouble with France. Week after week the administration was accused of dishonesty, misrepresentation, and malicious disloyalty. Without approving of censorship of the press, one can sympathize with Abigail when she wrote her sister, "Yet dairingly do the vile incendaries keep up in Baches paper the most wicked and base, violent & caluminiating abuse . . . . But nothing will have an Effect until congress pass a Sedition Bill . . . ."[24]

As noted above, when the Sedition bill was being debated in Congress its proponents argued that it was more lenient than recently passed British legislation, more protective of the rights of the accused than the common law, and that there were safeguards such as the necessity to prove "malice and intent" and the provision that allowed submission of the truth as evidence. Yet Borden pointed out that "in operation, these safeguards were of little value. Truth was never used as an effective defense." Furthermore, he indicated, "judges freely delivered blazing lectures to the jury" in "a climate of fear and defiance."[25]

During the period of hysteria that followed its passage, fourteen persons were sentenced under the Sedition Act. John Adams, without doubt, and despite protestations he made in later life, must take some of the blame for that hysteria, for he seems to have approved at least two of the major prosecutions.

This is certainly not a happy aspect of American history, and those who, through the years, have proclaimed it one of the most fearful and disgraceful episodes in our history have been quite correct. Most judges in 1798 and 1799 seem to have been linked both by politics and by social and economic class to the Arch Federalists, and few of those indicted under the Sedition Act seem to have received an impartial trial. Speaking of the alien and sedition legislation, DeConde wrote, "with Secretary of State Pickering as their chief enforcement officer, and Hamilton a leading advocate of their enforcement, the spirit of the black cockade became one of intolerant, oppressive, and, at times, hysterical native Americanism."[26]

It is quite proper to condemn the alien and sedition legislation, yet it should be recognized that the significance of that legislation has been overstated. There were Republicans, as well as Federalists, who supported at least part of the program. Some Americans defended the legislation as "war measures." When the Republicans were in power in certain states, Virginia among them, they used the state courts and English common law to inflict penalties for libel even more excessive than those meted out by federal courts under the Sedition Act.

Furthermore, the political effects of the legislation have been distorted and misrepresented. Even the most thorough student of the Jeffersonian newspaper press concluded, "Indisputably, the Sedition Law was a key issue in the 1800 campaign."[27] It has been pointed out, however, that in the elections of 1799, eight out of nineteen Virginians elected to the national House of Representatives were Federalists; and thus it would appear that in Virginia, seedbed of the Virginia and Kentucky Resolutions, stronghold of Jefferson and Madison, the Federalists did roughly twice as well as they had in the previous election. Nationalism, aroused by the XYZ fervor, seems to have been a much more potent political factor than any anger directed at the sponsors of the repressive legislation. Many of those who have studied the presidential election of 1800, especially the more recent scholars, tend to deemphasize the importance of the Alien and Sedition Laws in accounting for Jefferson's victory. In spite of the publicity that resulted from the abortive efforts of the Republicans to repeal the legislation, and the attention to these laws in the Jeffersonian press in 1800, most recent historians have tended to believe that both taxes and the issue of the army were more potent, politically, than the Alien and Sedition Acts.

By the spring of 1799 resentment against higher taxes made necessary by the defense preparations against France, especially by the increased army, spread throughout the United States. Opposition to the tax on whiskey, half a decade earlier, had centered in western Pennsylvania. This time it was eastern Pennsylvania, once a Federalist stronghold, where violence threatened. As early as December 1798 protest meetings were held in this section. The Germans or "Pennsylvania Dutch" were suspicious of their neighbors of English descent and viewed the increased military preparations as a pro-British move. Republican propaganda was also doing effective work in arousing the peoples' suspicion and distrust of the government. There was even a rumor that President Adams had mortgaged the entire state of Pennsylvania and that he would flee to England and purchase a title.

In the first months of 1799 there were numerous signs of opposition to the newer taxes, especially in Bucks and Northampton counties. Irate housewives poured scalding water on the heads of assessors who were measuring their windows for the "window tax." Some citizens refused to pay taxes.[28] Two Germans and a militia captain of unknown descent were jailed for such refusal. John Fries, described as a "county auctioneer," rallied an armed force of nearly 150 men, and on March 7 proceeded to Bethlehem. At the Sun Tavern there, he compelled a United States marshal, William Nichols, to free the three prisoners.

Great excitement followed. Some Federalists at least pretended to see in Fries's act the beginning of the long-expected attempt of the Jeffersonians to seize control of the government by force, and blamed all on the pro-French Republicans. Alexander Hamilton was sure that a large military force must be gathered at once to punish this threat against the sovereignty of the national government. "Whenever the government appears in arms," Hamilton proclaimed, "it ought to appear like a *Hercules* and inspire respect by the display of strength."[29]

On March 12 President Adams, ready to leave for Quincy that very day, issued a proclamation. Denouncing "certain acts which I am advised amount to treason," the President commanded "all persons being insurgents as aforesaid . . . to disperse and retire peaceably to their respective abodes . . . ."[30] Before the first of May, twenty-nine persons had been arrested, accused of resistance to the taxes, and taken to Philadelphia for trial. Opposition to the government then subsided as quickly as it had arisen.

John Fries was the acknowledged leader of the opposition to the government. On May 15, 1799, the trial of Fries was concluded and he and two principal aides were sentenced to death. On a technicality, however, Fries was granted a second trial. While waiting for this retrial, the three men who had been sentenced to hang appealed to the president for pardons.

Not all Federalists were happy at the sudden collapse of opposition. Oliver Wolcott wrote to the president, telling him that Fries and two of his principal associates had been tried in federal court and found guilty of treason. But, said Wolcott, certain "great men" were assuredly behind Fries.

When John Adams learned that Fries had been sentenced to death, he at once wrote to Pickering and Wolcott and to Charles Lee, the attorney general. He asked for all possible information about Fries, and the president undertook to read whatever the common law said about treason and to study the precedents he could locate. His May 19 letter to Oliver Wolcott suggests the thoroughness with which the president sought to familiarize himself with the most minute details of the case.

Adams could be firm but he could also be both charitable and reasonable. He failed to see a serious challenge to the survival of the national government in the spontaneous acts of a few back-countrymen who sought to "free" three friends from custody. On May 20, John Adams wrote of the Fries episode that it was a high-handed, dangerous riot, but that it was certainly not treason.

Late in the summer, John Adams received the official petitions asking for a presidential pardon. Adams, as was his usual custom, queried his cabinet for advice. On September 9 Pickering replied, noting that he had "the honor to inclose the opinions of the attorney general and heads of departments on the petitions of John Fries and others, insurgents in Bucks and Northampton counties in Pennsylvania, that no pardon should *now* be granted, nor any answer given."[31]

As late as May of 1800 John Adams still wrestled with the

problem of Fries and the sentence that hung over the latter's head. To Oliver Wolcott, the president wrote, "It highly concerns the people of the United States, and especially the federal government, that, in the whole progress and ultimate conclusion of this affair, neither humanity be unnecessarily afflicted, nor public justice be essentially violated, nor the public safety be endangered."[32]

The president would have been aware of the possibility that in the retrial Fries might be given a lighter sentence, thus obviating the necessity for him to take controversial action. Adams interpreted the conduct of Fries as the improper action of a hot-headed, impulsive man. He recognized the danger of identifying such isolated acts as high treason and was inclined to issue a pardon. Abigail left for Quincy on May 19. The president, however, planned to visit the new capital city that was rising on the banks of the Potomac.

The day after Abigail left, Lee, Wolcott, and Stoddert sent a communication to the president, urging him to issue no pardon. The next day the president replied, acknowledging receipt of their opinion but stating that since he disagreed he would assume the responsibility for pardoning Fries. The President also asked for a general pardon against treason in the three Pennsylvanian counties and suggested clemency for all who had been fined or imprisoned in the protest. Adams then asked that Lee prepare three pardons for his signature. It is possible that Lee still demurred, as we know that four days later the president repeated his request.

The president's action aroused fresh ire among the Arch Federalists. Some of them, men like Uriah Tracy, turned violently against the president. John Adams had frustrated their plans for alliance with Britain, for economic exploitation of the West Indies, for military action against both Spain and France; and he had begun to disband the new army, leaving their hero, Alexander Hamilton, without the means to realize the military glory he sought. Adams had overridden his advisers and sent another mission to France. He had dismissed Pickering and McHenry, and now he pardoned Fries. "Undue mercy to villains is cruelty to all the good & virtuous," Tracy exploded to McHenry. "Our people in this state [Connecticut], are perfectly astonished .... I am fatigued & mortified that our government, which is weak at best, would withhold any of its strength at a time when all its energies should be doubled."[33] The short, balding, much-criticized president had once more evaluated a situation and, convinced of what was right and best for his country, had opposed the strongest men in his party.

10

★★★★★

JOHN ADAMS ON THE DEFENSIVE

The threat of civil war, the growing antagonism between Federalist and Republican, the explosion over the hated taxes in eastern Pennsylvania, all were related to two aspects of Adams's presidency that have been often criticized and as often misunderstood. These were his absences from "the seat of government" and his replies to the "addresses."

Almost without exception, his own contemporaries and the historians of more recent times have assumed that John Adams, especially in the spring and summer of 1798, either desired or at least anticipated war against France. Thus the replies that he wrote in response to the hundreds of addresses that came to him have been interpreted as an effort to arouse nationalistic fervor and, in some quarters, support for war against France. An examination of these two areas, the absences and the replies to addresses, sheds light on Adams's four years as chief executive.

From the spring of 1798 well into the summer of 1799, President Adams was literally swamped with "addresses." They came occasionally from individuals but usually from groups: militia companies, legislative bodies, fraternal organizations, college students, fire companies, "inhabitants." Most of them offered support or praise for the president's foreign policy. Many of them indicated the strength of the nationalistic fervor that swept the nation after the reports regarding the XYZ affair were made public.

The president established the practice of answering every address. Both the address and his reply were usually printed in one or more newspapers serving the area from which the address came. Often these were widely reprinted by other editors. The composition of these replies was very time consuming. Abigail several times noted the enormous amount of time her husband spent in writing them and the physical demand they placed on his health and strength. On May 20, 1798, Liston, the British minister to the United States, wrote to Grenville, "Mr. Adams spends the whole morning from 6 o'clock till 12 or 1, in writing these answers, which are frequently as long as the addresses to which they apply."[1]

Contemporary reaction to Adams's replies varied with the bias of the observer. The Jeffersonians, interpreting Adams's words as evidence of a desire for war, often attacked them with vehemence. Recent historians seem to have been strongly influenced by such contemporary criticism and have written about the violence of Adams's recommendations and the intemperate nature of his language. It has been argued that the president's replies were a major factor in arousing the nationalistic fervor of the period, and thus that he had a hand in such repressive legislation as the Alien and Sedition Acts.

Such vigorous criticisms seem unwarranted. For example, in his undated reply to an address from Concord, Massachusetts, he wrote, "If Concord drank the first blood of martyred freemen, Concord should be the first to forget the injury, when it is no longer useful to remember it. Some of you, as well as myself, remember the war of 1755 as well as that of 1775. War always has its horrors, and civil wars the worst."[2]

The president was steadily pursuing a single goal. He did not want war with France, and he did not want an alliance with Britain. He believed, however, that the people must understand the seriousness of the situation with France, that his country must be prepared in the event that war came. If, as he came to believe, France wanted political dominance but not war, the United States must have enough naval strength to prevent such dominance. Equally aware of the pro-French attitude of most Jeffersonians and of the schisms within his own party, John Adams used words and logic, the only means at his command, to encourage unity, defiance toward French control, harmony within the country, and the support of those measures of defense that he believed essential.

Each reply was an individual matter; this was no mass production. Reading the addresses and the replies in turn shows John Adams's careful perusal of each address and the manner in which he directed each reply to a particular geographical area, age group, or point of view.

The president did not always agree with his addressors. Sometimes he lectured them and occasionally he chided them. He answered the addressors directly but he was also conscious of the people who would read his replies in their newspapers.

Admittedly Adams's language was sometimes strong; there were occasional intemperate attacks on the French government and on the evils of partisanship and factionalism at home. There certainly were statements that must have riled the political opposition. Yet Adams never advocated full-scale war, never denied an interest in peaceful and honorable settlement with France.

A perusal of 31 consecutive replies to addresses, all written by Adams at the peak of the XYZ anger, reveals eleven emphases, as follows: effort to promote nationalistic fervor, 30; criticism of the actions of France, 19; indications of a desire for peace, 13; criticism of partisan strife, 12; criticism of the philosophy of the French Revolution, 11; appeals for a stronger defense, 11; opposition to foreign alliances of any kind, 9; expressions of a love of liberty, 7; expressions of national danger, 7; attack on the Jacobins at home, 3; the probability of war with France, 1.[3] This summary seems to indicate that many of the comments in the secondary literature regarding Adams's replies are unjustified.

A few short extracts provide a sampling of some of the ideas and facts John Adams was emphasizing. On May 10, 1798, replying to the Inhabitants of the Town of Hartford, Connecticut, he played down the threat of war with France: "I have never considered the issue of our late endeavors to negotiate with the French republic as a subject either of congratulation or despondency; as, on the one hand, I should be happy in the friendship of France upon honorable conditions, under any government she may choose to assume; so, on the other, I see no cause of despondency under a continuance of her enmity, if such is her determined disposition. . . . if the spirit of independent freemen is again awakened and its force is combined, I agree with you that it will be irresistible."[4]

On the twenty-second of that month, he exhorted young Bostonians to arm and especially to go to sea in their country's defense. Yet, even here, he emphasized that being a good citizen of the United States was more important than being a soldier.

In April 1799, when John Adams was convinced that peace with France, on honorable terms, was possible, he still felt it necessary to maintain a stout defense. The president replied to the

Grand Jury of Morris County, New Jersey, in these words: "The end of even war is peace. . . . Whenever we have enemies, it will be their own fault; and they will be under no necessity of continuing enemies longer than they choose. In the present crisis, however, we ought to continue, with unabated ardor, all our preparations and operations of defence."[5]

Adams wrote for all the people and not from a partisan position. He seems to have looked upon his role as that of an educator or leader who must carefully think through situations and pass on information and evaluations to the people. He gave meticulous answers, sometimes calmly and again with vigor and strong emotions. His feeling of responsibility for the clarification of his point of view shines through his replies to the addresses quite as strongly as do his emotions, judgments, and prejudices.

One may learn much about John Adams, the problems he faced, the goals he had in mind, and his method of attempting to communicate with the people of the United States by reading his replies to the addresses sent him. It would seem that his replies have been misinterpreted by many. Or, perhaps, as with other aspects of his presidency, that too many have read what his enemies wrote and have accepted uncritically the judgments they made. It would seem that President Adams's replies are not the hot-headed rejoinders, calculated to lead to war, that many have labeled them. Rather they seem to bear testimony to the calculated, well-thought-out program of a dedicated leader who wanted, above all, an honorable peace, but who had determined that such peace could only be obtained by a strong, united nation. A leader who was prepared, if need be, to defend his position with vigor.

The president of the United States must maintain the confidence and be responsive to the needs of the general public. To the extent that he remains acceptable to the people, he must cultivate a "feel" for their moods, anxieties, hopes, and fears, must give them pertinent information and point out ways to alleviate or solve problems. Long after John Adams left the presidency, Harrison Gray Otis referred to "what old John Adams calls the tact of the feelings and passions of mankind."[6] Throughout his presidency Adams was concerned about the "feelings and passions" of his countrymen and spent much time reading and responding to letters from individuals and groups.

In the winter of 1799 increasing numbers of Americans, eighteen thousand from Pennsylvania alone, sent petitions for disbanding the army and repealing the direct taxes that had been levied to support it. John Adams was aware of and disturbed by this indication of popular unrest.

The president was always sensitive to the public pulse. Referring to the laudatory addresses that were flooding into the capital in the summer of 1798, he wrote to George Washington that "the approbatory addresses are very precious to me, as they discover more union among the States, and greater unanimity among the people, than was expected."[7] Hoping to present a bold front to France, in order to force that country to respect America's rights as an independent country, John Adams knew that the united support of the general public was essential.

There were more bitter attacks than praise, however, during Adams's four years at the helm. After May 1797 these attacks were most often mounted in the Jeffersonian press. In 1799 the Arch Federalists joined the cacophony—usually in their private correspondence. Sewart has noted, "As President, little that Adams said or did or refrained from doing escaped scathing denunciations."[8] The attacks also came in the form of resolutions and anonymous threats. "Take care, John Adams," read one such letter, "an evil day is approaching. Traitors will be punished."[9]

A more colorful but also anonymous threat mentioned the possibility of assassination. Probably written in October 1798, the letter read, "President Adams. *Myself and family are ruined by the French.* If you do not procure satisfaction for my losses, when a treaty is made with them, I am undone forever, and you must be a villain to your country!!! *Assassination* shall be your lot, if *restitution* is lost to America through YOUR means, or if ever you agree to a peace without it. The subsistence of thousands, who have lost their all, *depends upon it.* [signed] *A ruined merchant, alas! with ten children!!! made beggars by the French."*[10]

Many of his contemporaries and most historians have severely criticized John Adams for his absences from the "seat of government." Examination of such absences and such criticism is relevant to an understanding of how Adams regarded the presidency. It has been noted that during his four years in office he was absent from the national capital for a total of 385 days (approximately ninety-six days, or three months, a year), while Washington's total absence during his eight years in office was only 181 days. Examination reveals, however, that even allowing for the fact that each served eight years Thomas Jefferson and James Monroe were both absent from the capital more often than Adams, with James Madison not far behind.[11] Congress seldom met during July, August, September, and October and government slowed to a stand-still.

By the spring of 1799 most of the Arch Federalists were in bitter opposition to the president. It is always difficult to distinguish between a sincere criticism and a mere personal attack. But whatever its motivation, the letter Robert Troup wrote to Rufus King on May 6 reveals a frequently expressed contemporary attitude toward Adams's absences from the capital. Troup wrote, "The insurrection in Northern Pennsylvania [Fries Rebellion, discussed above] is suppressed . . . . The President suddenly, and without notice, left Philadelphia for Braintree [Quincy] just after this rebellion had broken out, and his departure at that crisis excited much dissatisfaction. His stay from the seat of Government, which is likely to continue till next November or December, is a source of much disgust. It embarrasses the public business and has the air of an abdication."[12]

Especially in those tense weeks of 1799, some of John Adams's close friends and supporters were equally disturbed by his stay in Massachusetts. General Uriah Forrest wrote from Georgetown at the end of April, apologetically pleading for Adams to return to Philadelphia:

> I feel how much the happiness of this country depends on the confidence the people have in the government, and I feel that yourself must be the rallying point of confidence. The public sentiment is very much against your being so much away from the seat of government, from a conviction that, when you are there, the public vessel will be properly steered; and that these critical times require an experienced pilot. The people elected you to administer the government. They did not elect your officers, nor do they (however much they respect them) think them equal to govern, without your presence and control. . . . I speak the truth, when I say that your real friends wish you to be with your officers, because the public impression is, that the government will be better conducted.[13]

About a month after John Adams received the above letter from General Forrest, Abigail wrote her youngest son, "When the president thinks it necessary for him to be at Philadelphia he will go, but not an hour before to please friend or silence foes—that was never his object."[14]

John Adams's absences from the capital first became a problem in the summer of 1797. When the special session of Congress, called because of the crisis precipitated by France in refusing to accept Charles C. Pinckney as American minister to that country, came to an end in July, John and Abigail at first thought they would look for a summer place outside of Philadelphia. Both preferred the quiet and relative coolness of the country to the hot and humid city with its threat of yellow fever.

After some hesitation, however, they decided to return home, and they left Philadelphia on July 19, a fortnight after the adjournment of Congress. Both were happy at the thought of being in their own home, with their neighbors and their old friends. John Adams found renewed strength as he tramped his fields or climbed Penn's Hill to scan the shoreline. Perhaps he sensed that both he and Abigail—the former no longer young and the latter never very robust—needed this renewal of physical and spiritual strength that being in their own home made possible.

In 1798 they again left Philadelphia in late July. During that summer and fall, Abigail lay critically ill and Adams found it difficult to wrench himself away from her bedside. Late in November he had to leave in order to be in Philadelphia before Congress convened, but he left reluctantly.

In 1799 John Adams left Philadelphia in mid-March, eight days after the adjournment of Congress. He timed his return to the urgencies of the foreign crisis. During the spring and summer of 1799 Adams may have realized his secretaries were disloyal and, protected by the distance between himself and his cabinet, may have deliberately waited for the completion of the new ships and the proper moment to dispatch the mission to France.

The summer and fall of 1800 were again marked by the Adams's absence from Philadelphia. John Adams's hopes and fears, his own view of the success or failure of his administration, hinged on the outcome of the negotiations taking place in Paris. If he had been primarily concerned with his chances for reelection, if personal compaigning by presidential candidates had been in vogue, he might well have returned to Philadelphia, or the new capital city in Washington, or even have gone on a southern tour. But Adams could wait for news from Paris as well in Quincy as in any other place.

Today it appears that Adams was remiss in absenting himself for such long periods from the capital, that he belonged where the action was. Certainly his own political career suffered from his absences. The Jeffersonians too often made hay while Adams was getting in his rowen in Quincy. The Arch Federalists in Congress, in his cabinet, in a New York law office, and in the embassy in London had opportunities to widen the breach between the Adams Federalists and themselves. It was most certainly during the summer of 1799 that the Federalist party, as an organization, began to come apart.

Yet, whenever John Adams was away from the capital he attended closely to government affairs, sometimes writing to the secretary of state as often as twice a day. The files of Adams's correspondence bear testimony to the effort of the president to keep on top of all developments. In an era when it took from four to seven or eight weeks to get word to or from Europe, the week or less needed for word to travel from the capital to the Massachusetts farmhouse seemed of little consequence.

In judging Adams it must be remembered that his absences from the seat of government were actually not of as long duration as has been charged, that several of the men who followed him as president were absent even more than he, that he sometimes had sound reasons for his absences, and that he does not appear to have allowed the affairs of state to suffer. At the same time it is also true that the absences were politically harmful to Adams and that they may have hastened or accelerated the schisms within the Federalist party.

11

★★★★★

INTRIGUE TO THE SOUTH: MIRANDA AND HAMILTON

Both France and Great Britain coveted the interior of North America. Neither country was willing to see the United States, then stretched precariously along the Atlantic seaboard, become master of the continent. France knew the wealth of Louisiana, and some French leaders dreamed of regaining this territory from Spain. As early as February 4, 1795, and again on the sixteenth, Fauchet, French minister to the United States, wrote to his government deploring the poor relations between his country and the United States and suggesting that Louisiana be regained as a means of forcing the United States to recognize French leadership. These dispatches fell into the hands of Britain and were given by the British to Secretary of State Pickering, already bitterly anti-French.

Spanish diplomats, however, were more fearful of an Anglo-American attack on Louisiana than of French intrigue. In 1795 Spain reversed its foreign policy and acceded to the request by the United States to arbitrate its southwestern boundary. In October 1795 Spain signed the Treaty of San Lorenzo, hereafter referred to as the Pinckney Treaty. By this treaty Spain promised to surrender the Yazoo Strip to the United States. This strip of land, reaching from the Mississippi River to Georgia, marked the border between the United States and Spanish territory and had been claimed by both countries since 1783. In addition, the treaty stipulated that Spain would withdraw from forts along the Mississippi and would grant Americans unlimited navigation of that river as well as the much coveted right of deposit (untaxed storage of commodities at New Orleans while awaiting reshipment).

As a result of the Pinckney Treaty, especially that part of it which granted citizens of the U.S. the right to navigate the Mississippi and deposit produce at New Orleans, Americans west of the Appalachians became more friendly to the Federalist party. The votes of westerners in Congress, especially their general support of the Washington administration in the voting on appropriations regarding the Jay Treaty, reflected this.

Andrew Ellicott, a surveyor who had left the Society of Friends to become a major of militia during the Revolution, was sent to Natchez by President Washington in 1796. He was assigned to assist the Spaniards in determining the southwestern boundary of the United States. Aware of the long-standing contention over that boundary, he was yet amazed at the crosscurrent of intrigue he found swirling through the area. Amidst a profusion of factions and interests, both political and economic, he detected three major conspiracies. In the first place, as President Washington had suspected, Spanish authorities were plotting with James Wilkinson (see chapter six), brigadier general in command of American forces in the Southwest, to detach the trans-Appalachian area from the United States and turn it over to Spain. Secondly, Ellicott found sentiment for a revolution against Spanish authority in Florida and Louisiana, and interest in making this area the base from which revolution would spread to South America. Finally, there were those who dreamed not only of driving Spain out of the New World but of adding her territory to either Great Britain or the United States.

It soon became apparent that Spain did not intend to honor all the provisions in the Pinckney Treaty. The Spanish governor, Carondolet, began to dismantle the Spanish forts along the Mississippi, then received orders from the home government to cease. Ambassador Yrujo, Spain's representative at Philadelphia, explained to an indignant Pickering that Spain must retain these fortified positions for fear of a British attack by way of Canada. Throughout the American Southwest the atmosphere of uncertainty and suspicion increased. Would Britain launch an attack on Louisiana from Canada? Would Spain retrocede Louisiana to France? Would the Spanish live up to their promises made in the Pinckney Treaty?

John Adams knew that the Spanish government was disregarding certain provisions of the Pinckney Treaty. Secretary of State Pickering believed the Spaniards were procrastinating in the expectation that a war between France and the United States would give then an excuse to abrogate the treaty. During this period of confusion and suspicion, General Victor Collot, suspected of being a secret agent of France, journeyed into the Mississippi Valley. There were disturbing reports about his apparent interest in political conditions there.

Meanwhile, as early as the summer of 1797, there were voices in the United States that cried out for war in the Southwest. In July, William Cobbett's *Porcupine's Gazette* carried the following comment: "A war with Spain is absolutely necessary to the salvation of this country, if a war with France takes place, or if the Spaniards have ceded Louisiana to France. They must both be driven into the Gulf of Mexico, or we shall never sleep in peace. Besides, a war with Spain would be so convenient! There is nothing but dry blows to be gotten from the pennyless sans-culottes; but the wealth of Spanish America would be a salve for every sore. It would be the cream of the war."[1]

Not long after John Adams assumed the presidency, Senator Blount of Tennessee was accused of intrigue, or attempted intrigue, against Spain. Owner of much land in the Southwest, he hoped to encourage settlement and land sales, and sought British and Cherokee support to drive the Spanish out of Florida and Louisiana. One of Blount's letters, containing evidence of his plan, was sent to Adams and he insisted on giving the incriminating papers to the Senate. Their disclosure caused political reverberations that not only forced Blount to resign but threatened American relations with England.

While the situation in the Southwest was frustrating, Adams proceeded according to the terms of the treaty with Spain. On June 12, 1797, the president asked Congress to enact legislation providing for territorial government in the Natchez area. The secretary of state, often imperious and antagonizing in his official capacity, was at his best in this crisis with Spain. Pickering disliked and distrusted the Spanish ambassador, Yrujo, and refused to compromise in his dealings with him. It seems probable that Pickering's firmness was instrumental in forcing Spain's eventual compliance with the terms of the treaty.

Into this complex situation, where national interests inevitably clashed and adventurous individuals recognized possibilities for personal gain, came a Venezuelan patriot, Francisco de Miranda. Born in Caracas, Venezuela, Miranda became associated with nationalist groups plotting for independence from Spain. In 1783 he avoided imprisonment by fleeing to the United States. For a year or more he visited many parts of the country and became acquainted with prominent Americans. He tried unsuccessfully to enlist aid to free South America from Spanish control.

In the winter of 1784–1785, Francisco de Miranda left the United States for France. Finding little support for his schemes in Paris, Miranda sailed for England. He remained there for a decade. The growing animosity between France and the United States, the pro-British sympathies that were so dominant in the Federalist party, and the increasingly close relations between France and Spain provided a fertile field for international intrigue, and Miranda made the most of it.

On January 16, 1798, Miranda visited Britain's Prime Minister Pitt. He outlined a plan, employing a United States army and a British fleet, by which he hoped to establish the independence of South America. Pitt is said to have indicated interest in such a project.

Just two weeks later Miranda called on Rufus King. When the Venezuelan had first met King, in 1783 or 1784, King had been a young Massachusetts congressman; now he was ambassador from the United States to the Court of Saint James. Ten days later, on February 8, King returned Miranda's call, even though England's Foreign Minister Grenville had expressed to King a distaste for the entire affair. Undoubtedly encouraged by the reactions of Pitt and King, on February 7 and again on April 6, Miranda promoted his plans in letters to Alexander Hamilton. The February letter was sent by messenger via South America and may not have reached Hamilton before summer. At that time Hamilton seemed uninterested, for he wrote on the cover of the letter the following comment: "Several Years ago this man was in America much heated with the project of liberating S. America from the Spanish Dominion. I had frequent conversations with him on the subject & I presume expressed ideas favourable to the object and perhaps gave an opinion that it was one to which the U States would look with interest. He went then to England upon it—Hence his present letter. I shall not answer because I consider him as an intriguing adventurer."[2]

Prime Minister Pitt was more receptive to Miranda's proposals. Pitt talked to Rufus King about him on February 7, 1798, the very day that Miranda sent his first long letter to Hamilton. (It would be interesting to know if the Venezuelan knew of Pitt's conversation with King before he wrote to Hamilton.) By the end of February the British cabinet reached an important decision. If Spain resisted France, Britain would take no military action against her. If, however, Spain succumbed to French inducements and became her ally, Britain would approach the United States with regard to a joint Anglo-American expedition against South America. At the end of February, King used his secret code to relay this information to Pickering, and the latter began to show enthusiasm for the idea.

Conscious of the success of French armies, disturbed by internal rebellion (Ireland) and the threat of financial disaster (the Bank of England had suspended specie payments), Britain was now inclined to accept aid from any quarter. Thus Liston would journey to Quincy to attempt to persuade John Adams that alliance with Britain was desirable. There were "offers of the protection of the British navy and vague hints of a future commercial partnership."[3] Always in the background, especially if Spain deigned to side openly with France, was the possibility of a joint attack on Spain's possessions in the Western Hemisphere.

So Miranda plotted, and England's government, not sure which way Spain would move, listened and waited. Rufus King became an ardent promoter of Miranda's plans, as did Arch Federalist George Cabot, who was in London in connection with the Jay Treaty arbitration.

Meanwhile, Alexander Hamilton and his friends in Adams's cabinet were meeting with delays in securing a dominant military role for the former. On August 22, 1798, Hamilton wrote to Rufus King. The letter clearly indicated that Hamilton was then ready to listen to Miranda:

> I have received several letters from General Miranda. I have written an answer to some of them . . . . With regard to the enterprise in question, I wish it much to be undertaken, but I should be glad that the principal agency be in the United States,—they to furnish the whole land force if necessary. The command in this case would very naturally fall upon me, and I hope I shall disappoint no favorable anticipation. . . . Are we yet ready for this undertaking? Not quite. But we ripen fast, and it may, I think, be rapidly brought to maturity if an efficient negotiation for the purpose is at once set on foot upon this ground.[4]

This letter to King contained a letter for Miranda, which King was to deliver or not, as he thought best. To Miranda, Hamilton wrote, "The plan in my opinion ought to be: A fleet of Great Britain, army of the United States, a government for the liberated territory agreeable to both co-operators, about which there will be no difficulty. To arrange the plan a competent authority from Great Britain to some person here is the best expedient. Your presence here will, in this case, be extremely essential."[5]

The above letters give evidence that Hamilton had been considering Miranda's proposal for some time, that he was enthusiastically in support of plans for attacking Spanish territory, that he desired British cooperation, and that he saw himself in the position of top military importance. The last sentence of the letter to Miranda may be interpreted as indicating that Hamilton desired Miranda near him—so he could be at the center of the planning.

On October 20, 1798, Rufus King replied to Hamilton, "I have received your letter of 22[d] August . . . . On that subject [Miranda and a possible attack on Spanish America] things are here as we could desire. There will be precisely such a cooperation as we wish the moment we are ready. The Secretary of State will show you my communication on this subject. Though I have not a word from him respecting it, your outline corresponds with what has been suggested by me, and approved by this [British] government. . . ."[6]

Three months went by, months in which John Adams not only refused to have any communication with Miranda but put off Liston and the possibility of a British alliance, months during which the possibility of a war with France seemed to fade further and further away. King had written repeatedly to Pickering, but had had no reply from Hamilton. In desperation, he pleaded with Hamilton to move rapidly against Spanish America:

> For God's sake attend to the very interesting subject treated of in my ciphered dispatches to the Secretary of State of the 10th, 18th, and 19th, instant. Connect it as it should be, with the main object, the time to accomplish which has arrived. Without superstition, Providence seems to have prepared the way, and to have pointed out the instruments of its will. Our children will reproach us if we neglect our duty, and humanity will escape many scourges if we act with wisdom and decision. I am more confirmed than before, that an efficient force will be confederated to act against France. The combination is *not yet completed,* but, as I have reason to believe, will soon be.
>
> That will be the moment for us to settle upon immutable foundations the extensive system of the American nation. Who can hinder us? One nation alone has the power; and she will cooperate in the accomplishment . . . ."[7]

Hamilton still dreamed of military conquest and continued his plans without the president's knowledge. At the end of January, about three weeks after King wrote the letter quoted above, he sent a message to Harrison Gray Otis indicating his objectives: a congressional authorization to use the army and navy against France, an increase in the expansion of the army, and plans for seizing Louisiana and the Floridas.

Late in December 1798 Hamilton wrote to General Gunn of Georgia about the need for military supplies, and he added, "This, you perceive, looks to offensive operations. If we are to engage in war, our game will be to attack where we can. France is not to be considered as separated from her ally [Spain]. *Tempting objects will be within our grasp.*" Hamilton went on to suggest the desirability of a draft of men between eighteen and forty-five to be continued until the army was increased to 50,000. Such a levy, Hamilton argued, would make it easier to draft even larger numbers of men in the event of war, and would "place the country in a very imposing attitude."[8]

Late in January, Hamilton wrote to Secretary of War McHenry in regard to a division of responsibility between himself and Major General Pinckney. Hamilton's proposal would give him complete control of the army west of the Appalachians. On February 12, 1799, Hamilton ordered General James Wilkinson, commander of all Federal troops in the West with his headquarters in Natchez, to report to him in New York. Hamilton indicated that he wished to consider ways of attacking the Floridas in the event of war with Spain. He also suggested that unless Wilkinson found it inconvenient the latter was to come by way of New Orleans. Whitaker, noting that "anyone journeying from the lower Mississippi to the Atlantic Coast at that time" would travel by way of New Orleans "if he could possibly do so," suggests that this was Hamilton's way of instructing Wilkinson to look into the defenses of that city as he passed through.[9]

The president as well as Hamilton was acutely conscious of conditions in the Southwest. The people west of the Appalachians had indicated no desire for an enlarged army. John Adams correctly assessed the attitude of the transmountain settlers; they wanted peace and prosperity, not war and expansion. On April 18, 1799, responding to an "address" of a group of citizens in the Mississippi Territory, the president wrote:

> As your situation on a frontier of the United States, near a nation under whose government many of you have lived, and with whose inhabitants you are well acquainted, qualifies you in a particular manner to maintain a benev-

olent, pacific, and friendly conduct towards your neighbors, and entitles you to a return of a similar behavior from them; it is to be hoped and expected that the peace and friendship between the two nations will be by these means preserved and promoted, and that the emissaries of no other nation that may be hostile, will be able to destroy or diminish your mutual esteem and regard.[10]

In mid-June, Alexander Hamilton wrote to General Washington, advocating Wilkinson's promotion to major general and asking Washington to support the promotion by a letter to McHenry. Arriving in New York City in August, Wilkinson at once conferred with Hamilton. There is no way of knowing all the matters they discussed, nor how frequently they conferred over a period of several months. We do know, however, that on September 4 Wilkinson submitted a written report, dealing with the defensive strength of the Spanish in New Orleans and the possible means of attacking Spanish positions in the two Floridas. Apparently Hamilton instructed Wilkinson to make plans for supplying an army, to stockpile food and ammunition, and to gather heavy cannon and mortars such as might be used in seige operations.

On September 7, 1799, Wilkinson left for Quincy, bearing a letter from Hamilton to the president requesting Wilkinson's promotion to major general. The effusiveness of Hamilton's endorsement of Wilkinson may indicate that the latter had given to him both information and promises of future support. Hamilton also urged the president to grant commissions in the new army to "leading characters" in the Southwest. This, he argued, would be "a powerful means of conciliating the inhabitants" of that area.[11]

Hamilton discussed his interest in the Southwest and his desire to lead an attack on Spanish territory with several other persons. In a letter to Secretary of War McHenry he stated, "Besides eventual security against invasion, we ought certainly to look to the possession of the Floridas and Louisiana and we ought to squint at South America."[12] Thus some four months after John Adams had nominated a new mission to seek a peaceful settlement with France and to maintain neutrality, Alexander Hamilton was still "squinting" at South America. To say the least, the president and the inspector general of his army were working at cross purposes.

Robert Palmer has noted that during the hysteria over the XYZ affair "some believed that the best way to allay democratic agitation in the United States was to launch a war of conquest against the American possessions of Spain."[13] Koch and Peden believed that

Hamilton and his supporters saw in a successful seizure of Spanish territory a means of justifying the army, forming a lasting alliance with Britain, and destroying the political opposition at home.[14]

John Adams was never a man to ignore his public responsibilities. During the long summer and fall of 1798 he did not ignore Miranda, nor Hamilton, nor the changing political kaleidoscope in Europe. The president knew that King, Hamilton, Pickering, and others were deeply involved in plans for action in the Southwest. Hamilton not only corresponded with King and Pickering and McHenry and General Gunn, but he tried to advance his point of view through frequent letters to the newspapers. "It was certainly apparent" to the president, Dauer has written, "by the time Liston took the unusual step of going to Massachusetts to see him, that there was a strange concurrence of opinion, even as to detail, among the ideas of Liston, the views of his cabinet, the recommendations of his minister to England, and the policy advocated by Hamilton in the press."[15]

Miranda had written to Adams, proposing his plan of a joint Anglo-American attack on the Spanish possessions, on March 24, 1798. It would seem that Miranda's letter should have reached Quincy by mid-summer. If so, Miranda may well have written again, for on October 3 the president sent the secretary of state some papers and wrote as follows, "Inclosed is a duplicate of a letter from Miranda, with some estimates. Read it and think of it. A number of questions and considerations occur. We are friends with Spain. If we were enemies, would the project be useful to us? It will not be in character for me to answer the letter. Will any notice of it, in any manner, be proper?"[16] Pickering replied on the eleventh, acknowledging receipt of the papers, but never mentioned, either then or later, the Miranda letter. Nor did he reply to the questions the president had raised. It seems highly probable, however, that the president's seeming lack of interest was at once conveyed to Hamilton.

The president kept his own counsel. Neither the secretary of state at the capital nor the inspector general of the army in New York knew what his reactions to Miranda's letter had been. The ambassador and the South American "liberator" in London knew as much as Adams's own cabinet about his reception of the proposal. In London, Rufus King continued to collect maps of South and Central America and probed for British intentions regarding South America. In New York, Hamilton wrote letters and newspaper "releases," advocating strong action against Spain. John Adams seemed to do nothing.

John Adams may have refrained from commenting on Miranda's proposals in order to avoid involvement in war with Spain. He did not wish to offend Great Britain, and thus make it more difficult to secure the naval cooperation that might become imperative if actual war with France should develop. If such war came, he would need all the help he could get from Hamilton and Washington. It seems, therefore, that Adams refrained from comment on the Miranda affair and made use of his distance from the capital, of his wife's illness, and of seeming indifference in order to delay a decision that might be harmful to his program of peace and neutrality for the United States.

One of the evidences of John Adams's excellence as a leader is the fact that he was so often successful in maintaining his own freedom of operation. By nature an impulsive man, tending to make quick decisions, he disciplined himself to delay those actions or decisions that would precipitate his country into war or restrict his later freedom of action or decision. At the same time he frequently upset his opponents with unexpected moves.

There were, of course, reasons for agreeing with Miranda, with Hamilton and King and Pickering. Alliance with Britain, either formal or informal, and a war against France and Spain might have brought the young nation to the threshold of power and influence. New Orleans and the Floridas would almost surely have fallen easy prey to a joint military and naval expedition. Mexico and Central America, even parts of South America, might have been separated from Spain, and independent nations established there. The Spanish and French West Indies might have been seized. Together with England, the United States might have established a commercial monopoly of the trade of the entire area. As Fisher Ames, sometimes described as the "High Priest of Federalism," wrote in July of 1798, "My faith is we [the United States] were born for high destinies."[17]

John Adams's ultimate goals for his country, however, were not power and influence but peace and neutrality. He believed his country needed time to gain strength and stability. Yet there were certain more immediate reasons for his rejection of Miranda's plan, for his antagonism to Hamilton's imperialistic dreaming. In the first place he distrusted Hamilton personally. Of more weight, however, was the fact that John Adams wished to avoid European entanglements. This was no new idea with the president. As far back as 1777 Adams had been fearful of an alliance with France, and in 1782, while negotiating for peace, he had demonstrated his distrust of bilateral diplomacy. The president realized that even an informal alliance, even the acceptance of temporary military or naval assistance (though such might be necessary in a real emergency), would limit America's independence and might inadvertently draw her into some European imbroglio.

There is no doubt that John Adams distrusted violent revolution, despite the fact that he had played a leading role in the Revolution by which his own nation was established. As an old man, looking back on the events of 1798 and 1799, John Adams indicated amazement that Pitt and Miranda had thought that he, who had witnessed the horror of colonial conflict, would "be desirous of engaging [himself] . . . in most hazardous and bloody experiments to excite similar horrors in South America."[18]

John Adams was a realist in his appraisal of the foreign situation. He felt that Britain's interest in alliance with the United States, or even in naval cooperation, was predicated on self-interest. He knew of the rebellion in Ireland and the reported mutiny in the British fleet. If Britain's position worsened, he felt, she might make peace with France. If it improved, she might no longer have need of American assistance. Even as Britain invited support and cooperation, commissions set up by the Jay Treaty were finding it difficult to reach agreement, and British agents were still intriguing with the Indians in the Northwest. Alliances and agreements were at best, John Adams knew, tenuous things.

In spite of the pressure from Arch Federalists, both within and without his cabinet, John Adams would not yield to the temptation to attack Spanish territories. He wanted no part of militaristic adventure and was alert to the danger of European involvement. War against a foreign aggressor might unite the nation, but he also knew that war for conquest and gain might precipitate civil war and the splitting of the nation.

12

★★★★★

ADAMS FACES GREAT BRITAIN AND THE FRENCH WEST INDIES

Not only did John Adams face serious problems with France and Spain, but throughout the four years of his presidency he had to be continually alert to the complexities of America's relations with Great Britain. Difficulties with that nation, of course, were but another aspect of the troubles with France. In both cases, the major question involved a choice between neutrality and involvement.

Since 1783 there had been a continuing dispute between the United States and Great Britain concerning their mutual obligations. There was little willingness on the part of Americans to pay debts owed to British subjects since before the Revolution. Until these were paid, Britain refused to surrender the forts along the northwestern border that had been granted to the United States by the Treaty of Paris of 1783.

There were other problems. The outbreak of England's war with France after 1793 resulted in a serious manpower shortage in the British navy and increasingly frequent impressment of American sailors. British policy at this time did not recognize the right of Englishmen to become naturalized citizens, and this increased the friction between the two nations.

As the British navy destroyed more and more French merchant ships, France became dependent upon American cargo ships to carry produce from the West Indies. This trade was as lucrative to American merchants and shipowners as it was necessary to the

French economy. Increasingly the British navy sought to prevent or at least decrease this use of American shipping to aid France and her allies. Even after the outbreak of the undeclared war against France in 1797, however, many American shipowners profited from this trade.

The Jay Treaty solved none of these problems. The treaty did prevent the immediacy of war, however, and created two arbitration commissions to attempt to resolve the economic disputes. These two commissions were to become a source of almost constant conflict and disagreement throughout much of John Adams's administration.

The onset of undeclared but actual hostilities with France found the United States woefully unprepared. Philadelphia was the only port with even the semblance of military defense. There was no navy; the army consisted of slightly over three thousand men. The U.S. requested British assistance, and military supplies were made available in what has been termed "the first lend-lease." Britain gave America some heavy canon, suitable for harbor defense. During the summer of 1798 the Royal Navy exchanged recognition signals with American warships. This cooperation was of great importance to both countries.

During the late spring and summer of 1797, however, other British actions became a major frustration for a new administration already deeply involved in the crisis with France. United States ships were stopped on the open sea, cargoes were searched, and week after week came the reports of the impressment of American sailors by the man-hungry British navy.

At roughly the same time, the Blount scandal was revealed. The British minister to the U.S., Robert Liston, had become involved with Senator Blount's plan to engage British assistance to force the Spanish out of Louisiana and Florida and thus increase the sale of his southwestern lands. Because of his involvement with foreign powers, Blount was expelled from the Senate in 1797. While investigation proved no official wrong-doing on the part of the British government, it seemed to many that Liston was guilty of intrigue.

Despite John Adams's desire to avoid alliances, he knew that if war with France developed, the naval resources of Great Britain would be essential to a successful American defense. Thus in the fall and winter of 1797–1798, while he waited for word from Marshall, Pinckney, and Gerry in Paris, he considered possible courses of action in relation to Britain.

In January 1798 Adams had sent a memo to the members of his cabinet asking for their judgment as to the proper course of action if the mission to France failed. If war with France occurred, the president asked, should the United States approach Great Britain regarding a military alliance? Or should the United States wait for a formal offer from Great Britain? The president's own thinking seems to have been that: (1) the U.S. should make no agreement with England that would limit America's right to make peace at any time, and (2) a formal alliance would bring no benefits that his country could not obtain without such an alliance.

Secretary of State Pickering desired a formal alliance with Britain. He apparently did not respond to the president's January 24 inquiry, but on March 25 he wrote to Alexander Hamilton, enclosing information from a report sent from France by John Marshall. This report was "top secret," and he indicated to Hamilton that he sent the information "without the privity of anyone." In this letter Pickering expressed approval of the idea of an alliance with Britain, and he also spoke of the ease with which the U.S. could seize Louisiana from Spain.

On June 9 Pickering wrote to Hamilton, "We cannot expect overtures from England. I very much suspect she is waiting to receive them from us."[1] By mid-July Robert Liston was sure that both Wolcott in the Treasury and McHenry in the War Department would support an alliance with England. On the nineteenth he wrote that these two cabinet members are "so staunch that I have no occasion to look after them; they are ready to go as fast and as far as I wish them to go."[2]

In the summer of 1798 Liston went to Quincy to approach the president regarding a formal military alliance between the United States and Great Britain. Such an alliance would offer Britain military and economic advantages in her war with France. The president skillfully avoided giving a definite answer, leaving Liston with the impression that he favored some agreement but felt it would take time to convince Congress and the general public of the desirability of such a move. All through the fall of that year, beset with worries about Abigail, with annoyances from Hamilton and from his cabinet, weighing the possibilities of peace with France, John Adams also assessed the advantages and disadvantages of alliance with Britain.

Largely because of continued impressment and interference with America's commerce, Anglo-American relations deteriorated still more in the winter of 1798–1799. One of the most dramatic events occurred in mid-November when a British squadron stopped an American warship, the *Baltimore*. This small sloop-of-war, commanded by Captain Isaac Phillips, was escorting a merchant convoy. Captain John Loring of H.M.S. *Carnatic* prevented the *Baltimore* from entering the harbor at Havana and ordered the latter ship to stand to and prepare to be searched. Phillips meekly complied and the British then removed fifty-five crew members, most of whom were later returned.

The impressment of sailors from merchant vessels, though irritating and costly, was far different from violating American sovereignty by intercepting a man of war. Secretary Pickering strongly protested the action of Captain Loring, and the British officer was transferred to another station. John Adams summarily dismissed Captain Phillips from the service, without trial, and ordered all officers of the navy to resist attempted impressment. In addition, in his official communications to the British government President Adams condemned impressment and insisted on the right of English citizens to become naturalized citizens of the United States.

As previously noted, on February 1, 1799, the *Aurora*, leading Jeffersonian journal, printed statistics compiled by the Insurance Company of North America covering the previous six-month period. The figures revealed that British warships had inflicted nearly 10 percent more damage on American shipping than had been done by French privateers. Writing to Rufus King, Pickering mentioned these statistics and suggested that King appeal to the British government to cease interfering with American shipping.

American merchants and shipowners complained bitterly, as evidenced by the following letter addressed to Oliver Wolcott, in early September:

> These good friends and allies of ours [the British] are again letting loose their corsairs against our commerce, and I do not see that we shall not soon be in as bad a predicament as we were in 1792–3. The judges at Jamaica and Providence have taken a lattitude of construction, that not only gives to their cruizers the right to our property, but as it authorizes carrying in our vessels, the vexation and expense to which we are subjected, even when we are acquitted, is sufficient to put a stop to our West India commerce . . . ."[3]

Rather than decrease their interference, after Davie and Ellsworth had set sail on their mission to France in November 1799 the British navy increased both impressments and economic harassment. Arch Federalists frequently claimed that this was a natural reaction to the fact that the president was again flirting with France.

Continuing depredations by the British furnished a source of propaganda ammunition for the Jeffersonian press. Thus, at the very time John Adams was having to stand fast against the war hawks (men who desired alliance with Britain and all-out war against France) in his own party, he was bombarded by Republicans who demanded action against Great Britain.

One of the more outspoken Jeffersonian newspapers was the Boston *Independent Chronicle*. Before Adams had been in office six months this paper named no less than twelve ships that had recently been seized by the British. On Christmas Day it listed five more. In many seaports large protest gatherings petitioned Congress to take retaliatory action. The historian Donald Stewart has concluded, "Throughout the entire Federalist period, British policy toward American shipping remained a major Republican issue."[4]

Two commissions had been provided for by articles VI and VII of the Jay Treaty. One, the Spoliations Commission, was established to resolve the question of property destroyed by the British during the American Revolution. The second commission was to deal with the debts owed British citizens by Americans. During and after the Revolution, some states had passed laws which made the collection of such debts illegal. Britain had justified her retention of forts in American territory by pointing out that these pre-Revolutionary debts had not been paid as promised. The acrimonious negotiations and continual disputes of these commissions demanded the attention and time of the president between 1797 and 1801. Perhaps in part because of Adams's basic honesty, but also because he realized the Americans beyond the Appalachians would never be satisfied until Britain had relinquished the forts in the Northwest, the president was determined that his country keep her promises and pay her honest debts.

The Jay Treaty had stipulated that each of the two commissions was to consist of five members, two appointed by each nation and a fifth chosen by agreement or, if necessary, by chance. Neither commission could agree on its fifth member; by lot the English secured the fifth member of the Debts Commission and the Americans the fifth member of the Spoliations Commission. The Debts Commission was designated to hold its meetings in Philadelphia and the other in London.

The discussions of the Debts Commission became very bitter,

apparently because the British majority constantly outvoted the Americans. Benjamin Stoddert wrote to the president in mid-September 1799, "No doubt their commissioners have for a long time been prejudiced & soured, and have in some instances acted as if it were their desire to plunge the two nations into War. If England insists on a quarrel, however we may lament the calamity, we need not fear the result if our own people are satisfied that the Government has acted in all instances right."[5] The contents of this letter were no surprise to the president. Two weeks earlier he had written to Pickering: "The dispute of the commissioners under the 6th Arti[cle] gives me much concern. I shall write you in a few days on that subject. My mind is made up thus far. The treaty, as far as it depends on me, shall be executed with candor & good faith. No unworthy artifice or chicanery shall be practised on my part. No, not though the consequence should be the payment of all the demands. We must however do our utmost to obtain an explanation, that may shelter our country from injustice."[6]

Three weeks later, probably after receiving Stoddert's letter, the president again wrote to Pickering, "I am determined as far as [it] depends upon me to execute the treaty in its full extent. If it costs us four million sterling when it ought . . . to cost us only one[,] I had rather pay it than depart from good faith or lie under the suspicion of it. . . . If we believe Britains less hungry for plunder than Frenchmen, we shall be deceived."[7]

In May 1800 John Marshall became secretary of state. On August 1 the president sent Marshall the following message from Quincy:

> I have twice read the dispatch of Mr. King No. 67, inclosed in your favor of the 21st of July. . . . The idea of paying a gross sum to the British government in lieu of & in satisfaction for the claims of British creditors, seems to me to merit attention & mature consideration. There will be great difficulties attending it no doubt. How can we form an estimate that will satisfy the American government & the British government? How shall the claims of British Creditors be extinguished or barred from recovery in our courts of Law? Shall the claim of the creditors be transferred to our government, & how—or shall it be a total extinguishment of debt & credit between the parties? How will the British government apportion the sum among the British creditors? This however is their affair. You ask an important question, whether such an arrangement will afford just cause for discontent to France? But

I think it must be answered in the negative. Our citizens arc in debt to British subjects. We surely have a right to pay our honest debts in the manner least inconvenient to ourselves & no foreign country has anything to do with it.[8]

There was no question about the president's position or his insistence on his country's meeting its debts and responsibilities.

Despite the president's efforts, however, little was being accomplished. The American commissioners at Philadelphia, indignant at the conduct of the British majority, boycotted the meetings. In retaliation, the British government ordered its members at the London parley on the Spoliations Committee to absent themselves.

When John Adams addressed Congress for the last session of his administration, November 22, 1800, he was forced to report, "The difficulties which suspended the execution of the sixth article of our treaty of amity, commerce, and navigation with Great Britain [the Jay Treaty] have not yet been removed. The negotiation on this subject is still depending [pending?]. As it must be for the interest and honor of both nations to adjust this difference with good faith, I indulge confidently the expectation that the sincere endeavors of the Government of the United States to bring it to an amicable termination will not be disappointed."[9]

Despite John Adams's insistence on America's meeting her just debts his hopes were not realized during the remaining months of his presidency. Believing that the British majority were misinterpreting the treaty, the two Americans withdrew from the debts commission and it ceased to function. Nearly a year after John Adams left office, the two governments finally agreed on a sum to be paid by the United States. After the Convention of 1802 had settled the problem of the debts payment to Great Britain, the Spoliations Commission reconvened and eventually completed its work.

How shall we evaluate John Adams's administration in terms of its handling of affairs with Britain? Despite Adams's continued efforts the problem of impressment was not solved. Bradford Perkins, however, has concluded that it was a less serious problem in 1801 than it had been in 1797. ". . . it can easily be argued," he stated, "that the policy of the Adams administration was every bit as successful as the one of bluster and recrimination later adopted by Thomas Jefferson. Even war was not enough to make the British government promise to end impressment."[10]

John Adams recognized, especially in 1797 and 1798, that British help might be necessary, that Britain must not be antagonized needlessly, and that Britain, like any other country, was chiefly concerned with its own problems and its own future. Adams, therefore, jealously guarded his country's independence and insisted that she be respected as an equal and a neutral.

This was not the position of the Arch Federalists, whom Joseph Charles has termed "colonials." To them, he concluded, "it seemed that we were being admitted into partnership with Britain; albeit as a junior partner. The fact that our whole position and prosperity as they envisaged it would be entirely dependent upon Britain appears not to have bothered them in the slightest degree." Charles also stated that "by 1800 the tendency toward nationalism and self-sufficiency was stronger than at any other time since 1789."[11] If Charles were right in that last estimate, Adams had, as he hoped, correctly felt the pulse of his country, strengthened and invigorated the nation, and turned her away from dependence on Britain.

While the continuing crises with France and England were central to John Adams's concern throughout most of his administration, he faced many other problems. One of the trouble spots was in the French West Indies, especially the island of Saint Domingue. In the 1790s the revolt of the blacks on this island, led by Toussaint L'Ouverture, ended all but nominal French control. Great Britain was toying with the idea of expansion in the West Indies. Adams, always conscious of the importance of the Caribbean trade to American merchants, was alarmed.

As early as the seventeenth century the English colonies on the mainland of America had developed profitable trade relations with the West Indies. Whether in authorized trade with the English colonies or illicit commerce with the possessions of Spain, Holland, and France, traffic in slaves, and increasingly numerous cargoes of fish and lumber and farm produce, all played an important role in the colonial economy.

America's independence, of course, halted all legal trade with the British islands. In the widespread war that followed the expansion of the French Revolution in 1793, Britain attempted to seize all French ships, thus opening lucrative markets to American shipping. By 1795 it was estimated that 90 percent of the foreign trade of the United States was carried in her own bottoms, and that more than six hundred American ships were trading with Saint Domingue alone.

Between July 1796 and June 1797 more than three hundred American ships were seized by the French. Some of these, of course, were released but often their cargo was retained. Prompted both by the deterioration of relations between the United States and France and by the need for Britain to move much of her naval strength to European waters, the seizure of American merchant ships by French privateers increased and became a major source of friction between the two nations.

This increased action against American merchant vessels stemmed from France's hope to pressure the United States into a pro-French position. In a life-and-death struggle between England and France, Talleyrand felt fairly confident that the United States would give in to French demands for cooperation, as had small European nations like Holland and Switzerland. Avarice on the part of French civilians in the West Indies, and their often desperate need for provisions due to the blockading actions of the British navy, also stimulated their seizure of U.S. vessels. Without American commerce, however, the economy of the islands would suffer. Louis-Guillaume Otto, a French diplomat and one-time *chargé d'affaires* in the United States, warned France of the danger of their depredations. He declared that if the United States should forbid all trade with the French colonies it would "destroy forever the French hope of reestablishing her colonial empire and her merchant marine."[12]

The effect of French attacks was nearly disastrous to American shipping. In mid-1796, before the increased activity of French privateers, an American merchant sending a cargo to the Caribbean could insure the shipment at 6 percent. By the end of the year the rate had doubled. By the spring of 1798, before the new American navy began to show its strength, a merchant often paid a premium equal to more than a third of the value of his ship and cargo.

Richest of the French islands in the Caribbean was Saint Domingue. It is said to have produced as much sugar as all the British islands combined. In 1793, when the slave revolt broke out, the island's exports declined rapidly. The effects of this revolt on the United States, over the next decade, were significant. In the first place, coming at a time when Whitney's cotton gin increased the profitability of slavery in the American South, the revolt on Saint Domingue stimulated fears of similar revolts on the mainland. Such fears were not unfounded; there were numerous slave insurrections after 1790, notably the so-called Gabriel's revolt in Virginia in 1800.

A second result of the black uprising on Saint Domingue was the emigration of thousands of Frenchmen from the Caribbean to the United States. Robert Palmer noted that "the French consul at Philadelphia estimated in 1797 that there were over 20,000 French refugees in the country. Almost all came from San Domingo and other French West Indian colonies."[13] These French, both directly and indirectly, added to the political agitation in the United States. They strengthened the pro-French Jeffersonian organization and their presence further inflamed the Francophobia of the Arch Federalists.

Saint Domingue was one of the principal bases from which privateers preyed on American shipping in the Caribbean. Yet this island, nominally still under French control although Toussaint L'Overture and his black supporters held most of the power, was largely dependent for much of its food on American merchants and shippers. The Non-Intercourse Act, passed by the American Congress in June 1798, made it illegal for Americans to trade with France or with French possessions. The U.S., therefore, could not legally send cargoes to Saint Domingue and the economy of the island began to suffer. In November, Toussaint sent a message to John Adams, asking that trade be resumed. He promised to protect American shipping and to pay for all cargoes delivered there, and said that French privateers had been ordered to leave. Both Adams and Pickering responded favorably, indicating that if French privateers were suppressed American trade would be resumed. Rufus King sent word from London that Britain's agent in Saint Domingue, General Thomas Maitland, had been ordered to Philadelphia to reach agreements with the United States regarding trade with the island.

Larger questions had arisen. Should Britain be allowed to take Saint Domingue? Should the United States go to war with France and Spain with the object of seizing their Caribbean territories? Should the United States recognize Toussaint as the ruler of the island? Robert Liston, British minister to the U.S., was much interested in obtaining an affirmative to the first two questions. By May 1798 he believed that Pickering, Wolcott, and McHenry were ready to accept the inevitability of war with France, of the American seizure of Louisiana and the Floridas, and of the British seizure of Saint Domingue. But the president, Liston found, did not agree.

John Adams was aware of the importance of trade to the development of his own country. As a neutralist he did not want war, but he would fight if it were necessary in order to protect either his country's honor or its economic position. Opposed to alliances, he would yet accept British aid and cooperation, even a temporary alliance if it were absolutely necessary, but he wanted neither

British control of Saint Domingue nor a British monopoly of the commerce of the West Indies.

Liston had been confident in May that Pickering, Wolcott, and McHenry would support the British policy in the Caribbean. By June 12, however, he wrote that Pickering was talking in terms of an independent Saint Domingue. In September 1798, when Liston went to the Adams's homestead in Quincy, he suggested that Louisiana be given to the U.S. while Great Britain should keep Saint Domingue. When Liston mentioned the latter, the president suggested that since time would inevitably draw the United States and the West Indies closer together, it might be best for Saint Domingue to remain independent. Adams explained that an agreement with Toussaint would have been reached already except for his concern over the possible apprehension of Britain. John Adams knew that an alliance with England would increase the possibility of war with France as well as give Saint Domingue to England.

Through the next spring and summer, Adams skillfully opposed both alliance with England and her expansion in the West Indies. When Britain suggested that she and the U.S. should jointly control Saint Domingue through a commercial company, Adams said that "it would be most prudent for us to have nothing to do in the business." Control of Saint Domingue by a jointly owned commercial company, the president believed, would "subject us more to the policy of Britain than will be consistent with our interest and honor." It was obvious that Adams wanted neither war with Spain and annexation of Spanish territory nor involvement in the diplomatic maneuvering of the European powers.[14]

Early in 1799 John Adams had appointed Edward Stevens as consul general to the port of Cap Francis in Saint Domingue. Stevens lived in Philadelphia but had been born in the West Indies, was a distant relative of Alexander Hamilton, and apparently was on familiar terms with both Hamilton and Pickering. The instructions to Stevens, written by Pickering in early March 1799, indicated that he was to attempt to increase the distrust between Toussaint and France; to end privateering from the ports of Saint Domingue; to aid Toussaint in defeating dissident groups that had not accepted his leadership, and encourage Toussaint in achieving independence from France. At the time Hamilton thought Adams inconsistent and could not understand how the latter could support Toussaint's revolt against France and at the same time oppose war with France. What Hamilton failed to understand was that the president hoped to maintain peace but believed it was to America's advantage to keep France from dominance in the Caribbean.

On April 17, 1799, the president wrote to Pickering. He mentioned that he had letters from Rufus King in London which stated the British desire for Anglo-American cooperation in freeing Saint Domingue. King indicated that Grenville, Liston's superior in England, wanted U.S. cooperation and that he was thinking in terms of a joint Anglo-American company that would receive exclusive trading rights in Saint Domingue. Adams indicated his preference for leaving the affairs of that island to its own people. He seems to have concluded that the French would never reestablish control there.

In late April, Pickering and Wolcott were in conference with Maitland, chief British agent for Saint Domingue, and with Robert Liston. The president had rejected the British suggestion for a jointly owned commercial company to "take over" the island. Stevens was already representing the United States in Saint Domingue. Fearing that he would complete an agreement with Toussaint that would grant exclusive trading rights to the U.S., Maitland and Liston made concessions to Pickering. These resulted in "an informal agreement called 'Heads of Regulations' to be proposed by Maitland to Toussaint . . . . Under this arrangement the direct trade with Saint Domingue would be opened to British and American ships but would be limited to one or two ports of entry."[15]

While John Adams waited for assurances that his new mission to France would be well received, and for the completion of new frigates, he anxiously watched the situation in the West Indies. The president believed that the United States needed the trade of this region and he preferred that the islands remain divided among several often jealous and suspicious powers. If Toussaint's revolt should spread, he knew that the results might be a take-over by a single, powerful European state such as Great Britain, or even the emergence of a strong and expansive independent nation.

What was the role of Alexander Hamilton in the developing situation in Saint Domingue? He and Secretary Pickering were in frequent communication, and often Hamilton's letters contained queries, suggestions, or recommendations regarding the islands in the Caribbean. In the winter of 1798–1799 Pickering went so far as to ask Hamilton to draw up a scheme of government for Saint Domingue. Pickering and Hamilton, perhaps without the president's knowledge, wished to place Toussaint in a position of nominal power but to leave him really controlled by the mercantile interests of New England.

The negotiations of Stevens, the presence of the British agent Maitland at Philadelphia, and the apparent interest of Liston in Anglo-American cooperation were of concern to the Jeffersonians. Southerners in general tended to oppose any support for Toussaint and his black revolutionaries. (The fear of slave revolts has already been noted.) The general suspicion of Hamiltonian motives, so prevalent in Virginia in 1798 and 1799, certainly developed in part from the apparent interest of the Arch Federalists in supporting Toussaint.

In July, in a letter to Pickering, the president indicated his basic feelings about the West Indies. He was suspicious of Toussaint, concerned lest the balance of power in the West Indies be disturbed, and desired to maintain cordial relations with Britain.

Always sympathetic to a demand for freedom, but equally distrustful of and opposed to the violence of revolution, John Adams declared to Stoddert, in May 1799, that "the mass of African bone and sinews" had gained little from the emancipation that had taken place in Saint Domingue. Yet his interest and concern about the West Indies situation remained intense because he recognized the connection between these problems and the possibility of a successful negotiation of peace with France.

After a protracted consultation, Maitland, Stevens, and Toussaint reached an agreement that was substantially similar to the Heads of Regulations, which had been approved by John Adams. By proclamation, on June 16, 1799, John Adams lifted the embargo on American trade with Saint Domingue. The presence of the American navy gave support to Toussaint and tended to inhibit French aggression in the Caribbean. American commerce again prospered.

13

★★★★★

THE ROAD TO PEACE:
MÔRTEFONTAINE

On November 3, 1799, Chief Justice Ellsworth and former Governor Davie sailed from Newport, Rhode Island, aboard the frigate *United States*. They were scheduled to meet Murray and proceed to Paris to conduct peace negotiations with the French government. Three and a half weeks later, on November 27, the frigate arrived at Lisbon and the envoys disembarked. It had been a cold, stormy, unpleasant voyage and Ellsworth and Davie decided to rest in Portugal. They learned that Napoleon Bonaparte had risen to power in France, and hoped to gain information relative to his attitude toward peace with the United States. Undoubtedly their decision to proceed cautiously was influenced by the reception Marshall, Gerry, and Pinckney had received two years before.

Unable to secure accurate information about political affairs in France, the two envoys decided to leave Lisbon and proceed to Holland to meet Murray. The latter was distressed as he had received no word from Davie and Ellsworth, although he knew their ship had arrived at Lisbon. Murray felt that Napoleon was friendly to the United States, a judgment that we now know was correct, and he was anxious to discuss terms for peace.

The weather along the western coast of Europe was uncommonly bad and the American envoys, stranded in Portugal, could not obtain passage for Holland. Therefore on December 21 they decided to proceed to Paris and try to meet Murray there. It would seem probable that they wrote to Murray but, if so, their letters must have been lost. After ten days at sea they landed at a Spanish port near La Corunna and from there went overland nine hundred miles to Paris. This was a tedious trip that required several weeks.

As the new year dawned, William Vans Murray was still unaware of the whereabouts or of the plans of his fellow envoys. On January 3, 1800, he wrote to his friend John Quincy Adams in Berlin, "I hear not from Messrs. Ellsworth and Davie at Lisbon. They probably wrote by London, and the Hamburg-English mail does not come, in consequence of the extreme cold and ice. Above a month has elapsed, however, since they arrived. . . . [I am] burning with impatience *to know what may be their intention.*"[1] Exactly four weeks later Murray received word from the other envoys, written in mid-December, that they would proceed to Paris at their first opportunity and meet him there.

On February 4 Murray received another message from Ellsworth and Davie to the effect that they had reached Corunna. Murray then wrote John Quincy in Berlin that he would leave for Paris "about the 18th; they cannot be there before the 20th."[2] On March 2 the three envoys met in the French capital and received a friendly reception. Both Napoleon and Talleyrand seemed eager for a settlement and the latter greeted the envoys three days after their arrival. They were presented to Napolon on the eighth.

Before their arrival news of the death of Washington reached Paris. Newspapers were lavish in their praise of the first president's accomplishments and his character. The attitude toward the United States was warm and friendly and the mission profited from it.

Talleyrand and Napoleon had disagreed on the choice of negotiators to treat with the American envoys. The former had suggested experienced diplomats, familiar with the United States. The latter overruled him, choosing to make political appointments to reward some of his friends and supporters. He selected Pierre Louis Roederer and Charles Pierre Claret Fleurieu, and to preside over the French delegation he named his eldest brother, Joseph Bonaparte. Murray was later to characterize the older Bonaparte as a man of "excellent character," amiable, well educated, mild mannered, and with "a correct but not very active mind."[3] The membership of the French delegation was announced soon after the arrival of the Americans in Paris.

American hopes for immediate negotiations foundered on Joseph Bonaparte's poor health. The talks began pleasantly enough, however, in early April, but it soon became apparent that agreement would be difficult. Each delegation had its precise instructions. The American envoys had been directed to press for a claims board to settle on the amount France was to pay for commercial damages. This was the "spoliation" factor that was to loom so large in their discussions. The claims board would estimate the damage done to American property by the French, especially by their privateers. The French government would be asked to recognize the legality, under international practice, of Congress's nullification of the treaties of 1778 and 1788, and a new treaty would be drawn up. The envoys had been instructed not to form any military alliance with France. There was to be no promise to help defend French territory in the Western Hemisphere. The Americans were also instructed that the special privileges that had been granted to French consuls by the treaty of 1788 were to be abolished as they were a restriction on American sovereignty.

The French envoys had been carefully briefed by Talleyrand, in accordance with Napoleon's overall diplomatic objectives. They were to seek to establish friendly relations with the United States; to foster American involvement on the side of France against England; and to draw up a new treaty in which the United States would go on record as supporting the concept of neutral rights commonly held by the small European neutrals. In addition, the instructions were to reaffirm previous treaties between France and the United States, to protect the rights of French consuls in the United States, and to gain any other possible advantages.

The French commissioners readily agreed to the principles of compensation for shipping losses but argued that the specifics could only be arranged after the question of the old treaties and the drafting of a new treaty had been settled. The Americans responded that they had no authority to discuss a new treaty until the matter of spoliations (commercial losses) was resolved. By the end of the first month the negotiations, friendly as they certainly were, had been stalemated.

It was now apparent that the French and American envoys held opposite attitudes about the desirability of concluding their assignment promptly. Napoleon was in Italy where the Austrians were badly defeated at the battle of Marengo on June 14. Pichon is said to have assured Napoleon that delay in the negotiations would make the Americans more amenable to French demands. Murray, however, believed the French were anxious to demonstrate to the world that the new French government was reasonable and just, and that they would eventually make concessions. At the same time he, and apparently Ellsworth and Davie as well, realized that an agreeable treaty would be a tremendous boon to Federalist success in the fall elections. It would seem, therefore, that it was the French who were chiefly responsible for the many frustrating delays and the difficulty in reaching agreements.

Through June and July the negotiations dragged on. Continued French military success alarmed the American envoys and probably made them more willing to make concessions. Murray, at least, was always conscious of the need for speed if a treaty were to improve John Adams's chances for reelection. Offer and counteroffer marked the snail's pace of the discussion. The Americans continued to demand both indemnities for shipping losses and an admission by the French that the United States had acted within its rights in abrogating the old treaties. The French countered that they would accept the latter only if the demand for indemnification for shipping losses was dropped. It seems probable, also, that Napoleon was not averse to delay while he worked secretly to acquire a new colonial empire in the heartland of the North American continent. Though the Americans were unaware of this, his bargaining with Spain would soon bear fruit in the reacquisition of Louisiana.

John Adams knew about the travels of Callot in the Mississippi Valley, and he may have seen King's letter of March 21, 1799, which had reached Philadelphia on June 4, informing the secretary of state of French interest in Louisiana. Darling has suggested that even the knowledge of Talleyrand's latest efforts to obtain Louisiana would not have changed Adams's instructions to the envoys, for "What the United States needed most at that time were peaceful relations with every power in Europe having interests or aspirations on the North American continent . . . ."[4]

Three days before the treaty was signed, Murray wrote to his friend John Quincy Adams, "My colleagues have acted from the first jump with the clearest and most pressing sincerity."[5] It seems probable, therefore, that the three men retained a high degree of respect for each other despite some disagreement and many frustrating moments.

Late in September the American envoys agreed to violate their instructions (they had, of course, already violated them by remaining in France after April 1) and sign a treaty that did not specifically renounce the former treaties nor provide for indemnification for U.S. losses. Wisely, it would seem, they reasoned that peace was the important thing. The French, while unwilling to accede to all the demands of the Americans, were equally anxious to reach a settlement. Possibly William Vans Murray expressed the feelings of the three American envoys when on September 27 he wrote to John Quincy Adams, "I confess my dear Sir to you that I am extremely rejoiced at it [the draft of a treaty then being proposed], even as it is—and I shall return to The Hague with more pleasure than I left it . . . . because at all events if our folks are as wise as they are honest, the storm will have been honorably passed & our country tranquil."[6]

So, leaving the matter of former treaties and previous losses for a possible later agreement, the representatives of the two nations, on September 30, 1800, brought the undeclared naval war to a close. The next day the envoys wrote to John Quincy Adams, "We have honor to inform you that a Provisional Treaty was yesterday signed between France and the United States, which if ratified reestablishes the relations of amity between the two nations."[7] On October 10 Murray wrote to John Quincy in Berlin, "By this time you have received my letters, and known that we have made a Convention— 30 September; that we were most handomsely feted four days after; that my colleagues set off so rapidly . . . . They are now at Havre— wind and tide bound."[8]

As a matter of fact the word "Convention," used meticulously in all official documents instead of the word "Treaty," was in itself an accommodation. The French were left free to argue that they had not recognized the voiding of the old treaties, while the Americans could claim that the old treaties were not operative.

While the mission worked in France, back in the United States John Adams delivered his Third Annual Address to the members of Congress on December 3, 1799. The message was even more moderate than that of the year before. This first session of the Sixth Congress opened in a calm and peaceful atmosphere. Before the end of the first month, however, partisan animosity was again on the upswing. Both Federalists and Republicans were anticipating the forthcoming presidential elections, and both sought every possible advantage. Jefferson, reluctant to leave his beloved home, finally arrived in Philadelphia in late December and assumed the presiding officer's chair in the Senate. On his arrival he learned that Bonaparte had seized power from the Directory. This marked the end of Jefferson's sympathy and support for France. He now turned his attention more and more to the domestic scene.

Throughout this first session, petty politics limited the productivity of Congress and constantly harassed the president. Late in February 1800 Adams sent the new Prussian Treaty, negotiated by John Quincy, to the Senate. A Republican senator demanded the correspondence between Secretary of State Pickering and young Adams that had preceded the drafting of the treaty, suggesting that it would reveal serious disagreement within the administration. John Adams was angry at the demand, but he acceded to the request and the treaty was eventually ratified.

Congress bickered over the disbanding of the army, over the proposed Bankruptcy Act, and over the increases in the federal judiciary requested by the president. The Republicans actually forced postponement of the judicial changes and eventually forced the discharge of the soldiers. The Speaker of the House broke the tie vote to give the Federalists victory in the passage of the Bankruptcy Act.

Every action or decision, it would seem, was appraised in terms of its effect on the forthcoming election. On April 24 the Library of Congress was established but apparently was not recognized as an act of significance. From John Adams's viewpoint, the one bright spot in all of this political in-fighting was the increasingly effective leadership of John Marshall in the House. More and more the Virginian demonstrated courage and resourcefulness in supporting the president's policies, and Adams came to respect both his judgment and his integrity.

The Arch Federalists, who had bitterly opposed the new mission to France from that February day when John Adams first announced it, had continued both to fear and condemn it. In April, Stephen Higginson, a Boston merchant, ship builder, and an Arch Federalist, had declared to Pickering, "The Jacobin influence is rising and has been ever since the mission to France was determined on. . . . if a treaty be made with France, their ascendancy will be sure."[9]

Two days after Ellsworth and Davie had set sail for France, Fisher Ames had written to the secretary of state that the peace mission was only "a measure to *make* dangers and to nullify resources; to make the navy without object; the army an object of popular terror." Ames went on to say that the mission would result in the national government being "weakened by the friends it loses and betrayed by those it will gain. It will lose . . . the friendship of the sense and worth and property of the United States, and get in exchange the prejudice, vice, and bankruptcy of the nation . . . ." The domestic result of "this miraculous caprice," Ames said, would

167

be "to embroil and divide," while on the international scene it would "irritate and bring losses and disgrace."[10]

A few weeks later Ames advised Pickering that the safety of the nation demanded the treaty negotiations with France be halted. This must be done, he believed, even if it meant ruining the Federalist party. (The actions of many Arch Federalists during the campaign of 1800 could have been predicted from this last statement.)

The bitterness and rigidity of the Arch Federalists increased as Jefferson's election seemed certain, and was reflected in the actions and writing of George Cabot, Theophilus Parsons, and Timothy Pickering as well as Ames. They not only deplored any negotiations with France but began to turn away from democracy as a form of government.

Adams disagreed violently. He believed in democratic government and in the Constitution, and he recognized the inevitability of change. Wise diplomat that he was, he knew that peace with France, not her form of government or her violence, was the important factor for America. He must have feared that the manipulations of the Arch Federalists, including Pickering in his cabinet, might still plunge the United States and France into war despite the peace mission in France.

There was no mistaking the growing rift between the president and three of his secretaries. In late December, Wolcott wrote to Fisher Ames that John Adams "considers Col. Pickering, Mr. McHenry, and myself as his enemies. His resentments against General Hamilton are excessive; he declares his belief of the existence of a British faction in the United States."[11]

A casual meeting between John Adams and the secretary of war in the late afternoon or early evening of May 5, 1800, may have developed into a very stormy session. The next morning, May 6, McHenry sent in his resignation to take effect June 1. If the session were as angry as McHenry reported, one may wonder that John Adams allowed him to remain in office for almost four weeks. Furthermore, our only record of what occurred was written by McHenry twenty-six days after the meeting took place.[12]

One may question McHenry's ability to remember, after three and a half weeks, exactly what was said in such an interview. Such accuracy is especially doubtful since the period between the incident and the time that McHenry seems to have recorded the conversation was filled with angry charges, heated denials, and hot-tempered attacks. McHenry was known to be highly emotional and at times dishonest.

On May 10, 1800, President Adams sent the following note to his secretary of state: "As I perceive a necessity of introducing a change in the administration of the office of state, I think it proper to make this communication of it to the present Secretary of State, that he may have an opportunity of resigning if he chooses."[13] John Adams asked Pickering to name such date as he would quit the post and indicated a hope that Pickering would respond before Monday morning so that the president could submit a successor's name to the Senate.

Two days later came Pickering's reply—a flat refusal. He wrote that he had a large family, many debts, and he would find it impossible to get along without his salary as secretary of state. If Jefferson were elected president, "an event which in your conversation with me last week," Pickering wrote, "you considered as certain," he had expected to leave the post. But at this time, the secretary insisted, he must refuse to leave.[14] In John Adams's handwriting, on the margin of Pickering's note, is this terse comment: "Rec^d at 9 o Clock May 12, 1800."

The same day the secretary of state received this reply: "Divers causes & considerations, essential to the administration of the government, in my judgment, requiring a change in the Department of State, you are hereby discharged from any further service as Secretary of State."[15]

Nowhere is there better evidence of Alexander Hamilton's insidious interference in the government, or of his curious use of the word "integrity," than in a letter written to Pickering a few days later (May 15, 1800), after Hamilton first learned of Pickering's dismissal from the cabinet: ". . . take with you copies and extracts to *explain* both *Jefferson* & *Adams*. You are aware of a very curious journal of the latter when he was in Europe, a tissue of weakness and vanity. The time is coming when men of real integrity & energy must unite . . . ."[16]

That the dismissal of the secretaries was not taken in a fit of anger but had long been considered is indicated by one of Abigail's letters. On December 11, 1799, five months before Pickering's dismissal, she wrote to her sister, Mary Cranch, that John would dismiss Pickering at once but for the fact that he was determined not to allow personal resentments to dictate government policy.

On May 16, from New York City, an old family friend named Sam B. Malcom wrote to Abigail, expressing regret at the outcome of the New York City elections in which Jeffersonians had won control of the next state legislature. He mentioned several reasons that were being suggested to explain Pickering's removal. Two days later, Abigail replied from Philadelphia, asking Mr. Malcome not to divulge the source of his information:

> With regard to the changes in the cabinet particularly in the office of State, if any Gentleman had a controversy to settle with his neighbour, would he choose to refer it to a person known and avowedly hostile to the parties; particularly if there was a degree of acrimony in their [his] disposition, and a prejudice that prevented their seeing objects in their true light? . . . no man's feelings were more seriously put to the test upon the occasion of the late removal than the presidents if popularity had been his object he would not have sought it by a measure that he knew must create two Enemies to one friend. But surely when a Gentleman is placed in a responsible situation, he has a right to engage such talents in his councils and such men as will cooperate with them.[17]

Three days earlier Abigail had written a long letter to her eldest son in Berlin. Much of the letter dealt with the political situation in New York and the recent election there, but one sentence is pertinent to the cabinet changes: "I could were it prudent, say many things to you which would satisfy you of the why and the wherefore—your own mind will suggest to you some."[18] The last phrase, "your own mind will suggest to you some," might well refer to Pickering's known anti-French bias and the inevitable delicacy of the forthcoming negotiations with that country. This is especially plausible in view of the fact that William Vans Murray had informed both John Adams, and John Quincy in Berlin of the correspondence he had had with Pickering, and of Pickering's almost irrational criticism of the mission to France.[19]

Writing to John Quincy Adams the next September, Abigail discussed the campaign then under way and again defended her husband's removal of the secretaries. "The mission to France has never met with there approbation," she declared, and went on to say, "the late Secretary of State took, whilst in office every possible occasion to excite the public sentiment against it. The removal of him became absolutely necessary . . . ."[20]

John Adams apparently came to see Pickering as incapable of understanding the need for peace with France and unable and unwilling to carry out the policies set by the president. Both Adams and Pickering were determined to the point of stubbornness, and their ideas on the foreign policy that the United States should follow were totally irreconcilable.

In the spring of 1800 John Adams had certainly made up his mind on two points: first, that Pickering disagreed with him on basic issues of foreign policy and the basic goals to be sought; and second, that Pickering would continue to do everything possible to prevent the successful termination of the misunderstandings and of the undeclared naval war with France.

It may be that John Adams lost his temper with McHenry on May 5, and thus precipitated the cabinet crisis without meaning to do so at that exact time. It seems certain, however, that Adams had determined to get rid of Pickering; that his primary reason dealt with the mission to France and that Abigail knew and implied this in her letter to Mr. Malcom above. It is also suggested that little exact information is available about the supposedly hot-tempered meeting with McHenry.

During the last nine months of Adams's presidency, with Samuel Dexter in the war office and John Marshall in the office of state, John Adams's official houschold was much more serene. Marshall, in particular, proved as loyal as he was efficient. The president had complete confidence in, and few if any disagreements with, his secretaries. It was a pleasant change for the chief executive.

Alexander Hamilton's interference, except for his role in the campaign of 1800, was minimal. Once bitterly opposed to the resumption of negotiations with France, he came to accept the fact that the people, as well as John Adams, wanted peace. As discussed above, he had favored both alliance with Britain and war against Spain or France. Yet on October 2, 1800, he wrote to John Marshall that "Of one thing I am sure, if France will slide into a state of Peace *de facto*, we must meet her on that ground. The actual posture of European Affairs and the opinions of our people demand an accommodating course."[21] He may have sensed the possibility but he could not have known that peace was already a reality.

The long weeks and dreary months prior to December 11, 1800, when Governor Davie returned with a copy of the Convention, were marked with uncertainty for both the president and his secretary of state, John Marshall. Both were well aware that the election of Jefferson to the presidency might be pleasing to France, and were ready to attribute some of the delay to French intrigue. The president, knowing that a successfully completed treaty might encourage his campaign for reelection, was especially suspicious of French delay. In a letter written to his secretary of state on the last day of July 1800, Adams commented on the news, or lack of news, from Paris: "But there are reasons to conjecture, that the French government may be inclined to explore, all the resources of their diplomatic skill, to protract the negotiation. The campaign in Europe may have some weight, but the progress of the election in America may have much more."[22] The president went on to suggest to Marshall that our envoys should stand firm on their original instructions.

Three and a half weeks later John Marshall sent the president reports that had left Paris as late as May 17, 1800. He suggested that the outlook was bleak and that the administration should not be surprised if the envoys returned without a treaty. Adams and his administration should, the secretary of state concluded, be prepared for such an emergency. Before Marshall's letter arrived in Quincy, a dispatch arrived there from Rufus King. The ambassador was deeply pessimistic about conditions in England; the French under Napoleon seemed unbeatable. On August 30 John Adams wrote to Marshall, "It will be our destiny, for what I know, republicans as we are, to fight the French republic alone. I cannot account for the long delay of our Envoys. We cannot depart from our honor nor violate our faith, to please the heroick consul [Napoleon]." Three days later, having received Marshall's note of the twenty-fifth and the papers of the envoys, the president noted that he "agree[d] with our gentlemen [meaning the envoys] that their success is doubtfull."[23]

The president's anxiety regarding peace continued but he still felt that sending the mission had been right. He wrote to John Trumbull, "These Federalists may yet have their fill at fighting. They may see our envoys home without peace, and if they do, what is lost? Certainly nothing, unless it be the influence of some of the Federalists by their own imprudent and disorganizing opposition and clamor. Much time has been gained."[24]

A week later the uncertainty still existed, but John Marshall had regained his poise. Writing to the president on September 17, 1800, he indicated his belief that France wanted better relations with all neutrals and his conviction that even if the envoys returned without a treaty there was neither need nor excuse for war. The secretary of state would soon leave the new capital at Washington for a vacation at his home in Virginia, and before long John Adams would take up residence in the unfinished White House. On September 27 Adams wrote to Marshall, "I wish you a pleasant tour to Richmond but I pray you to give such orders that if dispatches should arrive from our envoys they may be kept as secret as the grave till the Senate meets. On Monday the 13 Oct. I shall sett off from this place."[25]

On the evening of the very day on which the president wrote the above letter to Marshall, September 27, 1800, the work of the commission was completed. All that remained was to make the official copies of the agreement and sign them. The actual signing took place at two A.M. on the first day of October, but since the copies had been dated "September 30" this last date was accepted as the official one. The Convention of Môrtefontaine would now be submitted to the governments of France and the United States for final ratification.

William Vans Murray was in high glee over the conclusion of the negotiations. He wrote John Quincy in Berlin, "if we have not accomplished every object of the government of the United States, we have done all in our power—all I believe which any others would have done, or that could be expected in the present state of our relations, and of the world's affairs! We, at all events, put an end to the equivocal state of things, draw the government of the United States out of the quarrel with honour, and establish honourable rules for the future . . . . we have, I dare think, made a better treaty than the last mission might according to their instructions have made."[26]

When the voting for presidential electors took place in 1800 there was no official information that a treaty of peace with France had already been signed. On November 7, however, a Baltimore newspaper, *The Telegraph and Daily Advertiser,* carried on its front page such a statement. Six days later the *Maryland Gazette* of Annapolis made the same announcement under a Baltimore dateline of November 7. This latter paper indicated that the news had arrived by way of London.

Oliver Ellsworth, for reasons of health, decided to spend the winter in Europe. Governor Davie, bringing with him an official copy of the Convention of Môrtefontaine, arrived in the United States on December 11. On the fifteenth of that month the president submitted the Convention to the Senate along with the records kept by the envoys during the long negotiation, and added a special message asking for its approval.

As might have been expected, there were mixed reactions to the Convention. Leading Jeffersonians were critical of some provisions, but urged ratification. Arch Federalists outside of the government joined with members of Congress to damn the agreement that had been signed with the French. On December 17 Harrison Gray Otis expressed alarm in a letter to Hamilton. Sedgwick, Gunn, and Ames were furious; Rutledge and Morris were both amazed and angry. The secretary of the treasury, the only Hamiltonian remaining in the cabinet, wrote to Pickering at the end of December, denouncing the Convention.

In early January 1801 Rutledge wrote to Hamilton, "one part of the treaty abandons all our rights, and the other part makes us the dupes of France in the game she means to play against the maritime power of England . . . . We lose our honor, by restoring the ships we have taken, and by so doing, perhaps, make an implicit acknowledgement of the injustice of our hostile operations."[27]

Many moderate Federalists, including some far-sighted merchants, accepted the news with more equanimity. William Smith, a Federalist merchant in Lisbon, wrote to Rufus King in London that he was "pleased with the Convention; all the great points concerning navigation are settled to our advantage; they are extremely liberal & contain all we could require." He thought it an excellent bargain.[28] John Marshall, of course, supported the agreement and tried to calm the fears of those who doubted the wisdom of treating with France.

Arch Federalist strength in the lame-duck session of Congress, especially in the Senate, was great. The Convention was debated for over a month. A two-thirds majority, necessary for ratification, would have required twenty affirmative votes. On January 23 the vote was taken: sixteen yeas and fourteen nays. The Convention had failed of ratification.

John Adams never gave up easily. He resubmitted the Convention, urging the Senate to reconsider. Several minor changes were proposed, changes later accepted by Napoleon, and on February 3, by a vote of twenty-two to nine, the Convention was finally ratified.

How important was the Convention of Môrtefontaine? John Adams considered peace with France the greatest achievement of a long and eventful life. More than a dozen years after he left the White House, Adams wrote to Senator James Lloyd that he would defend his "missions to France, as long as I have an eye to direct my hand, or a finger to hold my pen. They were the most disinterested and meritorious actions of my life. I reflect upon them with so much satisfaction that I desire no other inscription over my gravestone than: 'Here lies John Adams, who took upon himself the responsibility of the peace with France in the year 1800.' "[29]

14

THE CAMPAIGN AND ELECTION
OF 1800

For a few months, in the spring and summer of 1798, John
Adams was highly popular with the Arch Federalists. Most of the
latter desired war with France, or at least an alliance with Britain,
and during this period they thought the president agreed with them.
Gradually, in the late summer and fall of that year, they developed
doubts about Adams. Was he, they asked themselves, really a
friend of Britain? Could he be counted on always to oppose France
and the revolution? They were dismayed by some of his statements,
disconcerted by what they considered his inconsistency, angry at
his attention to Gerry's entreaties for peace and his courtesy to
George Logan.

The president's nomination of a second mission to France, on
February 18, 1799, changed the doubts of the Arch Federalists to
downright dismay, complete distrust, and determined opposition.
From that time on they refused any cooperation with the president.
Now their only hope was that with McHenry's and Wolcott's assistance, Pickering would be able either to change John Adams's
mind or to delay and perhaps frustrate his plans for this second
mission to France.

During the spring and summer of 1799 Arch Federalists actively
sought a replacement for John Adams. They wished to rid themselves of a president who desired peace and whom they could not
control. Their early efforts were secret, almost furtive; eventually
they became blatantly open.

175

In April 1799 George Cabot wrote to Rufus King in London: "The jealousy which the P[resident] has felt of H[amilton], he now indulges toward P[ickering] to'd W[olcott] & to'd *very many of their friends* who are suspected of having too much influence in the Community, & of not knowing how to appreciate his merits." Cabot went on to suggest that they should turn to Washington to prevent the election of a *"French* President." Ten days later Troup wrote to King: "The President appears so whimsical and unsteady that I have no doubt that serious difficulties will be experienced if he be our candidate at the next election. The faux pas he commited in the late nomination of Minister to France [William Vans Murray] has so shaken the public spirit and the public mind, that he can never regain the ground on which he lately stood."[1]

On June 22, 1799, Jonathan Trumbull, in Lebanon, Connecticut, decided to ask George Washington about returning to the presidency. Trumbull was not quite sure this was the proper thing to do and so sent the letter to Oliver Wolcott. "I send it," Trumbull wrote, "open under cover to you, and pray you to read it with attention, and submit it to the view of our friend, Col. Pickering, and any others to whom you may think proper to make known the ideas of the writer."[2] In his reply Wolcott declared that he would not be a party to such a movement as long as he held an office under Adams. He did not really veto the suggestion, but indicated that it was dangerous and likely to promote discord within the party. It appears that Wolcott sometimes had qualms about deceiving his chief. Furthermore, it seems apparent that in mid-July the Arch Federalists were not yet ready to bring their opposition to Adams into the open.

Before the summer was over, however, the Trumbulls (both Governor Jonathan, and the poet and jurist, John) begged Washington to save the country by accepting another term as president. Washington not only refused, but implied his personal support of Adams and suggested that principles rather than men should occupy the attention of all good Federalists.

With the opening of the election year 1800, the plot of the Arch Federalists to get rid of Adams gathered momentum. Less than a month after Washington's death, Hamilton wrote to Rufus King in England, "At home everything is in the main well; except as to the perverseness and capriciousness of one [John Adams] and the spirit of faction of many [the Jeffersonians]." John Adams was, he asserted, subject to "momentary impulse," while "vanity and jealousy exclude all counsel" and "passion wrests the helm from reason." The loss of Washington had removed a "very salutary" control, and the "leading friends of government" were in a "sad dilemma." Should they risk a schism in the party by trying to change leaders? Or should they support Adams even though he was pursuing a course that might ruin the country? "In our councils there is no fixed plan," Hamilton lamented.[3]

There was a good deal of talk about Oliver Ellsworth for the Federalist nominee; the chief justice was considered "safe" by many of the Arch Federalists. They soon discovered, however, that Adams had too much support in New England, especially in Massachusetts, for him to be dropped from the ticket.

In some early state elections there seemed to be indications that the Adams Federalists and the Jeffersonians might cooperate. For example, Gerry ran for governor of Massachusetts as an independent, but widely proclaimed his loyalty to and respect for John Adams. He nearly won, frightening the Federalists in the process. With more than forty thousand votes cast, and the Jeffersonian candidate polling a mere two thousand, Gerry lost to the Federalist, Strong, by two hundred votes. In New Hampshire, Judge Walker, who had been a Federalist elector in 1796, ran for governor as a Republican. In Maryland a possible Adams-Jefferson ticket was discussed.

In April in New York City, Aaron Burr outwitted Hamilton and assured New York State's electoral vote for Jefferson. That ended talk of an Adams-Jefferson ticket. Republicans now smelled victory and Federalists sensed impending defeat.

Shortly after the New York City elections, so disastrous for the Federalists and for John Adams's chances for reelection, the Federalist members of Congress caucused. The meeting was apparently held at the suggestion of Hamilton, who had written to Senator Theodore Sedgwick on May 4 emphasizing the need to gather before the Federalists in Congress scattered to their homes. In this letter Hamilton asked for an endorsement of Adams and General Charles Cotesworth Pinckney, stating his belief that "to support *Adams* and *Pinckney* equally is the only thing that can possibly save us from the fangs of *Jefferson*." He demanded that Sedgwick inform him at once of the outcome of such a caucus.[4] Several letters written in the next few days bear testimony that the meeting agreed to Hamilton's request. Hamilton felt sure that if he could secure a unanimous vote for the two men by all northern electors there would be several southerners who would vote for Pinckney but not

177

for Adams. Thus was formalized Hamilton's attempt to by-pass John Adams and secure the presidency for General Pinckney.

Just when John Adams or his supporters realized the import of the May caucus and the fact that Hamilton was again planning to relegate Adams to the vice-presidency is difficult to establish. The following September, approximately two months before the choice of electors, the president's youngest son suggested that even at the time of the caucus Samuel Dexter of Massachusetts had been suspicious. At the end of May the same son had written to Joseph Pitcairn, "The Fed's have split. Some are resolved to abandon the present leader while some abide by him and resolve to see it out with the Anti's. Gen'l Pinckney will be run as V. P. in several of the Eastern States and as President in the Southern, which according to some calculations will put him in the chair."[5]

Meanwhile, Alexander Hamilton underwent a quick change of heart. On May 4 he had suggested to Sedgwick that the only way to save the country from Jefferson was to support Adams and Pinckney equally. Yet six days later, writing to the same Arch Federalist friend, Hamilton was ready to accept Jefferson as a means of saving the Federalist party. He wrote in part, "most of the influential men of that [Federalist] party consider him [Adams] as a very *unfit* and *incapable* character." Continuing, Hamilton declared, "I will never more be responsible for him by my direct support, even though the consequence should be the election of *Jefferson*. If we must have *an* enemy at the head of the government, let it be one whom we can oppose, and for whom we are not responsible, who will not involve our party in the disgrace of his foolish and bad measures. Under *Adams*, as under *Jefferson*, the government will sink. The party in the hands of whose chief it shall sink will sink with it, and the advantage will all be on the side of his adversaries."[6]

All through the summer of 1800 Cabot, Ames, Pickering, Wolcott, Sedgwick, and Hamilton were among the Arch Federalists doing all in their power to undermine John Adams and elect Pinckney president. On July 1 Hamilton wrote to Charles Carroll that John Adams "ought not to be the object of the federal wish . . . . His administration has already very materially disgraced and sunk the government. There are defects in his character which must inevitably continue to do this more and more. And if he is supported by the Federal party, his party must in the issue fall with him. Every other calculation will, in my judgment, prove illusory."[7]

In this same letter Hamilton suggested to Carroll that the

leaders of the middle states should threaten to ignore Adams. This, Hamilton thought, would make the "second class" leaders of New England aware that Adams could not win and make them willing to back Pinckney as the only way to stop Jefferson. The vicious attacks continued. Cabot called Adams a "Simple Individual," while Sedgwick screamed about Adams's "miserable jealousy" of those he ought to admire and emulate. Hamilton, over and over again, branded John Adams as "perverse," "capricious," and "vain."

Even before the May caucus Adams may have been aware of the scheming of the Arch Federalists. Twice in March, on the eleventh and again on the nineteenth, an anonymous writer signing himself simply "Yr Friend" warned the president against those who were plotting his downfall. The anonymous writer named names— Sedgwick, Dayton, Howell, Stockton, Hamilton, and the "secretaries"—and spelled out their plans. For example, he asserted that Hamilton and Wolcott were organizing the revenue officers to support Chief Justice Ellsworth. Adams was begged to dismiss the regiments or take other popular action that would make it impossible for the Hamiltonians to undermine his popularity with the people. No doubt John Adams recognized some truth in these warnings since his youngest son soon expressed similar suspicions.

Any attempt to understand John Adams's reactions to these attacks on him, which continued through the final weeks of the campaign, must depend upon answers to two questions. First, was reelection the chief object of John Adams's attention and effort? And second, how did the president react to the increasing likelihood of his defeat?

Although President Adams had many concerns in the summer and fall of 1800, his chief attention was centered on the peace negotiations going forward in Paris, not on the election. Would Murray and his associates be able to reach an understanding with Napoleon, and could the threat of all-out war be banished? Information was sketchy and it would be late fall before the president could be sure that he had won his gamble for peace, but this was always to be his main concern.

How did John Adams react to the increasing evidence of probable defeat? Historians disagree, but we do know that the president told John Trumbull in early September 1800 that if the Federalists lost the election the responsibility would rest squarely on the Hamiltonians. "For myself," he wrote, "age, infirmities, family misfortunes, have conspired with the unreasonable conduct of the jacobins and insolent Federalists, to make me too indifferent" to the outcome of the election.[8]

A year and a half earlier, on February 9, 1799, John had written Abigail, "I cannot converse much with the Ladies because I cannot Speak a word without Pain. If Robespierre were to cutt off my head I should not feel half the Pain that I suffer every hour. . . . Nevertheless I could be comfortable with my Wife upon my farm. Perhaps however I should see a Ghost or a Spirit. But it is time for me to bid farewell to Politicks. The Business of my office multiplies upon me to such a degree as to be very oppressive. I have got to the End of two years within a few days which I did not expect to do so well as I have. Possibly I may make it out two years more."[9]

There is evidence that John Adams continued to think in terms of retirement in 1801. In a letter to her sister in 1800, Abigail indicated that John himself must decide whether he would continue to serve the public or retire to his farm. Three months later Abigail discussed the forthcoming election with a family friend, revealing a resigned, objective attitude toward the outcome and the possibility of Jefferson's becoming president:

> If the people judge that a change in the chief magistracy of the nation is for its peace safety and happiness, they will no doubt make it, the station is an arduous and a painfull one, and may he who shall be calld to fill it have the confidence of the people and seek only their best interests—the rash imprudence of the federalist[s] injures their own cause more than their opponents. . . . I had rather see Mr. Jefferson president than any other man upon that side the question, and believe he would be as little disposed to do an injury to his Country. . . ."[10]

Abigail's comment does not suggest that John Adams did not wish to win a second term or that he made no effort to secure his reelection. While going to inspect the work on the new capital city on the Potomac, John Adams found time to address public gatherings in Lancaster, Pennsylvania, and Fredericktown, Maryland. Alexandria, Virginia, staged a four-day celebration to recognize the forthcoming transfer of the national capital, and John Adams was the guest of honor. Homeward bound, toward the end of June, the president made numerous appearances and impromptu speeches. The opposition press noted his frequent appeals to nationalism and patriotism as well as his references to his own role in the Revolution. Yet neither Adams nor Jefferson campaigned in the modern sense of the word.

In the heat of the summer the attack on Adams grew more torrid, and the most bitter attacks came from within his own party. When Harrison Gray Otis, Massachusetts Federalist, argued that the only way to avoid a fatal split in the party was to support Adams, he was angrily pounced upon by such fellow New Englanders as Cabot, Ames, and Higginson. As Arch Federalists increased the tempo of their attack on the president, much of it in private letters but increasingly in the press as well, Adams was branded as senile and too old for the responsibilities of public office. His tremor and failing eyesight were stressed.

In June 1800 Alexander Hamilton made a tour of New England, ostensibly to check on the army and the progress of recruitment there, but actually to assess Adams's strength and determine New England's support of Pinckney. Hamilton was very indiscreet in the openness of his attacks on Adams. Adams's supporters began to realize the game Hamilton was playing, and they rallied to the president's defense. In the middle of the next month John Adams wrote to his youngest son:

> I could fill a sheet with curious anecdotes of politicks & electioneering, but as this is a subject on which I ought not to permit myself to write[,] speak or even think you will convict me of error & transgressions if I say that Gen Hamilton has been [on] a tour through New England to persuade the people to choose electors who will give a unanimous vote for Gen. Pinckney. To be sure Mr. Adams will have an unanimous vote in Massachusetts but not one in Connecticut nor New Jersey. Thus imprudent and braze[ne]d faced is the style. My information is from Gentlemen of the best & first characters in more than one state to whom this language was held by Hamilton himself. You may shew this letter to Dr. Rush & to him alone —then burn it.[11]

George Cabot in Brookline, Massachusetts, and Oliver Wolcott at the Treasury Department in Philadelphia exchanged letters in mid-June. The former damned the president for his "caprice, ill humour, selfishness, and extreme vanity," and the latter indicated that "Whatever may be thought of my sentiments, I think it right to communicate them to my friends." His sentiments were that "no administration of the government by President Adams can be successful. His prejudices are too violent, and the resentments of men of influence are too keen, to render it possible that he should please either party."[12]

From July through October many of the Arch Federalists continued to ply the mails with their denunciations of John Adams, their expressions of fear for their party and the nation if he were reelected, and their belief that he was inefficient and untrustworthy. Typical, and by no means extreme, is a letter Bayard wrote to Hamilton on August 18. "What is the charm which attaches the East so much to Mr. Adams. It can be nothing personal. The escape we have had under his administration is miraculous. He is liable to gusts of passion little short of frenzy, which drive him beyond the control of any rational reflections. I speak of what I have seen. At such moments the interests of those who support him, or the interest of the nation, would be outweighed by a single impulse of rage."[18]

Hamilton was the real architect of the collapse of the Federalist party. Filled with pessimism and forebodings, he completed his tour of the northeastern states in June. Convinced that only the defeat of Adams and the election of Pinckney could save the nation and his party (and, perhaps unconsciously, his own schemes for military glory and adventure), Hamilton continued to plot for the election of Pinckney to the presidency. His New England tour had been bitterly disappointing. The lesser Federalists—"second class," Hamilton called them—were so solidly behind John Adams and so bitter at Hamilton's denunciation of the president that their response frightened him.

His scheme to elect Thomas Pinckney president in 1796 had failed because of New England. Now Hamilton was convinced that his only hope of defeating Adams in 1800 depended upon obtaining equal support for Charles C. Pinckney throughout the New England countryside. In his frustration he made public promises that he would soon convince Federalists that they should not support Adams. This was the background for his pamphlet attacking the president, which was to play such an unfortunate role in the affairs of Adams, the Federalist party, and Alexander Hamilton himself.

On July 1, 1800, Hamilton wrote two crucial letters. One was to Charles Carroll in which he denounced John Adams in the most bitter language he had used to date, and again stated his belief that support for Adams could only mean the destruction of the Federalist party. To Oliver Wolcott, in the new capital city in Washington, went a plea for information to be used in Hamilton's proposed denunciation of Adams.

Wolcott replied on July 7, "I will readily furnish the statement you desire, from a firm conviction, that the affairs of this government will not only be ruined, but that the disgrace will attach to the federal party, if they permit the re-election of Mr. Adams."[14]

Both Pickering and McHenry became involved in the intrigue. On July 22 the latter again denounced John Adams in a letter to Wolcott:

> I may possibly satisfy some of our most prominent characters that the peace and prosperity of our country have been brought into jeopardy by the present chief to answer electioneering purposes; that under a government dissimilar from that of the Prussians, and with talents of a very different cast from those of the Great Frederic, like him he would be everything, and do every thing himself; that he wants the prudence and discretion indispensable to enable him to conduct with propriety and safety even the collo- quial intercourse permitted between a President and forcign ministers; that he is incapable of adhering to any system, consequently must be forever bringing disgrace upon his agents and administration, that his foibles, pas- sions, and prejudices, arc of a stamp which must expose him incessantly to the intrigues of foreigners, and the unprincipled and wickedly ambitious men of cither party; and that the high and dearest interests of the United States cannot possibly be safe under his direction.[15]

At the beginning of August, Hamilton addressed the first of two demands to John Adams. He charged that the president had claimed the existence of a pro-British group and that Adams had named him as a member. Hamilton demanded proof to substantiate this. Did Hamilton perhaps expect to anger John Adams into a public confrontation? If so, he was disappointed. Adams must have been angry at Hamilton's insolence, but the president neither replied nor mentioned the matter publicly.

Years later Adams claimed he had not spoken of Hamilton as a member of a British faction—unless to his secretaries. (Yet certainly there *was* a "British faction," in terms of sympathy and interest, and who today would argue that Hamilton was not a member!)

Two days later, on August 3, 1800, Hamilton disclosed to Wolcott his matured plan for the previously discussed attack on Adams. After pleading for the "statement of facts," facts to de- nounce the Adams administration, which Wolcott had promised, Hamilton indicated he hoped to give the public, in the form of a letter to a friend, his opinions of the president. "What say you to this measure?" Hamilton queried. "I could predicate it, on the fact that I am abused by the friends of Mr. Adams, who ascribe my opposition to pique and disappointment, and would give it the shape of a defence of myself."[16]

By August 21 Cabot and Ames, who knew of his plans, were beginning to doubt the wisdom of Hamilton's attack. Would he go too far? Cabot wrote Hamilton that while he was in favor of some exposure of Adams he hoped Hamilton would not sign any statement he might make. On August 27 Hamilton appealed again for help in exposing Adams.

At the end of August, Fisher Ames seemed convinced that Jefferson would win. Opposed to Hamilton's plan to publish an attack on Adams over his own name, Ames emphatically stated that "the question is not how we shall fight, but how we and all federalists shall fall, that we may fall, like Antaeus, the stronger for our fall."[17] Early in September, Oliver Wolcott advised Hamilton against publishing a signed attack, yet he made it clear he had no sympathy for Adams and no respect for his abilities, and stated that the general public was coming to believe the president was unbalanced.

In spite of the warnings and the cautions of Cabot and Ames and Wolcott, Alexander Hamilton went ahead with the preparations of his attack on the president. On September 26 he sent Wolcott a finished copy, expressing his gratitude for the confidential information his friends had supplied, and asking for Wolcott's opinion of what he had written. He indicated that he expected the statement would provide two advantages: gain votes for Pinckney and "vindicate" Adams's opponents within the party. Hamilton indicated that he planned to send it to "so many respectable men of influence, as may give its contents general circulation," and said he was going to sign it because the press was so filled with anonymous statements that people no longer paid any attention to them.[18] Wolcott replied, praising the statement but expressing some doubt of the wisdom of publishing it. Wolcott was sure of Adams's popularity in Massachusetts and doubted that the letter could elect Pinckney, the only excuse, he thought, for its publication.

On October 1 Hamilton again wrote to President Adams. Referring to his letter of August 1 and the fact that Adams had neither replied nor acknowledged its receipt, he again demanded, in tones as insolent as in the first letter, that the president reply to his questions and accept or deny responsibility for rash statements about the British faction and Hamilton's membership in it. Adams did not reply.

Soon the "letter" was in print. It was true that Hamilton had said he intended only private distribution. Yet he had planned broad circulation. Somehow a copy reached Aaron Burr and was widely published by Jeffersonian editors in both newspaper and pamphlet form.

The attack on Adams produced violent reactions from the entire political spectrum. Noah Webster rushed to the president's defense with *A Letter to General Hamilton, occasioned by his letter to President Adams,* signed by "Aristides." Webster, who had long been associated with the moderate Federalists and had consistently supported President Adams in his handling of foreign affairs, charged that Hamilton's "ambition, pride and overbearing temper have destined . . . [him] to be the evil genius of this country." In far-off Holland, the next January, William Vans Murray read Hamilton's attack on the president and wrote to John Quincy Adams that he had "read it with sorrow, for I have always esteemed and vaunted Hamilton."[19] Other moderate Federalists rushed into print to defend John Adams.

The Arch Federalists were not interested in supporting the president, but many of them were unhappy with Alexander Hamilton and his public attack on Adams. Even Hamilton's good friend George Cabot wrote, "All agree that the execution [of the attack on Adams] is masterly, but I am *bound* to tell you that you are accused by respectable men of egotism; and some very worthy and sensible men say you have exhibited the same *vanity* in your book which you charge as a dangerous quality and great weakness in Mr. Adams. I should have left it to your enemies to tell you of the censures of your friends, if I was not persuaded that you cannot possibly mistake my motives or doubt of the sincerity of my affection or the greatness of my esteem."[20] In early November, Arch Federalist Troup wrote to Rufus King in London, "Our friends . . . lamented the publication [of Hamilton's "letter"]. . . . Not a man . . . but condemns it. . . . Our enemies are universally in triumph."[21]

The files of Adams's correspondence contain evidence of the large number of private citizens who rallied to his support. One of these was Colonel Tudor, and John Adams replied to him on November 14:

> I have received with great pleasure, your favor of the fifth. Of the book which my enemy has written, you shall hear more hereafter. My character shall not lie under that load. I will not write in newspapers nor in pamphlets, while I am in my present station, against that pamphlet—

Personal injuries! I cry your mercy. What personal injuries? Is making his nephew a Captain a personal injury? Is making his relation a Lt in the Navy a personal injury? Is making his brother Dr. Stevens Consul General at St. Domingo a personal injury? . . . I know not when, where or to whom I ever said, he was of a British party. If I ever did, it must have been to my confidential ministers, & has he betrayed them, to betray me & then betrayed both. . . . I never said, he was destitute of moral principle. I never said it of any man. . . .[22]

The next month the president wrote in a similar vein to Dr. Ogden Newark: "I dread neither his menaces of pamphlets nor the execution of them. It would take a large volume to answer him compleatly. I have not time & if I had, I would not employ it in such a work, while I am in public office. The public indignation he has excited is punishment enough."[23] So far as is known, John Adams kept his word not to take public notice of Hamilton's attack as long as he was president. It has been suggested that Hamilton's "letter" roused the pro-Adams wing of the party to more energetic and effective effort, and was thus actually of assistance to the supporters of the president.

In spite of the severity of Cabot's criticism and the evidence that his own charges were having little of the desired effect, Alexander Hamilton planned to publish a second attack. He wrote to McHenry, Pickering, and Wolcott, asking for new facts and new charges. Pickering was away and did not receive the request for nearly a month. McHenry agreed to help. Wolcott, however, did his best to persuade Hamilton not to make a new attack, and he seems to have succeeded.

Hamilton and the Arch Federalists were only a part of John Adams's political concern in the summer and fall of 1800. The entire campaign was bitter and scurrilous. All the criticism of John Adams published by the opposition press in 1796 was repeated: He was a monarchist! He had little respect for the United States Constitution! Although coming from a lower middle-class family, he was branded an aristocrat.

In rebuttal the Federalist press rang the old charges on Thomas Jefferson: He was an infidel! He was an atheist! He was a lover of France who would prostitute his own nation to the glory of a foreign country! Compared to Jefferson, however, John Adams's difficulties were complicated by the fact that his own party attacked him so bitterly. He must withstand not only the attacks of the

Jeffersonians but the even more bitter assaults of the Arch Federalists, or the "Pickeronians," as the Jeffersonian press sometimes called them.

John Adams was further embarrassed by the publication of the so-called Pinckney Letter. In 1792 John Adams had carelessly written a letter to Tench Coxe in which he had made disparaging remarks about Thomas Pinckney, the brother of Charles, who was the Federalist vice-presidential candidate. At that time Coxe was a Federalist officeholder, but in 1800 Coxe was a disgruntled man who had been dismissed from his office. Coxe, anxious for revenge, released Adams's letter and it was widely published, especially in the Jeffersonian press. John Adams was on his way to the new capital city when, stopping for the night at Francis's Hotel in Philadelphia, he received both a letter from Thomas Pinckney and a copy of the Charleston *Gazette* containing the old letter he had written to Coxe. Early the next morning Adams wrote a five-page letter of explanation to Thomas Pinckney. The entire matter was eventually smoothed over. Charles C. Pinckney was obviously not looking for trouble with Adams. In fact, most historians agree that Pinckney was without knowledge of Hamilton's plot to make him president. In the opinion of at least one historian, however, the episode cost Adams support in South Carolina.

Some of the attacks on John Adams were so ridiculous that the president could laugh or joke about them. There was, for instance, the report that Adams planned to marry one of his sons to a daughter of King George III and thus found a dynasty to unite Britain and the United States. This had only been prevented, according to reports, by the loyalty and courage of George Washington, who, dressed in a white uniform, called on the president and begged him not to unite Britain and the United States. Adams had been adamant. Washington had then returned, dressed this time in a black uniform, to plead with Adams to give up the scheme, and again the president had rejected his pleas. Washington, dressed in his old Revolutionary War uniform, had then called a third time. He had drawn his sword and threatened to run the president through; only then had John Adams renounced his secret plans to become king.

John Adams had been even more amused by the story that he had sent General Charles Cotesworth Pinckney, the Federalist vice-presidential candidate, to England to "procure four pretty girls as mistresses," two for each of them. Adams wrote to an old friend,

"I do declare upon my honor, if this be true General Pinckney has kept them all for himself and cheated me out of my two."[24]

One of the bitter crosses John Adams had to bear in the summer and fall of 1800 was the absence of old friends. Men like Cabot, Sewall, and Higginson, neighbors and friends for many years, failed to visit John and Abigail, and by their absence indicated their participation in the efforts of the Arch Federalists to by-pass Adams.

Yet there were bright spots, too. Conscious of his own heritage and interested in the preservation of the records of the past, John Adams was deeply moved by the invitation to become a member of the Massachusetts Historical Society. On August 20 he planned to attend a meeting of the Academy of Arts and Sciences, and Elbridge Gerry wrote to the president, inviting both John and Abigail to join the Gerrys for dinner that evening.

As the weeks went by, more and more men, both Federalists and independents, wrote Adams to pledge their loyalty and support. From Hartford in the late summer John Trumbull twice assured the president that while men in Connecticut had been disturbed in May when Pickering was dismissed, they had generally come to feel that it was the president's prerogative to select his secretaries. Furthermore, Trumbull claimed, Connecticut men had respect for John Adams's judgment and were sure he must have had good reasons for the dismissal. The president was promised that Connecticut would vote Federalist in the election. In early November, William Tudor wrote from Boston, denouncing Hamilton for his pamphlet and describing the large crowd that had celebrated the president's birthday on October 30, "Although there was not any of the *faction* there."[25] Five days later John Jay sent an assurance of his strong support. Such privately expressed sentiments of loyalty and confidence must have pleased crusty old John Adams.

Among the surprising number of men who rallied to Adams's support were personal friends and political moderates. Many were merchants or commercial lawyers. Some of the expressions of support reflected the loyalty of old comrades. Of such was the letter from old Dan Morgan of Revolutionary War fame. Writing from his Virginia home, "Soldier's Rest," General Morgan pledged his loyalty and vigorous support.

On Sunday, October 19, the youngest Adams son wrote to his mother. He described in great detail the sentiments he had discovered in Philadelphia. There were, he said, rumors of an Adams-Jefferson ticket. Such rumors, he realized, were harmful to his father. About three weeks later, Jedidiah Morse wrote to Oliver Wolcott, "There are very strong evidences . . . that the Jeffersonians intend to meet the President on his own ground, and it is much to be feared that he will accept their support."[26] Apparently the Arch Federalists were spreading rumors that Adams and Jefferson were having secret meetings.

By November 13, 1800, the president and his wife had received the unofficial word of the election results in South Carolina and were virtually certain that the Federalists had lost the election for the presidency. On that day Abigail wrote to her youngest son:

> Well, my dear son, South Carolina has behaved as your father always said she would. The consequence to us, personally, is, that we retire from public life. For myself and family, I have few regrets. At my age, and with my bodily infirmities, I shall be happier at Quincy. Neither my habits, nor my education or inclinations have led me to an expensive style of living, so that on that score I have little to mourn over. If I did not rise with dignity, I can at least fall with ease, which is the more difficult task. I wish your father's circumstances were not so limited and circumscribed, as they must be, because he cannot indulge himself in those improvements upon his farm, which his inclination leads him to, and which would serve to amuse him, and contribute to his health. I feel not any resentment against those who are coming into power, and only wish the future administration of the government may be as productive of the peace, happiness, and prosperity of the nation, as the two former ones have been. . . . My own intention is to return to Quincy as soon as I conveniently can; I presume in the month of January.[27]

Abigail knew how much her husband desired vindication by a victory at the polls, yet she also knew the physical and emotional strain under which he must constantly operate. She knew her own tenuous health. It was perhaps easier for her to accept defeat because of these factors. Yet Abigail, like her husband, did not give up easily and disliked defeat. By December 1, however, she was able to write calmly and objectively to her sister, Mary Cranch, as she included this expression of courage and public concern: "As to politicks; they are at present such a mere turn penny, that I believe it is best to leave all calculations to those who daily occupy themselves with them, and say what from the Sincerity of my Heart I do: that I hope the termination of the present contests will be such as will be most productive of the Peace, Liberty and happiness of our common Country, let who will be at the Head of the Government."[28]

Traditionally, many historians have assumed that a major factor in the outcome of the 1800 elections was the opposition to the Federalists generated by the fear and dislike of the Alien and Sedition Acts. Many mid-twentieth century critics, however, are of the opinion that the influence of these acts has been greatly overplayed. It has also been common to attribute the outcome of the election of 1800 to the president's determination to find a basis for peace, to the Murray appointment of February 18, 1799, and the second mission to France. Certainly this policy, and these actions, led directly to the breach in the Federalist party and the open effort of the Hamiltonians to get rid of Adams. In November, Adams wrote John Jay that "The last mission to France, and the consequent dismission of the twelve regiments, although an essential branch of my system of policy, has been to those who have been intriguing and laboring for an army of fifty thousand men, an unpardonable fault."[29] There are historians, however, who feel that John Adams's desire for peace won rather than lost votes.

It must be recognized, of course, that the final agreement or treaty with France had little if any effect on the outcome of the election. Most, if not all, ballots were cast before the agreement of Môrtfontaine was publicized in this country. If the agreement, bringing to an end the quasi-war, marking the renunciation of the alliance forged in 1798, and guaranteeing at least relative peace and harmony for several years in the future, had been signed in Paris three months earlier and the results had been known in the United States by mid-summer, the election results might have been more favorable to Adams.

Increasingly historians have come to see the issue of taxation as a major factor in the election of 1800. It is, of course, impossible to separate the issue of taxation from that of our relations with France. The navy that John Adams wanted, as well as the army that Hamilton and the Arch Federalists sought, required money. Congress passed several tax increases in 1798, during the XYZ frenzy. Ignoring the symbolism, a stamp tax was passed, thus providing a name quickly seized upon by the Jeffersonians and related back to the hated English tax of 1765. The Republicans worked for its repeal at the next session of Congress and the Federalists were able to retain it by a narrow margin in the Senate. The cost of operating the federal government nearly doubled during the four years of

Adams's presidency, and Secretary Wolcott estimated that the national debt had reached eight million dollars.

The rate of taxation on houses was made progressive, ranging from one-fifth of a percent on a house worth four hundred dollars to a full percent on a house valued at thirty thousand dollars or more. Yet even the people affected least by this tax were loud in their protests. In 1800, when agrarian counties in Pennsylvania, like Northampton, Bucks, and Montgomery, which had voted Federalist in 1796, swung sharply into the Jeffersonian camp, it was high taxes that could be blamed. This was the major factor leading to Fries Rebellion.

In November 1798, when the president and his secretary, Billy Shaw, returned to Philadelphia for the coming session of Congress, Adams had become aware of the growing resentment over taxes. He disagreed strongly with Wolcott over Treasury Department policy when, in late 1798, Wolcott negotiated a five million dollar loan at 8 percent interest. Adams insisted the money ought to be borrowed at no more than 6 percent. The president wrote to the secretary of war, "The system of debts & taxes is levelling all governments in Europe. We have a career to run to be sure, & some time to pass before we arrive at the European crisis—but we must ultimately go the same way."[30] But Wolcott, supported in his stand by Alexander Hamilton, had his way. Later this act became an important issue in the 1800 election.

Oliver Wolcott had differed with the president regarding the interest rate for the 1798 loan, but in general he was an economy-minded secretary. In December 1799 he had supported John Adams's pleas to cut government costs, showing Congress how the decline in customs revenue and the necessity of what we now know as deficit financing necessitated economy wherever possible. Despite Adams's concern, however, taxes rose and the country continued to blame him and the Federalists.

The army was inextricably connected with the matter of taxes, yet much of the trouble centered around the army as a symbol rather than the army per se. To the Jeffersonians, especially those in the South, the army was a symbol of the civil strife they feared, of the possibility that the Federalists might use force to retain their political supremacy. To the Adams Federalists, the army symbolized the desire of the Arch Federalists to involve the United States either in war with France or, at least, in an alliance with Britain, actions that neither they nor the president desired. To

Adams the army represented violence and was a symbol of the aggressive search for power that he distrusted in Alexander Hamilton.

The development of political party machinery also became a major factor in the election of 1800. The Federalists were quick to seize on techniques and patterns previously exploited by the Republicans, but the latter possessed much more initiative. "The victory which Republicans so enthusiastically hailed in 1801," Cunningham concluded, "was basically a party triumph. The election of Jefferson and of a Republican Congress had been accomplished through four years of party organizing, vigorous political campaigning, and realistic fashioning of party machinery, made effective by the ability of the Republican party to sense and to conform to the temper of the electorate."[31]

The Federalists, of course, suffered from an absence of effective organization and from disunity. A few weeks after the election returns were in, the president wrote to his youngest son, "The federal cause has been so imprudently managed, as well as so discordantly composed, that the overthrow of the party is no wonder. The federal cause had no head."[32]

While John Adams's second, and successful, mission to France returned too late to have any major effect on the outcome of the 1800 election, it did provide some negative influence. British efforts at collaboration were ended with the departure of Davie and Ellsworth for France, and Britain's seizure of ship and impressment of seamen increased steadily during 1800. Some have believed that the vote in New York City, in which the Jeffersonians won by a very narrow margin, was decisively influenced by British attacks on American commerce. Robert Liston did his best to persuade the British government to ameliorate its policy, warning that captures of American merchant ships and the manner of handling cases in the Courts of Vice Admiralty were arousing American indignation and might lead to a Jeffersonian political victory in the forthcoming elections, but his efforts were unavailing.

The election results clearly established three facts. When the electoral votes were finally counted they revealed that Jefferson and Burr both had seventy-three votes, John Adams had sixty-five, and Charles C. Pinckney had sixty-four—one Federalist elector in Rhode Island had failed to vote for Pinckney, thus guaranteeing that the two Federalist candidates would not be tied. Republican plans to accomplish the same result in their party were either not understood or malfunctioned. Now the House of Representatives would have to resolve the tie between Jefferson and Burr.

A second fact stands out clearly as the election results are assessed: the election for president was amazingly close. Outside of New York, Jefferson had fewer votes than in 1796, and the results in New York could have been changed by the switch of a few hundred votes in New York City. With the exception of this voting in New York City, John Adams ran better than in 1796. Although the new Congress was to be heavily Jeffersonian, Graber has pointed out that "The Federalist party did well . . . throughout the entire South . . . [And] Virginia and North Carolina elected more Federalists to office than ever before."[33] Finally, it is apparent from studying the votes for congressional seats that John Adams ran well ahead of his party, and Jefferson significantly behind his.

To determine the actual popular will is almost impossible. Federalists manipulated and may have taken votes to which they were not really entitled in New Jersey and Pennsylvania. New York's crucial electoral vote gave the victory to Jefferson, yet it was obtained as part of a power play between Burr and Hamilton. The Jeffersonians may have won because of Burr's astuteness in establishing the Manhattan Company Bank or because he managed to unite his party behind a distinguished ticket. Hamilton may have lost the election by his scheme to select a ticket of subservient second-raters in New York who would go along with his scheme to ditch Adams. Any one of the above may have been the crucial factor in giving the Republicans the presidency. Adams's foreign policy and the Federalist domestic policy seem to have had comparatively little influence on the outcome of the election.

John Adams had a double blow that December. He learned that he would not be reelected to a second term, and at almost the same time came the news of the death of his second son, Charles, who had become an irresponsible alcoholic. As a boy, Charles had been the gayest of the Adams children, always bringing joy and pleasure to the others in the family. Charles was established in a promising law practice, and had a lovely, loving wife and fine children. The realization of Charles's condition and then of his death was almost more than John and Abigail could bear. The agony of his son's death seems to have caused John Adams more concern than his political defeat. To his youngest son he wrote, "Oh! that I had died for him if that would have relieved him from his faults as well as his disease." However, John Adams went on, there was "nothing more to be said but, let the eternal will be done."[34]

On December 28 John Adams wrote two letters that reveal his

mental and emotional state of mind. To Dr. Cotton Tufts, Abigail's uncle, dear family friend, counselor, and agent, John Adams sent a long letter: Jefferson and Burr were tied, he wrote, the treaty with France was concluded—what should John Adams do now? "I have forgotten all my law," the president added, "& lost my organs of speech."[35] To F. A. Vanderkemp, a fairly new friend and frequent correspondent, he wrote despairingly of the loss of his son and then expressed the measure of his love for his country and his own evaluation of his administration. "Before this reaches you, the news will be familiar to you, that after the 3d of March I am to be a private citizen and your brother farmer. I shall leave the State with its coffers full and the fair prospect of a peace with all the world smiling in its face, its commerce flourishing, its navy glorious, its agriculture uncommonly productive and lucrative. Oh, my County! May peace be within thy walls, and prosperity within thy palaces."[36]

15

★★★★★

A NEW CAPITAL—
A RETIRING PRESIDENT

On October 13, 1800, before the presidential electors had been chosen, John Adams left Quincy for the new capital at Washington, D.C. He visited along the way and did not arrive until late Saturday, November 1. That evening he slept in the White House, the first president to occupy the building. The next day he wrote to Abigail. Describing the last stages of his journey, he told of his pleasure at finding that the executive mansion, although far from completed, was habitable. He was lonely, and he urged his wife to come on as soon as possible. As he closed his letter, he wrote, "before I end my Letter, I pray Heaven to bestow the best of Blessings on this House and all that shall hereafter inhabit it. May none but honest and wise Men ever rule under this roof."[1] His final sentence has since been chiseled on one of the White House mantlepieces.

Ten years earlier, the site of the capital had been covered with forest, fruit orchard, and a few fields of corn and tobacco, except for the part too swampy for cultivation. President Washington had selected the site after Congress had voted to establish the Federal District. L'Enfant, the French architect and engineer, and various commissioners wrangled over plans before it was decided to place the Capitol on a plateau near the eastern branch of the Potomac River. The executive mansion would be built a mile westward on a level plain. The city's main artery followed the course of a slow, muddy stream called Goose Creek. When John Adams arrived, however, Pennsylvania Avenue, like so much of the city, was only a plan and a hope. None of the official buildings were completely finished and the only thing in abundant supply was mud. In warm weather it was dust and mosquitoes.

From the vantage point of nearby Mount Vernon, George Washington had kept close watch on the developing community that had been named for him. In 1799 he wrote a friend in England that the new city would be grand and beautiful—in a century.

In June 1800 the government had begun to move offices and records to the new capital. From there Oliver Wolcott, Jr., the secretary of the treasury, wrote to a friend that the place was hardly fit for a man to live in. He found only one adequate tavern and could not imagine how Congress could secure housing when it assembled. He had an equally low opinion of the people he found living there, residing in "mean huts" scattered over the area. By August 1, however, both the secretary of state and the secretary of the treasury had found living quarters and were in frequent correspondence with the president at his Massachusetts home.

During the weeks of summer and early fall there was much activity in Washington. Various federal offices were opened and began to function, although often in crude and temporary quarters. Stagecoach companies increased the number of trips scheduled for the city. Fortunate travelers occasionally made the journey from Philadelphia to Washington in only thirty-three hours traveling time. A newspaper, *The National Intelligencer,* began publication and a theater managed to remain alive for a few weeks. Life in the new city, however, was drab and would remain so for many months.

The original plans for the city specified that all construction be of brick or stone and all houses be three stories high. Before his death the preceding December, George Washington had built a row of brick houses on North Capitol Street, hoping to encourage other men to invest in the city's future. Houses started by Robert Morris before his bankruptcy remained unfinished. Speculators had constructed two rows of houses west of the executive mansion. It was soon realized by the commissioners, however, that all residents could not afford such expensive structures, and that "mechanics" and members of the "lower orders" must have cheaper places in which to live. By the summer of 1800 numerous wooden houses appeared on a plateau beyond the Capitol. Other buildings dotted a ridge along New Jersey Avenue, some of them soon to become uncomfortable boarding houses for congressmen.

Upon receipt of her husband's letter indicating that the execu-

tive mansion was habitable, Abigail set out for the new capital city.
Beyond Baltimore the roads were not only almost impassable but
so poorly marked that the president's wife, or her driver, became
lost. When on Sunday, November 16, Abigail reached her new
home she was completely dismayed. She had managed the farm
and her family while John was at the Continental Congress; she had
faced the dangers of a stormy crossing of the Atlantic, accompanied
by small children (and the cow that they took along for butter and
milk). The rude stares and unkind remarks of English society had
not daunted her when John became the first minister to England.
But for once in her life, Abigail Adams was overwhelmed.

She wrote her favorite sister, "The establishment necessary is a
tax which can not be born by the present sallery: No body can form
an Idea of it but those who come into it. I had much rather live in
the house at Philadelphia. Not one room or chamber is finished of
the whole. It is habitable by fires in every part, thirteen of which
we are obliged to keep daily, or sleep in wet & damp places."[2] Abigail found that only six of the thirty rooms were plastered. At a
later date she wrote, "not a single apartment finished . . . the
principal stairs not up . . . not the least fence, yard, or other convenience without, and the great unfinished audience-room I make
a drying-room of, to hang the clothes in."[3] Abigail again spoke of
the damp cold and the difficulty of keeping warm. Firewood was
expensive and often impossible to obtain at any price.

Albert Gallatin reported to his wife, "Around the Capitol are
seven or eight boarding-houses, one tailor, one shoemaker, one
printer, a washing woman, a grocery shop, a pamphlets and sta-
tionery shop, a small dry-goods shop, and an oyster house."[4]

Members of Congress straggled into Washington, testimony to
the difficulties of travel and communication, the stories of poor
accommodations, and, perhaps, to the indifference with which some
members of Congress assumed their duties. Congressman James
A. Bayard of nearby Delaware did not arrive until January 2, 1801.
The next day he wrote, "I arrived here last evening after a very
tedious and fatiguing ride. [For] two nights I was but two hours
in bed and the roads being very bad we were intolerably jolted in
the stage. Nothing I may say has yet been done by Congress." Referring to the city itself, Bayard continued, "I have no lodgings yet
and am in no manner arranged. The City I have seen only from the
windows of the Capitol. The prospect furnishes a view of a few
scattered houses and a great deal of dreary rough country." Two
days later Bayard wrote, "I am at present lodged at Stelle's Hotel,

upon the following Moderate terms, 15 dollars p[er] week for my-self, 5 for my servant, 3 for wood and candles." At the end of the month Bayard noted, "Mrs. Bayard is not with me but at Dover. It was impossible to procure accommodations. I now stand at 23 dollars a week for self and servant including wood. A wife and additional servants would have been an enormous expense."[5]

The vice-president had secured lodgings at Conrad's boarding house. He had a separate drawing-room where he could entertain visitors, but when the more than thirty boarders sat down to eat, Thomas Jefferson was at the far end of the table, away from the fire and near the door. Apparently some congressmen did bring their wives, for Mrs. Brown, wife of a senator from Kentucky, was staying at Conrad's and described the manner in which her suggestion that the vice-president be accorded a seat nearer the fire was turned down by the other boarders.

Four years later the Irish poet Thomas Moore visited the capi-tal and wrote his oft-quoted jingle to ridicule the pretensions of the new city:

> Where tribunes rule, where dusky Davi bow,
> And what was Goose Creek once is Tiber now;
> This embryo capital, where Fancy sees
> Squares in morasses, obelisks in trees;
> Where second-sighted seers e'en now adorn
> With shrines unbuilt and heroes yet unborn
> Though now but woods—and Jefferson—we see
> Where streets sh'd run and sages ought to be.

Three weeks after his arrival, the president delivered his fourth and last annual address to the assembled houses of Congress in the new and uncompleted Capitol. Secretary of State Marshall had been especially helpful in the preparation of this message. The president paid his respects to his predecessor: "May this territory be the residence of virtue and happiness! In this city may that piety and virtue, that wisdom and magnanimity, that constancy and self-government, which adorned the great character whose name it bears be forever held in veneration! Here and throughout our country may simple manners, pure morals, and true religion flourish for-ever!"[6]

Other matters mentioned by the president in this address in-cluded the problems of the government of the District of Columbia, the discharge of the temporary army, and, as on December 3, 1799, an appeal for "a revision and amendment of the judiciary system." He announced the ratification of a treaty with Prussia, spoke of the problems still existing in connection with the "sixth article of our treaty of amity, commerce, and navigation with Great Britain," and mentioned the current mission to France. The president emphasized the need for a strong defense, praised the new navy, and called for improved fortification of the seacoast.

As Adams began his residence in the new capital city, there were two concerns central to his attention: the progress of his commissioners in Paris as they sought peace (for many weeks he would not know that the treaty had been signed on September 30), and the voting at home to determine whether or not he would be reelected. In addition, two major problems would soon claim the attention not only of the president but of all politically minded citizens: the expansion of the judiciary and, as soon as the election results were known, the resolution of the tie vote between Jefferson and Burr.

In 1799, when John Adams had first urged changes in the judiciary, the members of his own party were indifferent. As the 1800 election results became known, however, it was apparent that while John Adams had lost his bid for a second term by a rather narrow and perhaps inconclusive margin, the Jeffersonians had gained undisputed control of both houses of Congress. New judgeships and other court offices that could be filled by a Federalist president and confirmed by a lame-duck, Federalist-controlled Senate now became most appealing to the party.

Federalists in Congress went rapidly to work to draft such a bill as the president had requested. The proposal, as submitted and amended, reformed judicial districts, doubled the circuits to six, and created both twenty-three new federal judgeships and numerous subsidiary positions such as court marshals and justices of the peace. The bill was not passed by Congress until February 13, 1801, and was immediately signed into law by the president.

Position-hungry Federalists did not wait for passage of the bill to besiege the president with applications and recommendations. His correspondence, throughout January and February, was studded with such letters. Adams replied to many of them. For example, on January 23 he wrote to Richard Stockton of New Jersey, stressing his hope that he would be objective in making his nominations if the bill, then being considered, became law. "I may have been too indifferent to the smiles of some men & to the frowns of others," the president declared, "but neither will influence my judgment I hope in determining nominations of judges, characters at all times sacred in my estimation."[7]

With few, if any, exceptions, John Adams appointed Federalists to these new positions. Jefferson and many of his supporters were bitter, and considered it immoral for Adams to make such judicial appointments after his defeat for reelection. "Midnight judges," referring to Adams's engagement in making judicial appointments right up to the last moments of his term in office, and "packing the court" have become terms common to our textbooks and popular histories. Yet many years ago Koch and Peden concluded that the importance of these appointments was overemphasized, and they reminded their readers that John Adams had urged the expansion of the judiciary more than a year earlier. Furthermore, he had been reading and evaluating recommendations for these positions for many weeks.

John Adams usually did appoint men whose political thinking coincided with his own. Yet he did not confine his appointments to his own friends and supporters. Among the new appointees were both Oliver Wolcott, Hamilton's protégé and informer in Adams's cabinet, and Theophilus Parsons, an Arch Federalist who had ignored Adams during the campaign of 1800.

While numerous historians have written critically of Adams's "midnight appointments," one historian has pointed out that on Tuesday, March 3, 1801, Adams's last day in office, he submitted but two nominations for Senate approval, and both were for minor positions in Pennsylvania. The Senate did continue in session until nine that evening, acting on earlier nominations, but most of these appointments were army commissions or for unimportant judicial positions. Tuesday evening, John Adams signed but three commissions for judges, all in the courts of Washington, D.C. He must have been both pleased and relieved that the burden of expanding the judiciary was completed.

During this same period the chief justiceship became vacant, on the resignation of Oliver Ellsworth. It is interesting that the president received several letters urging him to "arrange" for himself to assume the chief justiceship on March 3. Elias Boudinot, asserting that he represented a group of New Jersey lawyers, wrote urging this action on January 20, 1801. Six days later the president replied, graciously thanking Boudinot for his suggestion but declaring that "the office of Chief Justice is too important for any man to hold of sixty-five years of age, who has wholly neglected the study of the law for six and twenty years." Adams continued by indicating that he had already nominated a "gentleman in the full vigor of middle age, in the full habits of business, and whose reading in the science is fresh in his head."[8] On February 4 Secretary of State Marshall accepted the appointment as chief justice, noting "I shall enter immediately on the duties of the office & hope never to give you occasion to regret having made this appointment."[9]

Determining whether Jefferson or Burr would become president on March 4 was another major problem during the final weeks of Adams's presidency. The Republicans had neglected to take the necessary precautions to prevent their two candidates, Jefferson and Burr, from receiving the same number of votes.

On December 28, 1800, John Adams wrote to Cotton Tufts, "Mr. Jefferson and Mr. Burr have equal numbers 73. Which will be chief?"[10] Two days later, writing to his old friend Gerry, the president suggested Jefferson was the worthy candidate and challenged Burr's pretensions to such high office. Abigail wrote her youngest son, "I presume mr. Jefferson will finally be agreed upon; *neither party can tolerate Burr,* tho he has risen upon stilts, they know it will be giving to America a president who was not thought of nor contemplated by any part of it for the office. . . . We are brought into a deplorable situation. God save the United States of America." A month later, writing to the same son, Abigail noted, "I am as perfectly at a loss to conjecture which of the candidates will be chosen one, as I was the day it was first known that there were two equals."[11]

Through January and into February the question of the succession was debated and argued in the House of Representatives. Some Federalists saw an opportunity to embarrass the Jeffersonians and perhaps remove Jefferson as a future opponent, by placing Burr in the presidency. To his credit, Alexander Hamilton tried to prevent such a questionable maneuver.

The actual voting began on February 11, 1801, during a wild blizzard that blanketed Washington with snow. Emotions ran high and few took the trouble to conceal them. The bitter fight continued for six days. A seriously ill congressman was carried into the Capitol on a bed so that he could cast his vote. One session lasted thirty-six hours. Then on the thirty-fourth ballot Thomas Jefferson won. On February 16 John Adams wrote to Abigail, "The election will be decided this day in favour of Mr. Jefferson as it is given out by good authority."[12]

John Adams has been criticized because he took no part in this conflict, made no public expression of opinion or choice. Some have seen this as an indication of his bitterness at defeat, have suggested that he really hoped Burr would win, and have branded him as

petty. Others have condemned his nonparticipation as a renunciation of his leadership responsibilities. Few seem to have looked at
the situation from John Adams's viewpoint. We know from their
correspondence that both John and Abigail thought Jefferson deserved to win and that they hoped he would. Jefferson himself was
aware of Adams's attitude, for as early as January 23 the former
indicated to his son-in-law that the president felt Jefferson deserved
the victory. How Jefferson learned this we are not sure. We do
know that while walking one evening, the two men met and briefly
discussed the current attempt to resolve the tie vote. Did John
Adams tell Jefferson of his preference? The only report of their
meeting was written by Jefferson and he did not mention such a
statement by Adams. Did Adams write to him, and has that letter
been lost? Or did some mutual friend like Rush or Gerry convey
the message? At any rate, Jefferson knew of Adams's good wishes.

While the president was concerned about the tie vote between
Jefferson and Burr, he never became a part of the Federalist attempt
to dictate the outcome. He knew it was the constitutional responsibility of the House of Representatives to resolve the situation.
Believing passionately, as he did, in the separation of the branches
of the government, he could not with intellectual honesty become
involved in the matter. A dozen years later Adams in a letter to
Jefferson wrote, "What pretensions had Aaron Burr to be President . . . ?"[13]

A close parallel would seem to exist between the role Adams
played in this dispute and his position during the debates on the
Jay Treaty in 1795 and 1796. He had been the presiding officer of
the Senate during those bitter debates, and he felt very strongly that
the treaty should be ratified and properly financed. He wrote to
Abigail, declaring that he wished he were a member of Congress
so he could speak out in favor of the treaty, but then, just as in the
winter of 1801, he would make no public pronouncement on a matter that he believed the House should decide. That Adams made
no public declaration in favor of Jefferson in January 1801 was evidence of the strength of his convictions and his self-control.

The closing weeks of John Adams's presidency were filled with
work and, especially after Abigail's return to Quincy in mid-Febru-
ary, loneliness. Two weeks before his term would be concluded,
John wrote his wife, "the Burden upon me in nominating judges and
Consuls and other officers, in delivering over the furniture, in the
ordinary Business at the Close of a Session, and in preparing for

my journey of 500 miles through the mire, is and will be very heavy. My time will be all taken up. I pray you to continue to write me."[14]

Was John Adams's defeat a crushing blow from which he would never recover? For more than a decade Adams had little communication with Jefferson. Was this evidence that he was bitter at his defeat and angry at the man who had bested him? Was Adams's hurried departure from the capital city, before daylight on March 4, 1801, a petty slap at Jefferson? How would John and Abigail spend the rest of their lives? Their correspondence sheds light on these questions.

Page Smith has portrayed John Adams as being absolutely crushed by his defeat in the election of 1800: "Deep down there was no assuaging the pain. He had been pierced and hurt terribly in his innermost self and he wished, like a stricken animal, to crawl away out of sight and die. . . . His rejection inflicted a raw wound that would never entirely heal, that he would carry to his deathbed, that would torment him in the dark hours of innumerable nights to come."[15] This is very effective writing, but it does not accurately describe John Adams. It is true that Adams "lived life . . . passionately, cared . . . intensely," had an unusually high level of aspiration, always challenged himself, repeatedly sought the hard answers, never found it easy to accept defeat. Self-critical he might be; hurt by rejection or defeat he certainly was. But John Adams was a fighter, a man who faced life too realistically and too selflessly ever to want "to crawl away out of sight and die." The death of Charles, the manner even more than the fact, seems to have caused both John and Abigail more torment than the political defeat in the election of 1800.

Adams seems to have been aware, through all his political life, of the vicissitudes, the disloyalties, and the hurts of public office. He had learned to steel himself to accept disappointments and reverses and to persevere in the face of criticism and bitter attack. Half-way through his presidency he had noted to Abigail that he thought he should soon be through with politics. In the fall of 1799 he commented in a letter to his wife, "An Election is approaching which will sett us at Liberty from these uncomfortable Journeys."[16]

Chinard believed that John Adams's third annual message to Congress, in December 1799, was meant to be his farewell message. The next May, in a letter to an old family friend, Abigail indicated her willingness to retire to Quincy. "If the people judge that a change in the chief magistracy of the nation is for its peace safety and happiness," Abigail adjured, "they will no doubt make it. The station is an arduous and painful one, and may he who shall be called to fill it have the confidence of the people and serve only their best interests . . . ."[17]

The correspondence of John Adams himself, whether letters written to political associates, old and intimate friends, or his wife and children, reveals little disappointment and no gnawing bitterness or deep anger at his defeat in the election of 1800. John Adams seldom tried to conceal his true feelings from his family. On December 17, 1800, he declared to his youngest son, "My little bark has been oversett in a squall of thunder & lightning & hail attended with a strong smell of sulphur. . . . Be not concerned for me. I feel my shoulders relieved from a burthen. The short remainder of my days will be the happiest of my life."[18]

Three weeks later he expressed to Colonel Tudor only one regret—a shortage of money to entertain friends as he would like, to offer hospitality, and to conduct agricultural experiments. He will be "John of Stonyfield & nothing more (I hope nothing less) for the rest of" life—"the happiest life it will be to me (at least I think so) that I ever led." Then John Adams continued, "I am not about to write lamentations or jeremiades over my fate nor panegyricks upon my life and conduct. You may think me disappointed. I am not. All my life have I expected it & you might be surprised perhaps to see how little it affects me."[19]

Abigail's correspondence also sheds light on the manner in which John Adams and his wife accepted this political rejection. In mid-November, when reasonably sure that Jefferson had won, Abigail wrote Thomas Boyleston that she felt "not any resentment against those who are coming into power." In the next January she indicated to the same son that she did not "mean to grow peevish, sour or discontented. I have not a regret at quiting my station personally. I believe it best both for your father and for me."[20] In that same month she indicated her belief that while the market was "down," it would not be wise to sell out, because she was confident times would improve.

Many historians have felt that John Adams left Washington in a very angry and bitter mood—especially angry at the man who had defeated him. It has been suggested repeatedly that Adams did not want to meet Jefferson, did not want to speak to him, did not want to congratulate him or wish him well. One wonders how closely those who drew the above picture of John Adams have read his correspondence, or that of Abigail, during the weeks between the election of 1800 and Adams's departure from Washington.

On January 3, 1801, Abigail wrote to her younger son. It was a long, personal letter, but buried in the middle was the following sentence that seems to have been unnoticed by those who evaluated the relationship between Adams and Jefferson: "Mr. Jefferson dines with us and in a card replie to the president's invitation, he begs him to be assured of his *Homage* and *high consideration.*" A month later, shortly before she left the new capital for home, she again wrote to Thomas. She explained that bad roads and weather had prevented her from leaving that day as she had originally planned. The previous day, she recounted, Thomas Jefferson "made me a visit . . . in order to take leave and wish me a good journey. It was more than I expected." Abigail went on to describe a rather long and obviously pleasant conversation. Jefferson had offered to retain all of the servants she recommended; he had indicated a hope that he might be of service to her or to her husband or to any of their family. He had "inquired particularly" for John Quincy and had seemed to suggest that he would be glad to have him remain in the embassy in Berlin, but Abigail had said she thought John Quincy planned to return to America.[21]

On February 20, 1801, the busy president took time to pen a short note to the president-elect. Adams informed Jefferson that he would have no need to purchase either horses or carriages; two carriages and seven horses, then in the White House stables, were the property of the United States. Perhaps this note was dictated by John Adams's staunch honesty; but it was also a personal note, warm and friendly. Less than a week after John Adams arrived back in Quincy he wrote to one of his cabinet members who had remained in Washington. One sentence of that letter read: "My respects to the President, and compliments to Messrs. Madison, Lincoln, Dearborn, and love to Mr. Stoddert."[22] It seems incorrect and unfair to write that Adams's "last months of office were months of gloom and petulance; the midnight judges were appointed, and in the cold dawn of March 4, 1801, a few hours before Jefferson's inaugural, Adams made an angry, unforgiving and ungracious exit from the still uncompleted presidential mansion in the far from completed Federal City."[23]

Dr. Cotton Tufts of Quincy, husband of Abigail's aunt, and their caretaker whenever John and Abigail were both absent, was a warm, personal friend of the Adams family, a frequent confidant of both husband and wife. A long letter to Dr. Tufts, written soon after John Adams had learned positively that he had been defeated for reelection, contains no bitterness, no recrimination, no attempt to question or justify or explain. "I shall be in Quincy," the president wrote, "as early in the spring, as the roads and weather will permit. The only question remaining with me is, what shall I do with myself." John's chief lament was that he had "forgotten all my law & lost my organs of speech." How could he use his time? For a starter, John suggests that he will "take a walk every noon to Pennshill" and "plant a potatoe yard with my own hand."[24]

About a month later, at the close of a letter dealing with public matters, John wrote, "The remainder of my days will probably be spent in the labors of agriculture and the amusements of literature in both of which I have always taken more delight, than in any public office of whatever rank. Far removed from all intrigues and out of the reach of all the great and little passions, that agitate the world, although I take no resolutions nor make any promises, I hope to enjoy more tranquility, than has ever before been my lot."[25]

A month after his return to Quincy, the ex-president replied to a letter from Christopher Gadsden, South Carolina Federalist, saying in part, "The only consolation I shall want will be that of employment. Ennui, when it rains on a man in large drops, is worse than one of our north-east storms; but the labors of agriculture and amusement of letters will shelter me. My greatest grief is that I cannot return to the bar. There I should forget in a moment that I was ever a member of Congress, a foreign minister, or President of the United States. But I cannot speak. . . . To Mr. Jefferson's administration I wish prosperity and felicity. . . ."[26]

John Adams's hasty departure from Washington, before daylight on Wednesday, March 4, 1801, has often been branded as the most petty action of his entire life. His apologists and supporters have often ascribed it to the bitterness and disappointment of defeat and the vindictiveness of his attitude toward Jefferson. His severest critics have seen it as further evidence of the man's jealousy, vanity, and hotheaded action. The late Clinton Rossiter, often understanding in his treatment of John Adams, wrote, "The most disquieting event [of his entire career] was a case of plain bad manners: the departure from Washington in the early hours of March 4, 1801."[27] Koch and Peden noted, "Adams was crushed by his grief at having been rejected by those he had served for over a quarter of a century, and he was not graceful in concealing his hurt."[28]

The relations between John Adams and Thomas Jefferson in the winter of 1801 were not as strained and bitter as has been suggested by many historians. It is true that there had been serious disagreements and misunderstanding between them ever since the

summer of 1797. It is also true that it would be more than a decade
before the two men resumed the friendly correspondence of earlier
years. Yet Jefferson could pay a friendly call on Abigail before she
left the federal city, and Adams could take time to remind Jefferson
that the horses and carriages in the White House stables were public
property. Just prior to March 4, he sent his faithful employee
Briesler to call on Thomas Jefferson, probably to acquaint him with
the operation of the White House. During the first three weeks of
Jefferson's administration the two men exchanged letters dealing
primarily with business yet revealing an attempt on the part of each
to be friendly. John Adams concluded one reply to Jefferson with
these words, "This part of the Union is in a state of perfect tranquility, and I see nothing to obscure your prospect of a quiet and
prosperous administration, which I heartily wish you."[29]

It seems to the present writer that the key to a proper evaluation of John Adams's hurried departure from Washington, on March
4, 1801, lies in the following facts. The new nation was to experience its first political change of command, and there was no established protocol to be followed. Today the president-elect drives to
the White House, is greeted by the retiring president, and they ride
together to the place of inaugural. No such procedure had been
established by 1801. (Four years earlier Chief Justice Ellsworth's
secretary had written John Adams to inquire what oath should be
used!) Secondly, not only was Jefferson's inaugural to be marked
by simplicity, but there is no indication that John Adams had been
invited to attend or participate in any way. The Jeffersonians had
taken over; the Federalists were out of power. What would John
Adams have done if he had remained in Washington until noon?

In the third place, while it is true that John Adams was a
sensitive as well as a proud man, and would have found it embarrassing to "stand around" while the man who had defeated him was
sworn in as his successor, it is equally true that throughout a long
life Adams always accepted the difficult when he saw it as his duty
or his obligation. There would seem to have been no thought on
Adams's part that it was his duty or his obligation to remain for the
inauguration. He had said and written repeatedly that his official
duties ended at midnight, March 3. He labored diligently to have
everything in order; then he left.

Finally, to have remained in Washington longer would have
been physically difficult as well as emotionally frustrating. Adams
no longer belonged in the White House or on the political scene.
Briesler had arranged passage for John Adams and his secretary,

Billy Shaw, on Maglanklin's Stage. In order to make the fourteen-hour trip to Baltimore in one day, the stage left at four in the morning. Evidently there were no adequate inns between Washington and Baltimore.

Well before daylight on March 4, the ex-president and his secretary were bumping along toward Baltimore. It must not have added to Adams's pleasure that a fellow passenger turned out to be the retiring Speaker of the House, Theodore Sedgwick. Although Adams's former friend and onetime social intimate, Sedgwick had followed Hamilton all the way. Welch has observed, "One wonders if Sedgwick and Adams passed a single word during the long cold journey north. Probably not, but each must have thought often of the other and blamed him for the fall of the Federalist regime."[30]

John Adams returned to Quincy with anticipation as well as with regret. Helping Billings, the hired man, rebuild a stone wall, or walking through his fields in the evening, the ground heavy with dew, the crops ripe for the harvest, Adams may have thought of politics and wondered about his defeat. But he never allowed himself the luxury of unmitigated self-pity. Years later he brought back into the circle of his close friendships the man who had defeated him in 1800. This, above all, would seem to disprove the picture of defeat and humiliation and unrelieved dismay that has often been painted.

After nearly three decades of public service, John Adams was back on his Quincy acres. Abigail was glad to be home; it is almost certain that John felt the same way. Although they grieved over the tragic death of their second son, Charles's children were with them and for the rest of his long life John Adams would be surrounded by grandchildren and great-grandchildren.

On May 3, 1801, Abigail wrote to her son-in-law, Colonel Smith: "My love to Mrs. Smith and the children. Tell her I have commenced my operations of dairy-woman; and she might see me, at five o'clock in the morning, skimming my milk."[31]

In mid-July, writing to Thomas, Abigail noted: "You will find your father in his fields, attending to his hay-makers, and your mother busily occupied in the domestic concerns of her family. I regret that a fortnight of sharp drought has shorn many of the beauties we had in rich luxuriance. The verdure of the grass has become a brown, the flowers hang their heads, droop, and fade, whilst the vegetable world languishes; yet still we have a pure air.

The crops of hay have been abundant; upon this spot, where eight years ago we cut scarcely six tons, we now have thirty."[32]

So the drought might come, but the air would be clear. And where once there had been but six tons of hay, there now were thirty.

16

★★★★★

A SUMMING UP: JOHN ADAMS
AND THE PRESIDENCY

The years from 1797 to 1801 were fraught with danger. The young nation's independence was threatened by France, by Great Britain, and by the possibility of civil war at home. John Adams clung tightly to his program to build a navy for protection, to negotiate for peace with France, to maintain neutrality, and to alleviate internal frictions and disputes. The country prospered, despite the increase in taxes and in government debt.

Adams, who had been instrumental in the birth of the country, as president strove to give his people breathing-space to determine the manner in which they would develop; to understand and improve the new government they had created. He did not look for personal glory nor did he desire the expansion of his country. He had no colonial concept. He forsook war and rebuffed alliance, and in so doing provided time for the country to grow strong. He believed in a government of law and order, in the separation of powers within the structure of government, in the authority of the courts and the protection of the individual—and these were the things he strove to promote.

Adams held definite convictions concerning the role of the executive and legislative branches in a democracy, and he refused to minimize the executive's responsibility. In his three-volume *A Defense of the Constitutions of Government of the United States of America,* written in 1786 and 1787, he had declared:

. . . you will be convinced that three branches of power
have an unalterable foundation in nature; that they exist
in every society natural and artificial; and that if all of
them are not acknowledged in any constitution of government, it will be found to be imperfect, unstable, and soon
enslaved; that the legislative and executive authorities are
naturally distinct; and that liberty and the laws depend
entirely on a separation of them in the frame of government; that the legislative power is naturally and necessarily sovereign and supreme over the executive; and,
therefore, that the latter must be made an essential branch
of the former, even with a negative, or it will not be able
to defend itself, but will be soon invaded, undermined, attacked, or in some way or other totally ruined and annihi-
lated by the former.

Furthermore, Adams argued in the same work:

If there is one certain truth to be collected from the history
of all ages, it is this: that the people's rights and liberties,
and the democratical mixture in a constitution, can never
be preserved without a strong executive, or, in other words,
without separating the executive from the legislative
power. If the executive power, or any considerable part of
it, is left in the hands either of an aristocratical or a democratical assembly, it will corrupt the legislature as necessarily as rust corrupts iron, or as arsenic poisons the human
body; and when the legislature is corrupted, the people
are undone.[1]

Adams believed that the two houses of Congress might be in
conflict and that it would require a strong executive to be a successful mediator between the aristocratical Senate and the more
democratic House. He felt that neither of these legislative bodies
should be allowed to become so strong that it could dominate the
other. If such a situation developed, the president should use his
leadership, his influence, and his prestige to effect a balance. Balance, or equilibrium, is one key to an understanding of John Adams's
philosophy of government.

Adams distrusted power because he felt all people strove to
secure influence. The only protection against such individual or
group drives, he believed, was a government that tried to balance
divergent forces and thus check excess build-up of power. A single
executive—for Adams believed executive power must never be
fragmented—must have authority enough to hold the legislature in

check, but not enough to totally dominate it. John Adams's fear was of *absolute* power.

Adams, however, argued that the executive's power to both appoint and remove was inviolable, that appointed officials were part of the executive branch of the government, "a sacred part of the constitution without which the government could not exist. If executive officers hold their offices independent of the head and can intrigue with members of the Senate and House to assist them in opposing the execution of the Laws, the executive authority must be a nose of wax."[2]

Yet Adams was concerned about the degree of power that accompanied presidential responsibility. An exchange of letters with Roger Sherman of Connecticut is especially enlightening. On July 18, 1789, Adams wrote, "Power naturally grows. Why? Because human passions are insatiable. But that power alone can grow which already is too great; that which is unchecked; that which has no equal power to control it."[3] He saw the presidency much as did Andrew Jackson thirty years later, as the one agent of government chosen by *all* the people and thus able to act in the best interests of the entire nation rather than of a faction, section, or special interest.

Besides believing in a strong, independent executive, Adams maintained that the executive power and responsibility must lie in the hands of one person; executive authority must not be divided. Writing from his daughter's home in East Chester, New York, the president stressed the need for a single executive by quoting the situation in France to Secretary of State Pickering: "By all the public Papers I received from abroad it appears, that the state of Things at present in France is exactly as I have many times written to particular Friends in Europe. The Executive Directory is divided into a Party of three and a Party of two. The two are the most popular, coincide best with the public Opinion and agree with a Majority in both Houses of the Legislature. This drives the three to the necessity of courting the Army and the Populace. And the question between three and the two can be decided only by a civil War."[4]

The laborious thoroughness with which John Adams sought correct answers in controversial matters is most impressive. This desire to find and recognize the truth was reflected in his letters to his secretaries after Fries was first sentenced to death. He demanded to know everything possible about the man, his background, and the climate in which he had operated. In the summer of 1799, anticipating the need to make a decision regarding Fries's punishment, he read feverishly in the literature of both the law and constitutionalism in order to be sure of the position he should take.

Adams believed that the president should seek the advice of his cabinet on matters of action but that the final decision was always the responsibility of the chief executive alone. Despite his differences with three of his secretaries, he continually pressed them for opinions, reactions, advice. His papers contain innumerable letters of inquiry written during his absences from the capital. Yet the final decisions made and the basic nature of the policy he pursued were, Adams believed, matters for the president alone to determine. Nor did he deem it necessary to keep his secretaries fully informed regarding all executive decisions.

A decade after his retirement from office, John Adams was to note that while in the British system the ministers had great power and responsibility, they did not in the United States: "Here, according to the practice, if not the Constitution, the ministers are responsible for nothing, the President for everything. . . . In all great and essential measures he is bound by his honor and his conscience, by his oath to the Constitution, as well as his responsibility to the public opinion of the nation, to act his own mature and unbiased judgment, though unfortunately, it may be in direct contradiction to the advice of all his ministers. . . ."[5]

While there is no doubt that Adams believed in a strong chief executive, he recognized the limitations of presidential power and was careful not to exceed them. For example, in late January 1799 Secretary Stoddert sent the following memorandum to the other cabinet officers: "Sir, the President requested me to consult the Heads of Departments, whether the President, in whom is vested the Executive Power of the Nation, possesses the Constitutional power of regulating the Exchange of Prisoners & all matters belonging to that subject."[6] He also accepted the necessity for obtaining legislative approval for appointments. To a distant relative, in 1799, the president wrote: "Our kinsman must apply to the senators and representatives of his own State for recommendations . . . . If I were to nominate him without previous recommendations from . . . [them], the Senate would probably negative him. . . ."[7]

A political scientist has pointed out that President Adams was "a believer in prudent, orderly, and stable government and in an ordered set of individual liberties and responsibilities, [and that as president he] dissolved many of the Hamiltonian arrangements and tried to carry out a model of government quite close to the hopes and expectations of most of the Framers."[8]

Strongly opposed to violence, fearful of any extreme or solely emotional reaction, John Adams believed that laws were passed to be obeyed, public officials should be respected, courts and law-enforcement agencies should be supported.

To the ideal of diligent thoroughness Adams added that of disinterested public service. He knew the president could function only from a position of strength and independence; that he must mediate and compromise between factions within the country and between the branches of Congress. He felt that the president must be able to retain or dismiss his appointees; that law and order were essential and must be maintained. Avidly seeking for better understanding and knowledge, he recognized the need for all the advice and information he could obtain and used this in arriving at his own decisions. The preservation of the new nation through the maintenance of peace and neutrality and unrestricted trade was high on Adams's list of presidential responsibilities. He devoted, as a matter of course, endless time and effort to the service of his country and accepted responsibility for his decisions and actions.

Adams's good friend Dr. Benjamin Rush wrote in his autobiography that John Adams "saw the whole of a subject at a single glance, and by a happy union of the powers of reasoning and persuasion often succeeded in carrying measures which were at first sight of an unpopular nature."[9]

Adams's philosophy of public service as above all personal interests was stated at the beginning of his eight years in the vice-presidency. He wrote to Mercy Otis Warren: "I should belie the whole course of my public and private conduct, and all the maxims of my life, if I should ever consider public authority entrusted to mc to be subservient to my private views, or those of my Family or Friends."[10] He never departed from that position.

In the last decade some historians of the American past have revealed a new willingness to ascribe strong and successful leadership to John Adams. Esmond Wright wrote that Adams "had a marked capacity for forming an independent and dispassionate judgment on events."[11] Smelser awarded high praise to Adams's leadership. "The big lesson for the rest of us," he wrote, "seems to be this: liberty was not preserved by argument, committee meetings, letters to the editor, nor generalized moral indignation. It was preserved by the action of a responsible statesman doing his duty to restore the tranquility of order in our foreign relations. Only when peace was assured was the infectious fever of the nation abated."[12]

To that responsible New Englander, being president meant doing a job with personal integrity and the greatest possible skill, not winning a popularity contest. The final assessment of Adams's presidency, therefore, should be not in terms of his defeat for reelection but in terms of his actual accomplishments, which were great.

John Adams believed that strong leadership was essential to the success of popular government. He believed that the people chose a leader because they trusted him, recognized his education, ideals, experience, knowledge, and self-control. It then became the responsibility of that leader to study and evaluate issues and situations, to fully inform the people and try to convince them of the best way to resolve such issues and situations. This he tried to do.

Adams interpreted the presidency not in terms of responding to or being manipulated by public pressure but as a lonely and difficult search for the correct answers, the best decisions and actions. Once convinced of the rightness of a course, he clung to it with great courage, using all his influence and power to inform the people of the facts and sway them to his point of view. If the public could not be persuaded, he believed the president must follow his own judgment regardless of popular reaction.

Adams managed to avoid internal conflict, to side-step involvement in the intrigues and disputes of Europe, to make peace rather than war, to prepare the way for important territorial expansion in the next administration. He worked diligently to support the Constitution, to avoid interference with the established division of powers, to uphold the laws, to expand the judiciary, to maintain the independence and integrity of the executive. In spite of serious divisions within his own party, disloyalty and intrigue within his cabinet, the misunderstanding and obstructionism of the political opposition, and the daring and forceful attacks of the most ambitious and charismatic individual among the Federalists, John Adams achieved his major goals.

The nation John Adams had helped to found, that he loved deeply, would grow and prosper and expand a continent in breadth. The short, balding, rotund president, retiring to his beloved acres on the Massachusetts coast, had served his country well.

Notes

CHAPTER 1

1. George W. Corner, ed., *The Autobiography of Benjamin Rush; His Travels Through Life; Together with His Commonplace Book for 1789–1813* (Princeton, N.J.: Princeton Univ. Pr., 1948), p. 140.
2. Quoted in Charles Francis Adams, ed., *The Works of John Adams, Second President of the United States; With a Life of the Author, Notes and Illustrations,* 10 vols. (Boston: Little, Brown and Co., 1856), 1: 496.
3. 3/12/1797, in Charles R. King, ed., *The Life and Correspondence of Rufus King, Comprising His Letters, Private and Official; His Public Documents and His Speeches,* 6 vols. (New York: G. P. Putnam's Sons, 1894–1900), 2: 158–159.
4. Charles Francis Adams, ed., *Letters of John Adams, Addressed to His Wife,* 2 vols. (Boston: Charles C. Little and James Brown, 1841), 2: 244–245.

CHAPTER 2

1. Adrienne Koch and William Peden, eds., *The Selected Writings of John and John Quincy Adams* (New York: Alfred A. Knopf, 1946), p. 153.
2. George W. Corner, ed., *The Autobiography of Benjamin Rush; His Travels Through Life; Together with His Commonplace Book for 1789–1813* (Princeton, N.J.: Princeton Univ. Pr., 1948), pp. 142–143.
3. Quoted in Zoltán Haraszti, *John Adams and the Prophets of Progress* (New York: Grosset and Dunlap, 1964), p. 1.
4. Esmond Wright, *Fabric of Freedom* (New York: Hill & Wang, 1961), p. 219.
5. Jefferson to William F. Gardner, 2/19/1813, in Paul Leicester Ford, ed., *The Works of Thomas Jefferson,* 10 vols. (New York: G. P. Putnam's Sons, 1892–1899), 9: 377–378.
6. Charles Francis Adams, ed., *Letters of John Adams Addressed to His Wife,* 2 vols. (Boston: Charles C. Little and James Brown, 1841), 2: 189–190.
7. Ibid., pp. 190–191; see also *The Microfilm Edition of The Adams Papers,* 608 reels (Boston: Massachusetts Historical Society, 1954–1959), reel 381.
8. Adams, *Letters to His Wife,* 2: 197–198.
9. Quoted in Page Smith, *John Adams* (New York: Doubleday and Co., 1962), p. 897.
10. Noble E. Cunningham, Jr., *The Jeffersonian Republicans; The Formation of Party Organization, 1789–1801* (Chapel Hill: Univ. of North Carolina Pr., 1957), p. 98.
11. Philadelphia, 11/2/1796, in John C. Fitzpatrick, ed., *The Writings of George Washington from the Original Manuscript Sources, 1745–1799,* 38 vols. (Washington, D.C.: Government Printing Office, 1931–1944), 35: 251–255.
12. Henry Cabot Lodge, ed., *The Works of Alexander Hamilton,* 10 vols. (New York: G. P. Putnam's

Sons, 1885–1886), 10: 195–196.

13. Ulrich B. Phillips, "South Carolina Federalist Correspondence, 1789–1797," *American Historical Review* 14 (1908): 782–783.

14. Quoted by John Alexander Carroll and Mary Wells Ashworth, *George Washington: Volume Seven: First in Peace* (New York: Charles Scribner's Sons, 1957), p. 411n.

15. Ibid., p. 425n.

16. *Adams Papers,* reel 382.

17. Philadelphia, 12/16/1796, ibid.

18. Ibid.

19. See Carroll and Ashworth, *George Washington*, p. 425n.

20. Charles Francis Adams, ed., *The Works of John Adams, Second President of the United States; With a Life of the Author, Notes and Illustrations*, 10 vols. (Boston: Little, Brown and Co., 1856), 8: 520–522; John Adams's response to Gerry's letter would indicate that Gerry may have implied a possible Jeffersonian involvement.

21. *Adams Papers,* reel 117; see also Paul A. Varg, *Foreign Policies of the Founding Fathers* (East Lansing: Michigan State Univ. Pr., 1963), p. 127.

22. Adams, *Letters to His Wife,* 2: 233–235.

23. Ibid., 235–237.

CHAPTER 3

1. Quoted in Morton Borden, *Parties and Politics in the Early Republic* (New York: Thomas Y. Crowell Co., 1967), p. 9.

2. L. H. Butterfield, ed., *The Diary and Autobiography of John Adams*, 4 vols. (Cambridge, Mass.: The Belknap Press of the Harvard Univ. Pr., 1961), 1: 7–8.

3. Quoted in John A. Schutz and Douglas Adair, *The Spur of Fame! Dialogues of John Adams and Benjamin Rush, 1805–1813* (San Marino, Cal.: The Huntington Library, 1966), p. 88.

4. Charles Francis Adams, ed., *The Works of John Adams, Second President of the United States; With a Life of the Author, Notes and Illustrations*, 10 vols. (Boston: Little, Brown and Co., 1856), 9: 47.

5. John Adams to John Quincy Adams, Philadelphia, 6/2/1797, in ibid., 8: 545; see also Samuel Flagg Bemis, *John Quincy Adams and the Foundations of American Foreign Policy* (New York: Alfred A. Knopf, 1949), p. 91. Also see *The Microfilm Edition of The Adams Papers*, 608 reels (Boston: Massachusetts Historical Society, 1954–1959), reel 117.

6. John C. Hamilton, ed., *The Works of Alexander Hamilton; Comprising His Correspondence, His Political and Official Writings, Exclusive of the Federalist, Civil and Military*, 7 vols. (New York: Charles S. Francis & Co., 1850), 6: 307.

7. Hamilton Papers in the Library of Congress, as cited in Broadus Mitchell, *Alexander Hamilton; The National Adventure, 1788–1804* (New York: Macmillan Co., 1962), p. 736, n63.

8. George Gibbs, *Memoirs of the Administrations of Washington and John Adams, Edited from the Papers of Oliver Wolcott, Secretary of the Treasury*, 2 vols. (New York: Privately Printed for the Subscribers, 1846), 2: 246.

9. Quoted in Gerard H. Clarfield, *Timothy Pickering and American Diplomacy, 1795–1800* (Columbia: Univ. of Missouri Pr., 1969), p. 97.

10. Stewart Mitchell, ed., *New Letters of Abigail Adams, 1788–1801* (Boston: Houghton, Mifflin Co., 1947), pp. 145–146.

11. Anne Hollingsworth Wharton, *Social Life in the Early Republic* (Williamstown, Mass.: Corner House Publishers, 1970), pp. 40–41.

CHAPTER 4

1. *The Microfilm Edition of The Adams Papers,* 608 reels (Boston: Massachusetts Historical Society, 1954–1959), reel 383.
2. Ibid.
3. Ibid., reel 382.
4. Ibid., reel 118.
5. Charles Francis Adams, ed., *The Works of John Adams, Second President of the United States: With a Life of the Author, Notes and Illustrations,* 10 vols. (Boston: Little, Brown and Co., 1856), 8: 537.
6. Ibid., p. 533.
7. [James D. Richardson, ed.], *A Compilation of the Messages and Papers of the Presidents,* 10 vols. (n. p.: Bureau of National Literature, 1913), 1: 225.
8. Henry Cabot Lodge, *The Life and Letters of George Cabot* (Boston: Little, Brown and Co., 1877), pp. 138–139.
9. Richardson, *Messages and Papers of the Presidents,* 1: 235.
10. Adams, *Works of John Adams,* 8: 547–548.
11. Quoted in Dumas Malone, *Jefferson and the Ordeal of Liberty* (vol. 3 of *Jefferson and His Time*) (Boston: Little, Brown and Co., 1962), p. 322.
12. Adams, *Works of John Adams,* 8: 549.
13. Quoted by Paul A. Varg, *Foreign Policies of the Founding Fathers* (East Lansing: Michigan State Univ. Pr., 1963), pp. 129–130.
14. Worthington Chauncey Ford, ed., *The Writings of John Quincy Adams,* 7 vols. (New York: Macmillan Co., 1913–1917), 2: 210–216.

CHAPTER 5

1. Stewart Mitchell, ed., *New Letters of Abigail Adams, 1788–1801* (Boston: Houghton, Mifflin Co., 1947), p. 125.
2. [James D. Richardson, ed.], *A Compilation of the Messages and Papers of the Presidents,* 10 vols. (n. p.: Bureau of National Literature, 1913), 1: 253–254.
3. Quoted by Bradford Perkins, *The First Rapprochement; England and the United States, 1795–1805* (Philadelphia: Univ. of Pennsylvania Pr., 1955), p. 93.
4. Charles Francis Adams, ed., *The Works of John Adams, Second President of the United States; With a Life of the Author, Notes and Illustrations,* 10 vols. (Boston: Little, Brown and Co., 1865), 8: 568; see also Alexander DeConde, *The Quasi-War; The Politics and Diplomacy of the Undeclared War with France, 1797–1801* (New York: Charles Scribner's Sons, 1966), p. 67.
5. The entire message is in Richardson, *Messages and Papers of the Presidents,* 1: 254–255; see also *The Microfilm Edition of The Adams Papers,* 608 reels (Boston: Massachusetts Historical Society, 1954–1959), reel 387.
6. Mitchell, *New Letters of Abigail Adams,* pp. 146–147.
7. Richardson, *Messages and Papers of the Presidents,* 1: 255, see also Clarence A. Berdahl, *War Powers of the Executive in the United States* (New York: Johnson Reprint Corp., 1970), p. 67.
8. Mitchell, *New Letters of Abigail Adams,* p. 152.
9. 4/9/1798, in Charles R. King, ed., *The Life and Correspondence of Rufus King, Comprising His Letters, Private and Official; His Public Documents and His Speeches,* 6 vols. (New York: G. P. Putnam's Sons, 1894–1900), 2: 311.
10. Quoted by James Morton Smith, *Freedom's Fetters; The Alien and Sedition Laws and American Civil Liberties* (Ithaca, N.Y.: Cornell Univ. Pr., 1956), p. 15.

11. Philadelphia, 5/3/1798, in *Liston Papers,* Library of Congress Box XII, reel 2.
12. Quoted by Winfred E. A. Bernhard, *Fisher Ames; Federalist and Statesman, 1758–1808* (Chapel Hill: Univ. of North Carolina Pr., 1965), p. 296.
13. 5/10/1798, in Mitchell, *New Letters of Abigail Adams,* pp. 171–172.
14. Philadelphia, 5/29/1798 and 6/11/1798, *Liston Papers,* Box XII, reel 2.
15. Quoted by Stephen G. Kurtz, "The Split in the Federalist Party," in Paul Goodman, ed., *The Federalists vs. The Jeffersonian Republicans* (New York: Holt, Rinehart and Winston, 1967), p. 99.
16. Quoted by Charles W. Upham and Octavius Pickering, *The Life of Timothy Pickering,* 4 vols. (Boston: Little, Brown and Co., 1873), 3: 423–424.
17. Henry Cabot Lodge, ed., *The Works of Alexander Hamilton,* 12 vols. (New York: G. P. Putnam's Sons, 1885–1886), 10: 277.
18. Ibid., 7: 97–98.
19. Richardson, *Messages and Papers of the Presidents,* 1: 256.
20. *Liston Papers,* Box XII, reel 2.
21. Quoted by Arthur Preston Whitaker, *The Mississippi Question, 1795–1803; A Study in Trade, Politics, and Diplomacy* (New York: D. Appleton-Century Co., 1934), p. 39.
22. E. Wilson Lyon, "The Directory and the United States," *The American Historical Review,* 43 (1938): 530.

CHAPTER 6

1. Henry Cabot Lodge, ed., *The Works of Alexander Hamilton,* 12 vols. (New York: G. P. Putnam's Sons, 1885–1886), 10: 286–287.
2. John C. Fitzpatrick, ed., *The Writings of George Washington from the Original Manuscript Sources, 1745–1799,* 38 vols. (Washington, D.C.: Government Printing Office, 1931–1944), 36: 324n; see also Broadus Mitchell, *Alexander Hamilton; The National Adventure, 1788–1804* (New York: Macmillan Co., 1962), p. 427.
3. Fitzpatrick, *Writings of Washington,* 36: 312n; and Charles Francis Adams, ed., *The Works of John Adams, Second President of the United States, With a Life of the Author, Notes and Illustrations,* 10 vols. (Boston: Little, Brown and Co., 1856), 1: 527–532.
4. 7/5/1798, in Fitzpatrick, *Writings of Washington,* 36: 318–320.
5. Quoted in John Alexander Carroll and Mary Wells Ashworth, *George Washington: Volume Seven: First in Peace* (New York: Charles Scribner's Sons, 1957), p. 520.
6. Washington to Pickering, 7/11/1798, in Fitzpatrick, *Writings of Washington,* 36: 323–327.
7. Ibid., pp. 327–329.
8. It will be noticed that the letter of acceptance addressed to John Adams the previous day contained no such stipulation. At the time of the final showdown with the president, Washington commented that he had left this stipulation out of his letter to the president in the expectation, later proved correct, that the president would release his letter to the press, and he did not think such a stipulation should be a matter of public record. But, said Washington at that time, he had instructed McHenry to inform the president of his stipulation. There is no evidence to show that McHenry did or did not comply with such an instruction.
9. Fitzpatrick, *Writings of Washington,* 36: 329–334. Mitchell suggests that in this letter Washington is indicating an intention to

place Hamilton second, and expressing the hope that Pinckney will "yield to measures which have a tendency to promote" the national welfare—and thus that McHenry *has* changed Washington's mind. Mitchell also says that McHenry *did* carry the letter to Hamilton. See *Alexander Hamilton, The National Adventure*, p. 428. Zahniser, on the other hand, believes that in this letter Washington is trying to get Hamilton to offer to take the third place, subordinate to Pinckney. (After much thought I am inclined to agree with Mitchell.) Zahniser writes, "Hamilton did not take the hint. Instead he returned a vigorous defense of his qualifications." Pinckney, Hamilton thought, "ought to be well satisfied" to serve under Hamilton. See Marvin R. Zahniser, *Charles Cotesworth Pinckney; Founding Father* (Chapel Hill: Univ. of North Carolina Pr., 1967), pp. 192–193. On July 17 Hamilton wrote to Pickering, indicating he would be willing to rank below Knox. Is it possible he had received Washington's letter of the fourteenth? It would seem doubtful, especially since McHenry seems not to have left Mount Vernon very early that day. At any rate, Pickering never relayed this information to either Washington or Adams, and later gave himself credit for concealing Hamilton's willingness to rank below the others, thus preserving Hamilton's claim to the second spot. See Richard Knollenberg, "John Adams, Knox, and Washington," *Proceedings of the American Antiquarian Society*, April 17, 1946–October 16, 1946, vol. 56,

pp. 235–237, and also Mitchell, *Alexander Hamilton, The National Adventure*, pp. 429–430.
10. See *The Microfilm Edition of The Adams Papers*, 608 reels (Boston: Massachusetts Historical Society, 1954–1959), reel 391.
11. Fitzpatrick, *Writings of George Washington*, 36: 453–462; also in *Adams Papers*, reel 391.
12. Ibid.
13. Adams to McHenry, Quincy, 10/12/1798, in ibid.
14. Adams's reply to the address of the Boston Marine Society, 9/7/1798, in ibid., reel 119.
15. [James D. Richardson, ed.], *A Compilation of the Messages and Papers of the Presidents*, 10 vols. (n. p.: Bureau of National Literature, 1913), 1: 241.
16. See Marshall Smelser, *Congress Founds the Navy, 1787–1798* (Notre Dame, Ind.: Notre Dame Univ. Pr., 1959), p. 179.
17. Quoted in Page Smith, *John Adams* (New York: Doubleday and Co., 1962), p. 967.
18. 8/31/1798, *Adams Papers*, reel 199; see also Nathan Sargent, "The Quasi-War with France," *The United Service. A Monthly Review of Military and Naval Affairs* 9 (1883): 10. Sargent says there were seventeen war vessels at sea by December 1798.
19. Quincy, 5/19/1799, in Adams, *Works of John Adams*, 8: 650–651.
20. See, for example, ibid., pp. 664 and 669.
21. Quincy, 4/25/1808, quoted by Joseph Charles, *The Origins of the American Party System; Three Essays* (Williamsburg, Va.: The Institute of Early American History and Culture, 1956), p. 61.

CHAPTER 7

1. Charles Francis Adams, ed., *The Works of John Adams, Second President of the United States; With a Life of the Author, Notes and Illustrations*, 10 vols. (Boston: Little, Brown and Co., 1856), 8: 612–613.
2. Stewart Mitchell, ed., *New Let-*

ters of Abigail Adams, 1788–1801 (Boston: Houghton, Mifflin Co., 1947), p. 192.

3. 9/11/1798, quoted by George Gibbs, *Memoirs of the Administrations of Washington and John Adams, Edited from the Papers of Oliver Wolcott, Secretary of the Treasury,* 2 vols. (New York: Privately Printed for the Subscribers, 1846), 2: 107.

4. "Letters to the Boston Patriot," no. 3, in Adams, *Works of John Adams,* 9: 246.

5. Charles R. King, ed., *The Life and Correspondence of Rufus King, Comprising His Letters, Private and Official; His Public Documents and His Speeches,* 6 vols. (New York: G. P. Putnam's Sons, 1894–1900), 2: 469.

6. *The Microfilm Edition of The Adams Papers,* 608 reels (Boston:

Massachusetts Historical Society, 1954–1959), reel 119.

7. Adams, *Works of John Adams,* 1: 534.

8. Adams to Pickering, Quincy, 10/29/1798, in *Adams Papers,* reel 391.

9. King to Hamilton, London, 9/23/1798, in King, *Life of Rufus King,* 2: 424.

10. Samuel Eliot Morison, *The Life and Letters of Harrison Gray Otis, Federalist, 1765–1848,* 2 vols. (Boston: Houghton, Mifflin Co., 1913), 1: 169.

11. See *Adams Papers,* reel 391.

12. Ibid., reel 392.

13. Albert Gallatin to his wife, Philadelphia, 12/7/1798, quoted by Henry Adams, *The Life of Albert Gallatin* (Philadelphia: J. B. Lippincott & Co., 1879), pp. 221–223.

CHAPTER 8

1. For the complete address, see [James D. Richardson, ed.], *A Compilation of the Messages and Papers of the Presidents,* 10 vols. (n. p.: Bureau of National Literature, 1913), 1: 261-265.

2. See Adams to Pickering, 1/15/1799, in Charles Francis Adams, ed., *The Works of John Adams, Second President of the United States; With a Life of the Author, Notes and Illustrations,* 10 vols. (Boston: Little, Brown and Co., 1856), 8: 621 and n1.

3. 1/25/1799, Madison Papers, Library of Congress, quoted by Stephen G. Kurtz, *The Presidency of John Adams; the Collapse of Federalism, 1795–1800* (New York: A. S. Barnes & Co., 1961), p. 347.

4. Paris, 2/10/1798, in *The Microfilm Edition of The Adams Papers,* 608 reels (Boston: Massachusetts Historical Society, 1954–1959), reel 393.

5. Robert R. Palmer, *The Age of the Democratic Revolution: A Political History of Europe and*

America, 1760–1800, 2 vols. (Princeton, N.J.: Princeton Univ. Pr., 1959), 2: 544.

6. Richardson, *Messages and Papers of the Presidents,* 1: 272-273.

7. Quoted in Samuel Eliot Morison, *Harrison Gray Otis, 1765–1848; The Urbane Federalist* (Boston: Houghton, Mifflin Co., 1969), p. 159.

8. Philadelphia, 2/19/1799, in Adams, *Works of John Adams,* 8: 624-625.

9. Quoted by Richard E. Welch, Jr., *Theodore Sedgwick, Federalist: A Political Portrait* (Middletown, Conn.: Wesleyan Univ. Pr., 1965), pp. 185–186.

10. 2/21/1799, in Henry Cabot Lodge, *Life and Letters of George Cabot* (Boston: Little, Brown and Co., 1879), pp. 221–222.

11. *Adams Papers,* reel 393.

12. Ibid.

13. Sedgwick to Hamilton, Philadelphia, 2/22/1799, in John C. Hamilton, ed., *The Works of Alexander Hamilton; Comprising His Correspondence, His Political*

and *Official Writings, Exclusive of the Federalist, Civil and Military,* 7 vols. (New York: Charles S. Francis & Co., 1850), 5: 217.

14. Pickering to King, 3/12/1799, in Charles R. King, ed., *The Life and Correspondence of Rufus King, Comprising His Letters, Private and Official; His Public Documents and His Speeches,* 6 vols. (New York: G. P. Putnam's Sons, 1895), 2: 558.

15. Peter P. Hill, *William Vans Murray, Federalist Diplomat: The Shaping of Peace with France* (Syracuse, N.Y.: Syracuse Univ. Pr., 1971), p. 148.

16. 8/6/1799, Quincy, in *Adams Papers,* reel 120.

17. 5/13/1799, Adams, *Works of John Adams,* 8: 645–646.

18. *Adams Papers,* reel 396.

19. Adams, *Works of John Adams,* 9: 19–20; see also, *Adams Papers,* reel 120.

20. Ibid., reel 396.

21. Adams, *Works of John Adams,* 9: 30.

22. Ibid., pp. 31–33, and 25–29.

23. Ibid., pp. 33–34.

24. *Adams Papers,* reel 120.

25. Ibid.

26. King, *Rufus King,* 3: 113.

27. Abigail Adams to Mary Cranch, 12/30/1799, in Stewart Mitchell, ed., *New Letters of Abigail Adams, 1788–1801* (Boston: Houghton, Mifflin Co., 1947), p. 224.

28. Hamilton to Washington, New York, 10/21/1799, in Henry Cabot Lodge, ed., *The Works of Alexander Hamilton,* 12 vols. (New York: G. P. Putnam's Sons, 1885–1886), 10: 356.

29. 10/24/1799, Pickering to Cabot, in Lodge, *George Cabot,* p. 249.

30. Pickering to Murray, Trenton, 10/25/1799, in Worthington C. Ford, ed., "Letters of William Vans Murray to John Quincy Adams, 1797–1803," *Annual Report of the American Historical Association, 1912* (Washington, 1914), pp. 610–612.

31. Morse to Wolcott, Charlestown, Mass., 11/8/1799, in George Gibbs, *Memoirs of the Administrations of Washington and John Adams, Edited from the Papers of Oliver Wolcott, Secretary of the Treasury,* 2 vols. (New York: Privately Printed for the Subscribers, 1846), 2: 287.

CHAPTER 9

1. Marshall Smelser, "The Jacobin Phrenzy: The Menace of Monarchy, Plutocracy, and Anglophilia, 1789–1798," *The Review of Politics* 21 (1959): 239–240.

2. Charles Francis Adams, ed., *Letters of John Adams, Addressed to His Wife,* 2 vols. (Boston: Charles G. Little and James Brown, 1841), 2: 207–209, 214–216, and 222–224.

3. Quoted in James Morton Smith, *Freedom's Fetters; The Alien and Sedition Laws and American Civil Liberties* (Ithaca, N.Y.: Cornell Univ. Pr., 1956), p. 13.

4. John C. Fitzpatrick, ed., *The Writings of George Washington from the Original Manuscript Sources, 1743–1799,* 38 vols.

(Washington, D.C.: Government Printing Office, 1931–1944), 36: 168–169.

5. Quoted in Alexander DeConde, *The Quasi-War; The Politics and Diplomacy of the Undeclared War with France, 1797–1801* (New York: Charles Scribner's Sons, 1966), p. 82.

6. Quoted in John C. Miller, *Crisis in Freedom; The Alien and Sedition Acts* (Boston: Little, Brown and Co., 1951), p. 14.

7. Samuel Eliot Morison, *The Life and Letters of Harrison Gray Otis, Federalist, 1765–1848,* 2 vols. (Boston: Houghton, Mifflin Co., 1913), 1: 158.

8. Robert Ernst, *Rufus King, American Federalist* (Chapel Hill:

Univ. of North Carolina Pr., 1968), pp. 266–267.

9. The account of this measure in *The Debates and Proceedings in the Congress of the United States . . . March 3, 1789 to May 27, 1827, inclusive,* 42 vols. or 536 microcards (Washington: Gales and Seaton, 1834–1856), microcard 101, does not contain this last phrase. It is perhaps significant that Sedgwick used the phrase and thus implied the possibility. See Richard E. Welch, Jr., *Theodore Sedgwick, Federalist; A Political Portrait* (Middletown, Conn.: Wesleyan Univ. Pr., 1965), p. 175.

10. See Alexander DeConde, "William Vans Murray and the Diplomacy of Peace, 1797–1800," *Maryland Historical Magazine* 48 (1953): 6–7.

11. Robert R. Palmer, *The Age of the Democratic Revolution: A Political History of Europe and America, 1760–1800,* 2 vols. (Princeton, N.J.: Princeton Univ. Pr., 1959), 2: 537.

12. Henry Cabot Lodge, ed., *The Works of Alexander Hamilton,* 12 vols. (New York: G. P. Putnam's Sons, 1885–1886), 10: 340–342.

13. Esmond Wright, *Fabric of Freedom, 1763–1800* (New York: Hill & Wang, 1961), pp. 224–225.

14. Quoted in Henry Adams, *The Life of Albert Gallatin* (Philadelphia: J. B. Lippincott & Co., 1879), pp. 221–223.

15. New York City, 1/5/1800, in Lodge, *Works of Hamilton,* 10: 358–359.

16. *The Microfilm Edition of The Adams Papers,* 608 reels (Boston: Massachusetts Historical Society, 1954–1959), reel 398.

17. To James Lloyd, 2/6/1815, in Charles Francis Adams, ed., *The Works of John Adams, Second President of the United States; with a Life of the Author, Notes and Illustrations,* 10 vols. (Boston: Little, Brown and Co., 1856), 10: 114–116; Palmer, *The Age of the Democratic Revolution,* 2: 526.

18. Paul Leicester Ford, ed., *The Works of Thomas Jefferson,* 10 vols. (New York: G. P. Putnam's Sons, 1892–1899), 8: 411, 414.

19. Quoted in Smith, *Freedom's Fetters,* p. 110.

20. Charles R. King, ed., *The Life and Correspondence of Rufus King; Comprising His Letters, Private and Official; His Public Documents and His Speeches,* 6 vols. (New York: G. P. Putnam's Sons, 1894–1900), 2: 425.

21. Quoted in Smith, *Freedom's Fetters,* pp. 94–95.

22. *The Annals of Congress,* 1797–1799, 2: 1992.

23. Frank Malloy Anderson, "The Enforcement of the Alien and Sedition Laws," *Annual Report of the American Historical Association, 1912* (Washington, 1914), pp. 115 and 119.

24. Abigail Adams to Mary Cranch, 4/26/1798, in Stewart Mitchell, ed., *New Letters of Abigail Adams, 1788–1801* (Boston: Houghton, Mifflin Co., 1947), pp. 164–166.

25. Morton Borden, *Parties and Politics in the Early Republic, 1789–1815* (New York: Thomas Y. Crowell Co., 1967), p. 36.

26. DeConde, *The Quasi-War,* p. 100.

27. Donald H. Stewart, *The Opposition Press of the Federalist Period* (Albany: State Univ. of New York Pr., 1969), p. 486.

28. I am indebted to Professor Peter Levine of Michigan State University for assistance in understanding the background of this episode and for the loan of an unpublished manuscript titled "John Adams and the Fries Rebellion."

29. Hamilton to William McHenry, 3/18/1799, in Lodge, *Works of Hamilton,* 1904 edition, 7: 69.

30. [James D. Richardson, ed.], *A Compilation of the Messages and Papers of the Presidents,* 10 vols. (n. p.: Bureau of National Lit-

erature, 1913), 1: 276–277.
31. *Adams Papers*, reel 396.
32. Adams, *Works of John Adams*, 1: 572.

33. Quoted in Albert J. Beveridge, *The Life of John Marshall*, 4 vols. (Boston: Houghton, Mifflin Co., 1916–1919), 2: 430.

CHAPTER 10

1. Quoted in Alexander DeConde, *The Quasi-War; The Politics and Diplomacy of the Undeclared War with France* (New York: Charles Scribner's Sons, 1966), p. 403, n15.
2. Charles Francis Adams, ed., *The Works of John Adams, Second President of the United States; With a Life of the Author, Notes and Illustrations*, 10 vols. (Boston: Little, Brown and Co., 1856), 9: 211.
3. Ibid., 9: pass.
4. Ibid., pp. 192–193.
5. Ibid., p. 232.
6. Quoted by David Hackett Fischer, *The Revolution of American Conservatism; The Federalist Party in the Era of Jeffersonian Democracy* (New York: Harper & Row, 1965), p. 40.
7. Adams to Washington, 6/22/1798, in Adams, *Works of John Adams*, 8: 572–573.
8. Donald H. Stewart, *The Opposition Press of the Federalist Period* (Albany: State Univ. of New York Pr., 1969), p. 537, and see also p. 457.
9. Quoted by Eugene Perry Link, *Democratic-Republican Societies, 1790–1800* (New York: Columbia Univ. Pr., 1942), p. 205.
10. Adams, *Works of John Adams*, 8: 652n.
11. See [James D. Richardson, ed.], *A Compilation of the Messages and Papers of the Presidents*, 10 vols. (n. p.: Bureau of National Literature, 1913), 7: 361 ff.
12. Charles R. King, ed., *The Life and Correspondence of Rufus King, Comprising His Letters, Private and Official; His Public Documents and His Speeches*, 6 vols. (New York: G. P. Putnam's Sons, 1894–1900), 3: 14.
13. Adams, *Works of John Adams*, 8: 637–638.
14. Abigail Adams to T. B. Adams, Quincy, 6/2/1799, in *The Microfilm Edition of The Adams Papers*, 608 reels (Boston: Massachusetts Historical Society, 1954–1959), reel 395.

CHAPTER 11

1. Arthur Preston Whitaker, *The Mississippi Question, 1795–1803: A Study in Trade, Politics, and Diplomacy* (New York: D. Appleton-Century, 1934), p. 121.
2. Quoted by Broadus Mitchell, *Alexander Hamilton: The National Adventure, 1788–1804* (New York: The Macmillan Co., 1962), p. 444.
3. Joseph Charles, *The Origins of the American Party System; Three Essays* (Williamsburg, Va.: The Institute of Early American History and Culture, 1956), p. 133.
4. Two slightly different versions of the letter appear in print. The extract given here is from Henry Cabot Lodge, ed., *The Works of Alexander Hamilton*, 12 vols. (New York: G. P. Putnam's Sons, 1885–1886), 10: 314–315; with a few variations but the same meaning, the letter appears in Charles R. King, ed., *The Life and Correspondence of Rufus King; Comprising His Letters, Private and Official, His Public Documents and His Speeches*, 6 vols. (New York: G. P. Putnam's Sons, 1895), 2: 658–659.
5. Quoted by Richard B. Morris, *Alexander Hamilton and the*

Founding of the Nation (New York: The Dial Pr., 1957), p. 435.

6. London, 10/20/1798, in King, *Life of Rufus King,* 2: 662.

7. London, 1/21/1799, King to Hamilton, in John C. Hamilton, ed., *The Works of Alexander Hamilton, Comprising His Correspondence, His Political and Official writings, Exclusive of the Federalist, Civil and Military,* 7 vols. (New York: Charles S. Francis & Co., 1850), 6: 389-390.

8. 12/22/1798, New York, Hamilton to Gunn, in ibid., 5: 184-185.

9. Whitaker, *The Mississippi Question,* p. 124.

10. 4/8/1799, in Charles Francis Adams, ed., *The Works of John Adams, Second President of the United States; With a Life of the Author, Notes and Illustrations,* 10 vols. (Boston: Little, Brown and Co., 1856), 9: 232.

11. *The Microfilm Edition of The Adams Papers,* 608 reels (Boston: Massachusetts Historical Society, 1954-1959), reel 396.

12. Hamilton, *Works of Hamilton,* 5: 283-284.

13. Robert R. Palmer, *The Age of the Democratic Revolution: A Political History of Europe and America, 1760-1800,* 2 vols. (Princeton, N.J.: Princeton Univ. Pr., 1959), 2: 328-329.

14. Adrienne Koch and William Peden, eds., *The Selected Writings of John and John Quincy Adams* (New York: Alfred A. Knopf, 1946), pp. xxii-xxiii.

15. Manning J. Dauer, *The Adams Federalists* (Baltimore: The Johns Hopkins Pr., 1953), p. 187.

16. Quincy, 10/3/1798, in Adams, *Works of John Adams,* 8: 600.

17. Quoted in Charles, *The Origins of the American Party System,* p. 63.

18. Quoted in Bradford Perkins, *The First Rapprochement; England and the United States, 1795-1805* (Philadelphia: Univ. of Pennsylvania Pr., 1955), pp. 111-112.

CHAPTER 12

1. Pickering to Hamilton, 6/9/1798, in John G. Hamilton, ed., *The Works of Alexander Hamilton; Comprising His Political and Official Writings, Exclusive of the Federalist, Civil and Military,* 7 vols. (New York: Charles S. Francis & Co., 1850), 6: 307.

2. Quoted in Charles R. King, ed., *The Life and Correspondence of Rufus King, Comprising His Letters, Private and Official; His Public Documents and His Speeches,* 6 vols. (New York: G. P. Putnam's Sons, 1895), 3: 213.

3. Thomas Fitzsimmons to Oliver Wolcott, Philadelphia, 9/3/1799, in George Gibbs, *Memoirs of the Administrations of Washington and John Adams, Edited from the Papers of Oliver Wolcott, Secretary of the Treasury,* 2 vols. (New York: Privately Printed for the Subscribers, 1846), 2: 262.

4. Donald H. Stewart, *The Opposition Press of the Federalist Period* (Albany: State Univ. of New York Pr., 1969), p. 241.

5. Dudley W. Knox, ed., *Naval Documents Related to the Quasi-War Between the United States and France,* 7 vols. (Washington, D.C.: Government Printing Office, 1935-1938), 4: 181-182.

6. Quincy, 8/29/1799, in *The Microfilm Edition of The Adams Papers,* 608 reels (Boston: Massachusetts Historical Society, 1954-1959), reel 120.

7. 9/23/1799, ibid.

8. Ibid.

9. [James D. Richardson, ed.], *A Compilation of the Messages and Papers of the Presidents,* 10 vols. (n. p.: Bureau of National Literature, 1913), 1: 296.

10. Bradford Perkins, *The First Rapprochement; England and the United States, 1795–1805* (Philadelphia: Univ. of Pennsylvania Pr., 1955), p. 69.

11. Joseph Charles, *The Origins of the American Party System; Three Essays* (Williamsburg, Va.: Institute of Early American History and Culture, 1956), pp. 132 and 137.

12. See Rayford W. Logan, *The Diplomatic Relations of the United States with Haiti, 1776–1891* (Chapel Hill: Univ. of North Carolina Pr., 1941), p. 60.

13. Robert R. Palmer, *The Age of the Democratic Revolution: A Political History of Europe and America, 1760–1800*, 2 vols. (Princeton, N.J.: Princeton Univ. Pr., 1959), 2: 514.

14. See Charles Francis Adams, ed., *The Works of John Adams, Second President of the United States; With a Life of the Author, Notes and Illustrations*, 10 vols. (Boston: Little, Brown and Co., 1856), 8: 634 and 657.

15. Alexander DeConde, *The Quasi-War; The Politics and Diplomacy of the Undeclared War with France, 1797–1801* (New York: Charles Scribner's Sons, 1966), p. 139.

CHAPTER 13

1. Worthington C. Ford, ed., "Letters of William Vans Murray to John Quincy Adams, 1797–1803," *Annual Report of the American Historical Association, 1912* (Washington, 1914), p. 635.

2. Murray to John Quincy Adams, 2/7/1800, ibid., p. 641.

3. Ibid., p. 657.

4. Arthur Burr Darling, *Our Rising Empire, 1763–1803* (New Haven, Conn.: Yale Univ. Pr., 1940), p. 380.

5. 9/27/1800, *The Microfilm Edition of The Adams Papers*, 608 reels (Boston: Massachusetts Historical Society, 1054–1959), reel 398.

6. Murray to John Quincy Adams, 9/27/1800, ibid.

7. Paris, 10/1/1800, ibid., reel 399.

8. Ford, "Letters of William Vans Murray," pp. 656–657.

9. "Letters of Stephen Higginson, 1783–1804," *Annual Report of the American Historical Association, 1896*, 2 vols. (Washington, 1896), 1: 836.

10. Seth Ames, ed., *Works of Fisher Ames with a Selection from His Speeches and Correspondence*, 2 vols. (New York: DeCapo Pr., 1969), 1: 260-261.

11. George Gibbs, *Memoirs of the Administrations of Washington and John Adams, Edited from the Papers of Oliver Wolcott, Secretary of the Treasury*, 2 vols. (New York: Privately Printed for the Subscribers, 1846), 2: 314–315.

12. *Adams Papers*, reel 397; I refer also to my unpublished article, "Did John Adams Know of His Cabinet's Disloyalty?"

13. *Adams Papers*, reel 120.

14. Ibid., reel 397.

15. Ibid., reel 120.

16. Pickering Papers, Massachusetts Historical Society, quoted by Broadus Mitchell, *Alexander Hamilton, The National Adventure, 1788–1804* (New York: Macmillan Co., 1962), p. 735n.

17. *Adams Papers*, reel 397.

18. Ibid.

19. See Worthington C. Ford, ed., "Letters of William Vans Murray to John Quincy Adams, 1797–1803," *Annual Report of the American Historical Association, 1912* (Washington, D.C: Government Printing Office, 1914), pp. 600–602 and 610–612, for Pickering's letters to Murray, and pp. 629–630 for Murray's report of having received "a most flogging and harsh letter from the Colonel."

20. Abigail to John Quincy, 9/1/ 1800, in *Adams Papers,* reel 398.
21. Quoted by Clinton Rossiter, *Alexander Hamilton and the Constitution* (New York: Harcourt, Brace and World, 1964), p. 313n.
22. Adams to Marshall, Quincy, 7/ 31/1800, *Adams Papers,* reel 120.
23. Ibid.
24. 9/10/1800, quoted by Stephen G. Kurtz, "The French Mission of 1799–1800: Concluding Chapter in the Statecraft of John Adams," *Political Science Quarterly* 80 (1965): 557.
25. *Adams Papers,* reel 120.
26. See Ford, "Letters of William Vans Murray," pp. 653 and 666.

27. John C. Hamilton, ed., *The Works of Alexander Hamilton; Comprising His Correspondence, His Political and Official Writings, Exclusive of the Federalist, Civil and Military,* 7 vols. (New York: Charles S. Francis & Co., 1850), 6: 511.
28. Quoted in Alexander DeConde, *The Quasi-War; The Politics and Diplomacy of the Undeclared War with France, 1797–1801* (New York: Charles Scribner's Sons, 1966), p. 288.
29. Quoted in Zoltán Haraszti, *John Adams and the Prophets of Progress* (New York: Grosset & Dunlap, 1964), p. 263.

CHAPTER 14

1. Charles R. King, ed., *The Life and Correspondence of Rufus King, Comprising His Letters, Private and Official; His Public Documents and His Speeches,* 6 vols. (New York: G. P. Putnam's Sons, 1894–1900), 3: 7–10 and 14–15.
2. George Gibbs, *Memoirs of the Administrations of Washington and John Adams, Edited from the Papers of Oliver Wolcott, Secretary of the Treasury,* 2 vols. (New York: Privately Printed for the Subscribers, 1846), 2: 243.
3. 1/15/1800, in King, *Life of Rufus King,* 3: 173–175.
4. Henry Cabot Lodge, ed., *The Works of Alexander Hamilton,* 12 vols. (New York: G. P. Putnam's Sons, 1885–1886), 10: 371; and Noble E. Cunningham, Jr., *The Jeffersonian Republicans; The Formation of Party Organization, 1789–1801* (Chapel Hill: Univ. of North Carolina Pr., 1957), pp. 164–165.
5. Quoted in ibid., p. 186.
6. Lodge, *Works of Hamilton,* 10: 375.
7. John C. Hamilton, ed., *The Works of Alexander Hamilton; Comprising His Correspondence, His Political and Official Writings, Ex-

clusive of the Federalist, Civil and Military,* 7 vols. (New York: Charles S. Francis & Co., 1850), 6: 445–446.
8. Charles Francis Adams, ed., *The Works of John Adams, Second President of the United States: With a Life of the Author, Notes and Illustrations,* 10 vols. (Boston: Little, Brown and Co., 1856), 9: 83–84.
9. *The Microfilm Edition of The Adams Papers,* 608 reels (Boston: Massachusetts Historical Society, 1954–1959), reel 393.
10. Abigail Adams to Mr. Malcom, 5/18/1800, in *Adams Papers,* reel 397.
11. 7/14/1800, in ibid., reel 120.
12. Cabot to Wolcott, 6/14/1800, in Gibbs, *Memoirs of the Administrations of Washington and John Adams,* 2: 370–371; and Wolcott to Cabot, 6/15/1800, in ibid., pp. 371–372.
13. Quoted by Morton Borden, *The Federalism of James A. Bayard* (New York: Columbia Univ. Pr., 1955), pp. 34–35.
14. Hamilton, *Works of Hamilton,* 6: 447.
15. Gibbs, *Memoirs of the Administrations of Washington and John Adams,* 2: 384–386.

16. Ibid., 2: 397; and Lodge, *Works of Hamilton*, 10: 383–384.
17. Quoted by Winfred E. A. Bernhard, *Fisher Ames; Federalist and Statesman, 1758–1808* (Chapel Hill: Univ. of North Carolina Pr., 1965), pp. 326–327.
18. Gibbs, *Memoirs of the Administrations of Washington and John Adams*, 2: 421–422.
19. Worthington C. Ford, ed., "Letters of William Vans Murray, to John Quincy Adams, 1797–1803," *Annual Report of the American Historical Association, 1912* (Washington, D.C.: Government Printing Office, 1914), pp. 674–675.
20. Quoted in Henry Cabot Lodge, *Life and Letters of George Cabot* (Boston: Little, Brown and Co., 1877), pp. 298–300.
21. See King, *Life of Rufus King*, 3: 331.
22. *Adams Papers*, reel 399.
23. 12/9/1800, in ibid., reel 120.
24. Quoted in Page Smith, *John Adams* (New York: Doubleday and Co., 1962), p. 1034.
25. 11/5/1800, in *Adams Papers*, reel 399; Adams's birthday was actually on October 19.
26. 1/8/1800, in Gibbs, *Memoirs of*

the *Administrations of Washington and John Adams*, 2: 287.
27. Charles Francis Adams, ed., *Letters of Mrs. Adams, The Wife of John Adams*, 2 vols. (Boston: Charles C. Little and James Brown, 1851), 2: 237–239.
28. Stewart Mitchell, ed., *New Letters of Abigail Adams, 1788–1801* (Boston: Houghton, Mifflin Co., 1947), p. 261.
29. 11/24/1800, in Adams, *Works of John Adams*, 9: 90–91.
30. Quincy, 7/27/1799, in *Adams Papers*, reel 120.
31. Noble E. Cunningham, Jr., "The Sources of Republican Supremacy," in Paul Goodman, ed., *The Federalists vs. The Jeffersonian Republicans* (New York: Holt, Rinehart and Winston, 1967), p. 114.
32. 1/16/1801, in *Adams Papers*, reel 400.
33. Doris A. Graber, *Public Opinion, the President, and Foreign Policy* (New York: Holt, Rinehart and Winston, 1968), p. 79.
34. Quoted by Smith, *John Adams*, p. 1053.
35. *Adams Papers*, reel 120.
36. Ibid.; see also Adams, *Works of John Adams*, 9: 576–577.

CHAPTER 15

1. *The Microfilm Edition of The Adams Papers*, 608 reels (Boston: Massachusetts Historical Society, 1954–1959), reel 399.
2. Washington, 11/21/1800, in Stewart Mitchell, ed., *New Letters of Abigail Adams, 1788–1801* (Boston: Houghton, Mifflin Co., 1947), pp. 259–260.
3. Quoted in James Sterling Young, *The Washington Community, 1800–1828* (New York: Columbia Univ. Pr., 1966), p. 45.
4. Henry Adams, *The Life of Albert Gallatin* (Philadelphia: J. B. Lippincott & Co., 1879), p. 252.
5. 1/3/1801, in Elizabeth Donnan, ed., "The Papers of James A. Bayard, 1796–1815," *Annual Re-*

port *of the American Historical Association, 1913*, 2 vols. (Washington, D.C.: Government Printing Office, 1915), 2: 116–122.
6. [James D. Richardson, ed.], *A Compilation of the Messages and Papers of the Presidents*, 10 vols. (n. p.: Bureau of National Literature, 1913), 1: 295.
7. *Adams Papers*, reel 120.
8. Washington, 1/26/1801, in Charles Francis Adams, ed., *The Works of John Adams, Second President of the United States; With a Life of the Author, Notes and Illustrations*, 10 vols. (Boston: Little, Brown and Co., 1856), 9: 93–94; also see Bond to John Adams, 1/20/1801,

Adams Papers, reel 400, and Adams to Boudinot, ibid., reel 120.

9. Ibid., reel 400.

10. Ibid., reel 120.

11. 1/3/1801 and 2/3/1801, Abigail to Thomas Boyleston Adams, ibid., reel 400.

12. Ibid.

13. Adams, *Works of John Adams,* 10: 43.

14. John to Abigail, Washington, 2/16/1801, *Adams Papers,* reel 400.

15. Page Smith, *John Adams* (New York: Doubleday and Co., 1962), p. 1056.

16. Trenton, 10/25/1799, *Adams Papers,* reel 396.

17. Abigail to Mr. Malcom, 5/18/1800, ibid., reel 397.

18. John Adams to Thomas Boyleston Adams, 12/17/1800, in ibid., reel 399.

19. Adams to Colonel Tudor, Washington, 1/20/1801, in ibid., reel 400.

20. Abigail to Thomas Boyleston Adams, 11/13/1800 and 1/15/1801, in Charles Francis Adams, ed., *Letters of Mrs. Adams, The Wife of John Adams,* 2 vols. (Boston: Charles C. Little and James Brown, 1851), 2: 237–239; and *Adams Papers,* reel 400.

21. Abigail to Thomas Boyleston Adams, Tuesday, 1/3/1801 and 2/3/1801, in ibid.

22. Adams to Samuel Dexter, Quincy,

3/23/1801, in Adams, *Works of John Adams,* 9: 580–581.

23. Esmond Wright, *Fabric of Freedom, 1763–1800* (New York: Hill & Wang, 1961), p. 229. Dumas Malone, far more accurately, recognized that Adams's departure was not necessarily as petty as has often been implied; see *Jefferson the President; First Term, 1801–1805* (Boston: Little, Brown and Co., 1970), pp. 3–4.

24. 12/28/1800, *Adams Papers,* reel 120.

25. Adams to Boudinot, Washington, 1/26/1801, in ibid.

26. 4/16/1801, in Adams, *Works of John Adams,* 9: 584–585.

27. Clinton Rossiter, "The Legacy of John Adams," *The Yale Review* 46 (1957): 530–531.

28. Adrienne Koch and William Peden, eds., *The Selected Writings of John and John Quincy Adams* (New York: Alfred A. Knopf, 1946), p. xxiv.

29. See Adams, *Works of John Adams,* 9: 581.

30. Richard E. Welch, Jr., *Theodore Sedgwick, Federalist; A Political Portrait* (Middletown, Conn.: Wesleyan Univ. Pr., 1965), p. 230.

31. Adams, *Letters of Mrs. Adams,* 2: 245.

32. Abigail to Thomas Boyleston Adams, 7/12/1801, in ibid., pp. 246–247.

CHAPTER 16

1. Adrienne Koch and William Peden, eds., *The Selected Writings of John and John Quincy Adams* (New York: Alfred A. Knopf, 1946), pp. 84, 100.

2. 5/3/1797, in *The Microfilm Edition of The Adams Papers,* 608 reels (Boston: Massachusetts Historical Society, 1954–1959), reel 117.

3. Charles Francis Adams, ed., *The Works of John Adams, Second President of the United States;*

With a Life of the Author, Notes and Illustrations, 10 vols. (Boston: Little, Brown and Co., 1856), 6: 431.

4. *Adams Papers,* reel 119.

5. Leonard D. White, *The Federalists; A Study in Administrative History* (New York: Macmillan Co., 1948), pp. 44–45.

6. Quoted by Edward S. Corwin, *The President, Office and Powers, 1789–1957, History and Analysis of Practice and Opinion* (New

York: New York Univ. Pr., 1957), p. 449.

7. Quoted in White, *The Federalists*, pp. 85–87.

8. James MacGregor Burns, *Presidential Government* (Boston: Houghton, Mifflin Co., 1965), p. 28.

9. George W. Corner, ed., *The Autobiography of Benjamin Rush; His Travels Through Life; Together with His Commonplace Book for 1763–1800* (Princeton, N.J.: Princeton Univ. Pr., 1948), p. 140.

10. White, *The Federalists*, p. 267.

11. Esmond Wright, *Fabric of Freedom, 1763–1800* (New York: Hill & Wang, 1961), p. 219.

12. Marshall Smelser, "The Jacobin Phrenzy; Federalism and the Menace of Liberty, Equality and Fraternity," *The Review of Politics* 13 (1951): 482.

Bibliographical Essay

This bibliographical essay provides brief annotations for those sources most helpful to an understanding of the presidency of John Adams. There is no attempt to be exhaustive; neither are all sources listed in the footnotes cited here. Full bibliographical data are provided the first time each work is cited in each chapter.

PRIMARY SOURCES—JOHN ADAMS

For many decades the voluminous papers of the Adams family—John Adams, his son John Quincy, the latter's sons and grandsons—were kept at Quincy in a lovely little stone building erected to house the family's books and papers. Later they were transferred to the safer keeping of the Massachusetts Historical Society in Boston. Access to the papers was gained only by permission, and over the years this was seldom granted. Now, in process of being carefully and skillfully edited by Lyman Butterfield and his staff, these papers have been arranged and microfilmed. The 608-reel *Microfilm Edition of the Adams Papers* (Boston: Massachusetts Historical Society, 1954–1959), available in major libraries throughout the country, guarantees for the first time that this vast treasure chest of historical data can be widely used.

Prior to 1955 most scholars doing research on John Adams had to rely on the ten-volume compilation made by the president's grandson: Charles Francis Adams, ed., *The Works of John Adams, Second President of the United States: With a Life of the Author, Notes and Illustrations* (Boston: Little, Brown and Co., 1856). Edited with care, and apparently with a high degree of integrity, this work was of course only a selection, and the bias of the editor inevitably showed in both the selection and the editorial comments.

Several briefer and more specialized selections of the writings of John Adams have been of help in the preparation of this book. Adrienne Koch and William Peden edited a one-volume *Selected Writings of John and John Quincy Adams* (New York: Alfred A. Knopf, 1946). The selections are excellent, and the long introduction provides some unusual insight into John Adams and his time. Yet I must disagree with its evaluation of Adams's presidential

leadership. Among the already published volumes of Adams Papers under Butterfield's supervision, *The Diary and Autobiography of John Adams,* 4 vols. (Cambridge, Mass.: The Belknap Press of Harvard Univ. Pr., 1961), is of value to anyone interested in the developing personality and character of John Adams.

Nearly a quarter century ago Stewart Mitchell, then director of the Massachusetts Historical Society, where the Adams Papers reposed, edited a fascinating collection of the letters of John Adams's wife: *New Letters of Abigail Adams, 1788–1801* (Boston: Houghton, Mifflin Co., 1947). Most of the letters deal with the decade of the 1790s and many of them are pertinent to the present study. I disagree with some of the editor's conclusions and interpretations—for example, with Mitchell's analysis of the relations between John Adams and Oliver Wolcott, Jr.—but there is no denying the interest or the importance of these letters.

In the second quarter of the nineteenth century, prior to the preparation of the ten-volume work cited above, Charles Francis Adams prepared two groups of Adams correspondence. Long out of print and not always readily available, this writer found both of real assistance: *Letters of John Adams, Addressed to His Wife* (Boston: Charles C. Little and James Brown, 1841), and *Letters of Mrs. Adams, The Wife of John Adams,* 2 vols. (Boston: same publisher, 1851).

Several books containing selections of the correspondence between John Adams and friends have proved helpful. The same "editing grandson" mentioned above was responsible for the "Correspondence Between John Adams and Mercy Warren, Relating to Her 'History of the American Revolution'" (*Collections* of the Massachusetts Historical Soc., vol. IV, Fifth Series, 1878; pp. 317–491). This group of letters is largely devoted to Adams's criticism of his old friend's statements and interpretations in her three-volume history of the War for Independence and have little direct bearing on the events of the late 1790s. The letters do, however, reveal much about Adams's thinking and personality. Worthington C. Ford edited *Statesman and Friend, Correspondence of John Adams and Benjamin Waterhouse, 1784–1822* (Boston: Little, Brown and Co., 1927). Adams's continuing interest in, concern with, and frequent explanation of his controversial presidential decisions and actions are apparent in many of his letters written after leaving public office. John A. Schutz and Douglas Adair edited *The Spur of Fame: Dialogues of John Adams and Benjamin Rush, 1805–1813* (San Marino, Cal.: The Huntington Library, 1966), a selection of

the body of Adams correspondence that is second only to Adams's correspondence with Thomas Jefferson for interest and significance.

PRIMARY SOURCES—NOT DIRECTLY RELATED TO JOHN ADAMS

Since Alexander Hamilton was a major figure during Adams's presidency, his letters and other writings are of importance. The edition of his papers being currently carried forward by Dr. Harold Syrett and his staff, and published by the Columbia Univ. Press, has not yet reached the second half of the 1790s, therefore the older collections were used in writing this volume: John C. Hamilton, ed., *The Works of Alexander Hamilton; Comprising His Correspondence, His Political and Official Writings, Exclusive of the Federalist, Civil and Military*, 7 vols. (New York: Charles S. Francis and Co., 1850); and Henry Cabot Lodge, ed., *The Works of Alexander Hamilton*, 12 vols. (New York: G. P. Putnam's Sons, 1885–1886; also slightly revised in 1904). Neither edition is complete and both are somewhat marred by the strong pro-Hamilton bias of their editors.

Two other collections of source material, both from the Arch-Federalist point of view, are George Gibbs, *Memoirs of the Administrations of Washington and John Adams, Edited from the Papers of Oliver Wolcott, Secretary of the Treasury*, 2 vols. (New York: Privately Printed for the Subscribers, 1846), and Charles R. King, *The Life and Correspondence of Rufus King, Comprising His Letters, Private and Official; His Public Documents and His Speeches*, 6 vols. (New York: G. P. Putnam's Sons, 1894–1900). The two volumes by Gibbs consist of an interweaving of the letters and papers of Oliver Wolcott with the editor's extensive comments, interpretations, and summaries. The editor hews sharply to the accepted line of the Arch Federalists, making extremely partisan comments and highly questionable, sometimes false, generalizations and interpretations. Yet the volumes are indispensable to anyone working in this period, both because of the typically Arch-Federalist position they represent and because of the many letters and documents apparently reproduced with accuracy. The King volumes are well edited and useful.

Starting in 1931 and finishing in 1944, the United States Government Printing Office published, in thirty-eight large volumes, *The Writings of George Washington from the Original Manuscript Sources, 1745–1799*, edited by John C. Fitzpatrick. These volumes remain, four decades later, the most readily available, competently edited, and complete source of George Washington's writings. They have been frequently and profitably used in writing this book. In presenting the *Life and Letters of George Cabot* (Boston: Little, Brown and Co., 1877), Henry Cabot Lodge reveals a bitterly anti-Adams conviction and a tendency to defend and support Alexander Hamilton; the editorial comments read like an Arch-Federalist exhortation of 1799.

Julian Boyd's *Papers of Thomas Jefferson* have not yet progressed to the point where the volumes are useful in a study of the late 1790s. Paul Leicester Ford, *The Works of Thomas Jefferson*, 10 vols. (New York: G. P. Putnam's Sons, 1892–1899), and Andrew A. Lipscomb and Albert Ellery Bergh, eds., *The Writings of Thomas Jefferson . . .*, 20 vols. (Washington: The Thomas Jefferson Memorial Assn., 1904–1905), have been of much help. Gaillard Hunt's *The Writings of James Madison; Comprising His Public Papers and His Private Correspondence, Including Numerous Letters and Documents Now for the First Time Printed*, 9 vols. (New York: G. P. Putnam's Sons, 1900–1910) has occasionally proved helpful. George W. Corner's *The Autobiography of Benjamin Rush; His Travels Through Life; Together with His Commonplace Book for 1789–1813* (Princeton, N.J.: Princeton Univ. Pr., 1948) provides contemporary data on people and events. Worthington C. Ford edited two collections of source material very useful in gaining an understanding of John Adams's opinions in regard to France: *Writings of John Quincy Adams*, 7 vols. (New York: Macmillan Co., 1913–1917) and "Letters of William Vans Murray to John Quincy Adams, 1797–1803," *Annual Report of the American Historical Association, 1912* (Washington, D.C.: Government Printing Office, 1914). Anyone who has ever struggled with Murray's atrocious handwriting will appreciate the difficulty of Dr. Ford's work on the last-mentioned letters.

Agents and diplomatic representatives of both Britain and France remained privy to important events in John Adams's administration. Nearly seventy years ago Frederick Jackson Turner edited *Correspondence of French Ministers to the United States, 1791–1797*, vol. II, *Annual Report of the American Historical Association, 1903* (Washington, D.C.: Government Printing Office, 1904). More recently Patricia Holbert Menk has provided "D. M. Erskine: Letters from America, 1797–1799," *William and Mary Quarterly*, 3rd series, VI, no. 2, April, 1949; pp. 251–284. The Library of Congress has microfilmed some of the Robert Liston correspondence.

Two other works containing primary material must be mentioned for their usefulness in connection with the preparation of the current study. Almost half a century ago James Brown Scott edited *The Controversy Over Neutral Rights Between the United States and France, 1797–1800* (New York: Oxford Univ. Press, 1917). Many of the official records of the period are to be found therein. James Richardson's edition, *A Compilation of the Messages and Papers of the Presidents*, 10 vols. (n.p.: Bureau of National Literature, 1913), is an indispensable work.

SECONDARY SOURCES—CLOSELY RELATED TO THIS TOPIC

Of the many biographical studies bearing on the 1790s, two stand out as especially valuable for those who work with the present topic. Page Smith's *John Adams*, 2 vols. (New York: Doubleday & Co., 1962) is the most recent, the most extensive, and the soundest biographical study of John Adams that has been made. Not only is this study carefully researched, well organized, and effectively styled, but it is marked by unusually thoughtful analysis: witness the author's disagreement with Kurtz in regard to the possible political aspects of Adams's nomination of William Vans Murray (pp. 1001–1002). The older biography by Gilbert Chinard, *Honest John Adams* (Boston: Little, Brown and Co., 1933), remains, after forty years, a brilliant portrayal of personality and an expert analysis of events.

Samuel Flagg Bemis's *John Quincy Adams and the Foundations of American Foreign Policy* (New York: Alfred A. Knopf, 1949) offers assistance to anyone exploring the influence of the son on his father during the tempestuous negotiations of 1798 and 1799.

For a decade Stephen G. Kurtz's *The Presidency of John Adams; The Collapse of Federalism, 1795–1800* (New York: A. S. Barnes & Co., 1961) has remained the most authoritative study of these years. I gladly acknowledge my great debt to Professor Kurtz. I have differed with Kurtz on some particulars, but only after much thought and considerable reluctance. In the space of ten pages, three of our more distinguished living historians have given us deep insight into the leadership of John Adams and the perplexing problems of his times: Merrill Jensen, Samuel Flagg Bemis, and David Donald, "The Life and Soul of History" [an essay review of the microfilm edition of the Adams Papers], *New England Quarterly* 34 (1961): 96–105.

Peter P. Hill's *William Vans Murray, Federalist Diplomat; The Shaping of Peace with France, 1797–1801* (Syracuse, N.Y.: Syracuse Univ. Pr., 1971) is a careful and well-written study of this important young Federalist and his role in achieving peace with France.

One of the best known monographs dealing with the years of Adams's presidency is Alexander DeConde's *The Quasi-War: The Politics and Diplomacy of the Undeclared War with France, 1797– 1801* (New York: Charles Scribner's Sons, 1966). This book represents an exhaustive examination of the topic; yet in terms of its lack of understanding of President Adams and the number of unsupported generalizations, it must be somewhat suspect.

Manning J. Dauer's *The Adams Federalists* (Baltimore, Md.: Johns Hopkins Univ. Pr., 1953) is a most important monograph. Dauer stresses the economic bases for the split in the Federalist party, and might be considered Beardian in his general approach. In his understanding of John Adams, Dauer ranks very high. In *The Changing Political Thought of John Adams* (Princeton, N.J.: Princeton Univ. Pr., 1966), John R. Howe, Jr., has set forth some provocative thoughts about the ideas and philosophy of John Adams. Zoltán Haraszti's *John Adams and the Prophets of Progress* (New York: Grosset & Dunlap, 1964) contains occasional insights into John Adams's personality and character that proved especially helpful to this writer. Among the more penetrating monographs dealing with the political crosscurrents of the late 1790s, none surpasses Joseph Charles's *The Origins of the American Party System; Three Essays* (Williamsburg, Va.: Institute of Early American History and Culture, 1956) for originality and suggestiveness.

The partisan strife of 1797 was in large part a carry-over of the rabid debates around the Jay Treaty, thus the importance of Jerald A. Combs's study of *The Jay Treaty: Political Battleground of the Founding Fathers* (Berkeley: Univ. of California Pr., 1970). Sixty-five years after its first publication, John Spencer Bassett's *The Federalist System, 1789–1801* (New York: Harper & Row, 1906) remains helpful to a general understanding of the period, but it is deficient in its analysis of Adams's character and personality. Noble E. Cunningham, Jr., in *The Jeffersonian Republicans; The Formation of Party Organization, 1789–1801* (Chapel Hill: Univ. of North Carolina Pr., 1957), provides the finest analysis and description of Republican party strategy and tactics during the 1790s. Jonathan Daniels's *Ordeal of Ambition: Jefferson, Hamilton, Burr* (New York: Doubleday and Co., 1970) is an interesting personality study of three men who loom large on any canvas of the 1790s. The lack of documentation and the confusing chronology are damaging weaknesses.

BIOGRAPHIES OF LEADING FIGURES
OF THE TIME

Broadus Mitchell's two-volume biography of Alexander Hamilton is the most recent as well as the most complete of the many biographical studies of this man, and it is generally considered to be the best of all Hamilton lives. The second volume, covering the period under consideration in this study, is *Alexander Hamilton: The National Adventure, 1788–1804* (New York: Macmillan Co., 1962). I find the overall appraisal of John Adams fair and understanding; with regard to specific encounters between Adams and Hamilton, however, the study is often biased and sometimes inaccurate. Five other volumes on Hamilton that were used more or less extensively in the preparation of the present book, arranged alphabetically by author, are: Ralph Edward Bailey, *An American Colossus; The Singular Career of Alexander Hamilton* (Boston: Lothrop, Lee & Shepard Co., 1933); Louis M. Hacker, *Alexander Hamilton in the American Tradition* (New York: McGraw-Hill Book Co., 1957), a book that is severely biased and inaccurate in its treatment of Adams; Henry Cabot Lodge, *Alexander Hamilton* (Boston: Houghton, Mifflin Co., 1882); Richard B. Morris, *Alexander Hamilton and the Founding of the Nation* (New York: Dial Pr., 1957); and Saul K. Padover, *The Mind of Alexander Hamilton* (New York: Harper & Bros., 1958).

Among many biographical studies of Republican leaders, five proved especially helpful. First in importance is Dumas Malone's *Jefferson and the Ordeal of Liberty* (Boston: Little, Brown and Co., 1962). The third of five published volumes in Dr. Malone's monumental study of our third president, representing a long lifetime of study and analysis, this may well remain the all-time standard by which other lives of Jefferson are measured. Irving Brant's six-volume *James Madison* (Indianapolis: Bobbs-Merrill, 1941–1961) does nearly as well by Jefferson's first lieutenant. Frederick B. Tolles's life of *George Logan of Philadelphia* (New York: Oxford Univ. Pr., 1953) is a brilliant job of recreating the life and character of a second-line figure. Raymond Walters's *Albert Gallatin: Jeffersonian Financier and Diplomat* (New York: Macmillan Co., 1957) supplements the older but still useful study by Henry Adams, *The Life of Albert Gallatin* (New York: Peter Smith, 1943), and both proved very useful.

239

Among innumerable studies of George Washington, two were of primary assistance: John Alexander Carroll and Mary Wells Ashworth's *George Washington: Volume Seven; First in Peace* (New York: Charles Scribner's Sons, 1957), which was completed after Dr. Freeman's death and was indispensable. James Thomas Flexner's *George Washington and the New Nation, 1783–1793* (Boston: Little, Brown and Co., 1970) provided valuable background information.

Eight biographical studies of as many Federalist leaders are listed alphabetically by subject, as follows: Winfred E. A. Bernhard's *Fisher Ames; Federalist Statesman, 1758–1808* (Chapel Hill: Univ. of North Carolina Pr., 1965) helps greatly in any attempt to understand the Arch Federalists; careful and critical in many respects, it is somewhat marred by frequent misunderstanding of Adams. Morton Borden's *The Federalism of James A. Bayard* (New York: Columbia Univ. Pr., 1955) is a fine study of the tough Delaware Federalist; Robert Ernst's *Rufus King; American Federalist* (Chapel Hill: Univ. of North Carolina Pr., 1968), especially when used in conjunction with the older collection of King's writings, is extremely useful. Samuel Eliot Morison's *Harrison Gray Otis, 1765–1848; The Urbane Federalist* (Boston: Houghton, Mifflin Co., 1969) is a brilliantly written and understanding account of one of the Federalists who frequently seemed to straddle the divisions between the Arch Federalists, who opposed so much of what Adams tried to do, and such Adams supporters as William Vans Murray and John Marshall. Gerard H. Clarfield's *Timothy Pickering and American Diplomacy, 1795–1800* (Columbia: Univ. of Missouri Pr., 1969) is a remarkably objective study of this prickly, irascible, self-righteous Yankee; Clarfield seems to have misunderstood John Adams's position in early 1798, but he is never blindly partisan. Marvin R. Zahniser's *Charles Cotesworth Pinckney; Founding Father* (Chapel Hill: Univ. of North Carolina Pr., 1967) is an important study of the South Carolina Federalist. Richard E. Welch, Jr., in *Theodore Sedgwick, Federalist; A Political Portrait* (Middletown, Conn.: Wesleyan Univ. Pr., 1965), gives an interesting picture of Sedgwick. The book contains an excellent bibliographical essay on the sources of Federalism but is flawed by its interpretation of Adams's policies and personality. *Evolution of a Federalist; William Loughton Smith of Charleston (1758–1812)* (Columbia: Univ. of South Carolina Pr., 1962), by George C. Rogers, Jr., proved helpful in understanding the role of southern Federalists during this period.

PERTINENT MONOGRAPHS

In his *Fabric of Freedom, 1763–1800* (New York: Hill & Wang, 1961) Esmond Wright, a British historian, provides an excellent distillation of the major events and actions of these years. Surprising to this writer was the fact that, even more than America's own scholars, Professor Wright seems to understand and appreciate the role John Adams played in these years. Thirty years ago Dixon Ryan Fox and John A. Krout published a social history of these years that remains the best such study of this period: *The Completion of Independence, 1790–1830* (New York: Macmillan Co., 1944). Bradford Perkins's fine analysis of Anglo-American relations, *The First Rapprochement: England and the United States, 1795–1805* (Philadelphia: Univ. of Pennsylvania Pr., 1955), is a most important work. Nathan Schachner's *The Founding Fathers* (New York: G. P. Putnam's Sons, 1954) offers stimulating and often provocative appraisals of many of the people dealt with in the present study. Kenneth Umbeit's *Founding Fathers: Men Who Shaped Our Tradition* (New York: Harper & Bros., 1941) needs to be used with some caution.

James E. Pollard's *The Presidents and the Press* (New York: Macmillan Co., 1947) offers an interpretation of Adams that is more conventional than correct. By contrast a more recent and somewhat comparable book by Doris A. Graber, *Public Opinion, The President, and Foreign Policy* (New York: Holt, Rinehart & Winston, 1968), is marked not only by interesting conclusions but by considerable insight into Adams's philosophy and personality.

Unusually perceptive when it comes to understanding Adams's policies and ultimate goals, Paul A. Varg's *Foreign Policies of the Founding Fathers* (East Lansing: Michigan State Univ. Pr., 1963) is an admirable study that deserves more recognition than it seems to have received. Gilbert L. Lycan's *Alexander Hamilton & American Foreign Policy; A Design for Greatness* (Norman: Univ. of Oklahoma Pr., 1970) provides a detailed study of Hamilton's thinking and action in regard to foreign policy and perhaps the most careful appraisal ever made of Washington's Farewell Address. It is scarred, in my opinion, by a pro-Hamilton bias and an almost total failure either to understand or to appreciate John Adams. Alexander DeConde's *Entangling Alliance; Politics & Diplomacy Under George Washington* (Durham, N.C.: Duke Univ. Pr., 1958) provides a detailed study of foreign policy under President Washington. It is, however, subject to some of the same criticisms directed at

DeConde's *The Quasi-War* above. Arthur Burr Darling's *Our Rising Empire, 1763–1803* (New Haven, Conn.: Yale Univ. Pr., 1940) is interesting and valuable.

Two monographs dealing with the Alien and Sedition Acts were used extensively, but with growing care and suspicion. James Morton Smith's *Freedom's Fetters; The Alien and Sedition Laws and American Civil Liberties* (Ithaca, N.Y.: Cornell Univ. Pr., 1956) has been widely commended. I was distressed by numerous, though usually minor, errors and inaccuracies. John C. Miller's *Crisis in Freedom; The Alien and Sedition Acts* (Boston: Little, Brown and Co., 1951) is marred by frequent misunderstanding and misinterpretation of both actions and policies.

Leonard D. White's *The Federalists; A Study in Administrative History* (New York: Macmillan Co., 1948) remains after a quarter century a uniquely valuable study of the manner in which Federalists administered the national government between 1789 and 1801. The concluding chapter is a superb summing up of the achievements as well as the failures of these twelve years. Yet White seems to have completely misunderstood the relationship between Adams and Wolcott.

An exhaustive study of the newspaper propaganda of these years became the basis for Donald H. Stewart's massive *The Opposition Press of the Federalist Period* (Albany: State Univ. of New York Pr., 1969). Eugene Perry Link's *Democratic Republican Societies, 1790–1800* (New York: Columbia Univ. Pr., 1942) is valuable for understanding partisan maneuvering as well as party organization.

Arthur Preston Whitaker's *The Mississippi Question, 1795–1803; A Study in Trade, Politics, and Diplomacy* (New York: D. Appleton-Century Co., 1934) provides a careful and full-bodied study of the topic. It is indispensable to an understanding of Miranda and of Hamilton's interest in the Southwest. Robert R. Palmer's *The Age of Democratic Revolution: A Political History of Europe and America, 1760–1800,* 2 vols. (Princeton, N.J.: Princeton Univ. Pr., 1959), provides not only an admirable study of events in France in the 1790s but of their interaction with forces and events in the New World. Palmer's insight into political events and climate in the United States is very keen.

Edward Hake Phillips's unpublished dissertation, "The Public Career of Timothy Pickering, Federalist; 1745–1802," (Harvard, 1950), contains a wealth of material on Pickering but is flawed by a multitude of factual errors, a strong anti-Adams bias, and no apparent awareness of the nature of Hamilton's political scheming. Edmund P. Willis has edited a thin volume of intriguing papers: *Fame and the Founding Fathers* (Bethlehem, Pa.: Moravian College, 1967). Most controversial of the papers is Jacob E. Cooke's "Country Above Party: John Adams and the 1799 Mission to France," somewhat limited by a general unawareness of John Adams's long-range goals.

Andrew Oliver's *Portraits of John and Abigail Adams* (Cambridge, Mass.: The Belknap Press of Harvard Univ. Pr., 1967) is a fascinating and valuable volume, marked by careful scholarship, thorough and competent editing, and excellent reproduction of a large number of portraits.

Index